Arduino for Projects in Scientific Measurement

Taking your Arduino to the Frontiers of Science!

Randy A Normann

Publication Date: Jan 31, 2018

ISBN-13: 978-0-9997536-1-3

Publisher: On Measurement 4U LLC

Author, Randy A. Normann, Pattonville, Texas

Print 1.02

Dedication

To my mom for still placing my meager accomplishments on the refrigerator and to my dad for telling me, "Most people are limited by their lack of integrity", Jeane and Charles B. Normann

Credits

Reviewers

Both of these technical reviewers have retired from long careers in electronic measurement. They took on this project for the sole purpose of benefiting the next generation of instrumentation developers. I am grateful for their help and insight.

Charles Egbom: Charles has 30 years' experience designing aerospace telemetry systems at Sandia National Labs. He was the technical lead for 18 of those years.

Joe Henfling: Joe worked in the geothermal research department at Sandia National Labs as a logging and drilling tool designer. Joe worked with Randy on various geothermal tool design projects while both were working at Sandia and after retiring from Sandia. Also, special thanks to the three women on Joe's support team: Cindy, Allison and Kaithlyn.

Randy A Normann nor any of the reviewers of this literary work have taken any fees or other compensation from any company whose name or trademark is used within. Randy is owner of On Measurement 4U LLC, www.onmeasurement.com.

Table of Contents

Chapter 1: Introduction

Author Goals and Expected Readers of This Publication

If you want to take your Arduino sensor measurement skills to the next level…..
If you want to publish your findings in scientific publications….
If you want to design a data collection system as part of a research team….
If you're a geologist, physicists, volcanologist or any science driven person wanting to learn how to make
your own electronic measurements…..
Then I wrote this book for you.

I have been making electronic measurements supporting research and development for more than 30 years. In this book, you will NOT need CAD software. I assume the reader is armed with an Arduino Uno, Mega or Due, a handheld scientific calculator, and with some experience with running Arduino sketches (programs).

- ✓ I provide simple analog circuits for interfacing most sensors to the Arduino.

- ✓ I provide insight for avoiding trouble spots when making electronic measurements.

- ✓ I provide some easy to use digital filters and explain why you should not use the "moving average".

- ✓ I tried to provide real world considerations on sampling strategies so the reader can have these discussions with other members on their research team.

- ✓ I provide insight into my considerations when reviewing a technical research proposal.

Finally, I provide complete program sketches using the Arduino to capture electronic measurement data, filter it and time tag it. Complete sketches with an SD card, SRAM, 22 bit ADC, 12 bit DAC and more. Sketches based on easy to reference instructions found on the Arduino.cc web site. I want to: Keep it simple, empower the reader to explore where they want to go and embolden the reader publish their results with confidence.

Please feel free to contact me with suggestions on including more topics, corrections in my writing and hopefully your success stories. My email is: randy@onmeasurement.com

1.1 Author's Background

I have been in the research and development business for over 30 years. I have a MS EECE in Signal Processing. I started my career at Sandia National Labs in the telemetry department monitoring both aircraft and missile systems. Our electronic data collection systems measured a wide variety of environmental factors such as vibration, shock, and temperature. We also monitored system performance signals which fired the flight correction rockets. That work afforded me the unique chance to work on a project monitoring the temperature of each tooth of a drill bit while drilling into huge underground waste tanks. Old waste tanks containing solid waste and potentially combustible gases located on government sites. That project lead to my first patent, "Downhole Telemetry System", #5363095. I then transferred to the Geothermal Research Department developing well drilling, well logging and well monitoring instrumentation for extreme temperatures and pressures. I have been a technical reviewer of over 100 research proposals. I have been the technical advisor for scientific experiments with budgets over $10M USD. I have been involved in research for the US Department of Energy (US DOE) and the National Aeronautics and Space Administration (NASA). I have participated in creating standards for commercial aircraft electronic systems under the Society of Automotive Engineering (SAE).

During my career, I have worked alongside researchers with a wide range of backgrounds -- geologists, physicists, reservoir engineers, mechanical engineers, volcanologist and (dare I use the term? yes) rocket scientists. I have never met an engineer or scientist I did not like.

I'm sharing what I've learned over the years with the reader and want to speed up their understanding of how to make great electronic measurements, how to avoid the embarrassment of reporting false information and how to understand the language of a professional in the electronic measurement world supporting scientific research.

I have targeted this book for **non-electrical engineers** wanting to know how to make excellent scientific electronic measurements. And I chose the Arduino system because it's an easy place for almost anyone to start. The Arduino systems provide a relatively simple platform to build scientific measurement systems.

1.2 Expected Level of the Reader

The Arduino is an inexpensive microcontroller with world-wide support. The author's assumption is that the reader owns an Arduino Uno, Mega 2560 or Due and has some experience with running public domain example code on it. Even if this isn't true, there are many books directed at getting users started with the Arduino as well as a number of Arduino 'cookbooks' directed at getting the user to make useful measurements and work with low cost sensors. This book moves the user from being just good to being professional.

I have attempted to create examples of the ideas presented in this book to read like real world researchers talk. I want the reader to have the ability to work with others in team projects, the ability to discuss what is needed and how they can meet those needs. Cost is always a major issue for any research project. The data collection system is not normally the priority of the project but a much needed means to capture the true result of the experiment. Without high quality, reliable, data the experiment could result in no reportable results or worse false assumptions.

This book provides 'cookbook' programming and example applications for anyone wanting to make scientific electronic measurements. It also provides the user with tools for better understanding how digital sampling of sensor data is done to support the scientific processes. Where I can, I offer lessons learned from my experience.

Using the techniques presented here, anyone with a calculator and desire can learn how to get the most out of data logging with the Arduino. This book will extend abilities of the Arduino with shields developed to extend the precision and resolution of the Arduino.

1.3 Reader Hardware

All the hardware to get started is an Arduino Uno, a proto plug-in board, a scientific calculator, some passive components (i.e. resistors, capacitors, diodes) and a low cost sensor to measure. The photo shows the author's basic set up.

In future applications, the Mega (Mega 2560 R3) or Due might be better suited for your use since they offer more program space. There are some low cost (check Ebay) shields and other useful items.

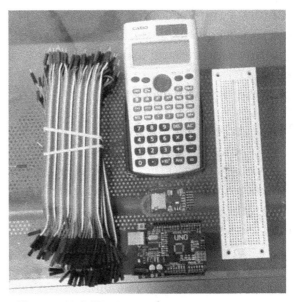

1. An SD card shield (either micro or standard) is really useful for saving your collected sensor data

Figure 1.1 Basic reader system

2. High resolution analog-to-digital converters in the 16bit to 22bit range

3. A 9V battery pack using "AA" batteries and connection to your Arduino

4. Access to Microsoft Excel or other spreadsheet program for viewing and processing your captured data

5. Button switch and 5K or 10K potentiometer

1.4 Microcontroller vs Microprocessor (or Why Arduino?)

The popular Arduino Uno is an 8 bit microcontroller running at 16MHz. How can it compete with the Raspberry Pi or BeagleBone Black running at GHz with 32bit digital buses? Those others are full credit card sized computer systems. They have the benefit of a large operating system with video output, mouse and keyboard input and complex memory systems. Microprocessor based systems are great for running complex computational software and interfacing with humans. The microprocessor is designed to run executable software with timer interrupts to multiplex processing tasks and human interface functions such as monitoring the keyboard while updating the video. Microcontrollers like the Arduino are poor at performing those activates.

However, microcontrollers are complete micro-processing systems on a chip, (SOC). They contain integrated RAM, EPROM (or flash) memory and Analog- to- Digital Converters (ADC) they are compact and self-sufficient. Executable code stored and read from microcontroller memory is run serially one statement after another. No program background multi-tasking like microprocessors. This makes programming interfaces with other external electronic devices or systems more user controllable.

Another reason a microcontroller is attractive is they simply run on far less power. The Arduino Uno can run on a 9v battery, while the GHz microprocessor machines require large batteries or wall power since they typically require 200 to 500mA. For this reason, 8 bit microcontrollers may not be sexy but the electronics industry sells (perhaps 100X) more of them than GHz microprocessors. In this book, we look at the Arduino Uno, Mega 2560 and Due. The Due has a 32bit, 84MHz microcontroller. The Due runs on the same basic code under the Arduino IDE as the Uno and Mega.

1.5 Standard Data Logger

After completing this book, the reader should be able to create their own data logger to best suited for their particular application. They will gain an understanding the engineering trade-offs when designing a measurement system such as resolution versus speed and analog filtering versus digital filtering. Through this process the reader will begin to see how to maximize their results using the Arduino. They should have a greater awareness of how false or misleading data is inadvertently created. Maximizing your data while avoiding misleading results is the goal of anyone designing scientific electronic data collection systems.

The standard Arduino based data logger records electronic measurements or events to a memory system. The data must be recorded with some type of timer to allow the user to correlate measured data with other events of the experiment. Figure 1.2 is the standard data logger for this publication.

Signal conditioning can mean anything needed to interface a sensor to the Arduino,

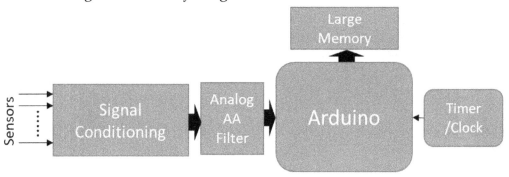

Figure 1.2 This is a standard data logger. By the end of this book, the reader will be introduced to the functions and circuits of each block.

Chapter 4. Signal conditioning circuits are maximizing the Arduino's internal Analog-to-Digital Converter (ADC) resolution. The analog AA (Anti-Aliasing) filter is a low pass filter needed to meet the digital sampling requirements, Chapter 5. Once the Arduino has made an analog reading from its internal ADC, digital signal processing can start, Chapter 7. Since the Arduino ADC has limited resolution, there are examples of increasing the resolution of the Uno by dithering the incoming signal, section 6.6. Example code for interfacing to a 22bit ADC allows the user to increase system resolution as needed for many scientific experiments, Chapter 10.

Higher measurement resolution requires building low noise measurement circuits, Chapter 9. This book will aid budget constrained engineers/scientists in making valid and accurate electronic measurements supporting their research.

1.6 Extra Details

In many of the sections of this publication, I have included "Tech Notes". These are for advanced concepts the reader might be interested in. They are in the form below.

[**Tech Note:** Additional information going past where most readers need to know.]

Also included are a few stories from my past. Hopefully they demonstrate the reason for writing a section in this publication or some lesson learned. They are in the form below.

[STORY: I used a UPS to power the ......]

Finally, the last pages of the book include a reference sheet. This sheet is called the, "Oh Yea, I was Right Sheet". It is intended to help reinforce the reader's memory and provide a quick reference when looking at circuits covered within.

Chapter 2: The ADC

Basic how to for sampling analog voltages

There are several different types of Analog-to-Digital Converters, ADCs. The ADC converts an analog voltage to a digital sampled value which we store. The Arduino use a successive approximation converter, SAC. We will take a short look at the SAC and a couple of other common types of ADCs for background information. Knowing these options is important when discussing future electronic measurement projects. The Arduino can be interfaced with any type of ADC.

2.1 Flash Converter

I'm starting with the flash ADC because it is the simplest. The flash converter is called the flash because it is fast. The flash conversion time is in microseconds or faster but their resolution is limited to 8 bits or less. The natural tradeoff for speed is a loss of resolution.

The flash is composed of a voltage reference (as all ADCs), a voltage ladder and comparator circuits. Let's look at the 1 bit flash circuit in Figure 2.1. Don't worry about the R1 or R2 resistors, these will be explained in section 4.1.

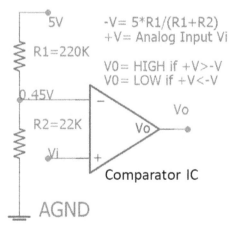

Figure 2.1 A comparator circuit

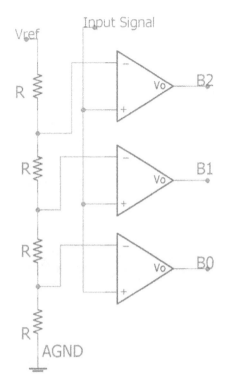

Figure 2.2 A 2 bit flash ADC

A comparator circuit is a simple analog logic device. The comparator is a fast circuit comparing two inputs, +V pin and the –V pin. If the +V input is greater than the –V input voltage, the output of the comparator is HIGH (5V in this case). For +V less than the –V input, the output is LOW or 0V. In this circuit, the voltage reference is the 0.45V created by the voltage divider (R1&R2) from the 5V supply. If the analog input is < 0.45, the output is 0 and 1 for an analog input > 0.45. Since the gain of the comparator is so high, there is no analog input exactly equal to the reference voltage. All the uP has to do is constantly read in the 1 bit (Vo) to monitor the input voltage level. Now, let's look at a higher resolution flash converter of 2 bits.

With three comparators, a 2 bit flash ADC can be built. A 2 bit ADC has only 4 possible values. The three comparator flash ADC circuit is shown in Figure 2.2. Each comparator compares the input (+V) to the fixed –V input. The resistor ladder has 3 equal voltage steps between 0 and Vref. The comparator outputs B0, B1 and B2 can be converted to ADC readings shown in Table 2.1.

In section 4.1, the flash voltage ladder in Figure 2.2 will be calculated. With that information, the ADC counts in Table 2.1 are: 00 for 0V to 1.25V, 01 for 1.25 to 2.5V, 10 for 2.5V to 3.75V and 11 for above 3.75V.

For a 3 bit flash ADC, seven comparators are needed and a 4 bit flash ADC requires 15 comparators. The flash ADC is simple and fast but quickly becomes hardware intensive and power hungry. The good news, a 6-8 bit flash ADC device is less than $10.

Table 2.1 2Bit flash logic

B2	B1	B0	ADC
X	X	0	00
X	0	1	01
0	1	1	10
1	1	1	11

2.2 Successive Approximation Converter, SAC

The successive approximation converter (SAC) is implemented internally in the Arduino. This is perhaps the most common type of ADC. They are slower than a flash converter but offer lower power operation and higher resolution. The Arduino Uno and Mega have 10bit ADCs and the Due has a 12 bit ADC.

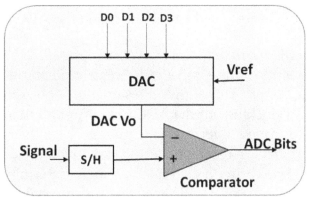

As with the flash converter, the SAC begins with a voltage comparator. However, in the SAC the –V input of the comparator is the output voltage from a Digital-to-Analog Converter (DAC). The DAC converts a binary input to an analog voltage using a voltage reference. A 10 bit DAC is needed to make a 10 bit SAC. (This will become clearer in a moment.)

Figure 2.3 Block diagram of a SAC type ADC

The analog signal voltage is sampled and held constant by a sample & hold circuit (labeled S/H). Sampling and holding the input static is needed to give time for the conversion process. The comparator is comparing the DAC output with the analog input voltage held in the sample and hold circuit. The SAC is changing the DAC digital input value until the DAC output best matches the analog input signal. One by one, each bit of the DAC is tested until all bits have been determined.

Operating the 4 bit ADC successive approximation converter in Figure 2.3 is illustrated in Table 2.2. Note the column labeled "DAC Vo" is the input to the –V pin of the comparator. The first setting of the DAC is 0,0,0,1 for D0 to D3. The DAC output is 2.5V. The comparator indicated the DAC output is higher than the 1.65V input. This results in the first SAC

Table 2.2 The 4 bit SAC Internal DAC Function, Vref = 5.0V							
Signal	D0	D1	D2	D3	DAC Vo	Comp Out	Bits
1.65V	0	0	0	1	2.5V	0	ADC3
1.65V	0	0	1	0	1.25V	1	ADC2
1.65V	0	1	1	0	1.875V	0	ADC1
1.65V	1	0	1	0	1.5625V	1	ADC0

output bit, ADC3 is LOW. The SAC output is MSB (Most Significant Bit) first, ADC3 in this case. Next the DAC D2 bit is tested by the comparator for ADC2. Each bit of the SAC ADC is determined and shifted out serially.

A final value for our 4 bit SAC is a digital reading of 0101 binary or the integer 5. The result in our example is $5*Vref/2^4 = 1.5625V$. This is the closest estimate of the input voltage 1.65V the 4 bit SAC can make. For the remaining book, the Arduino internal SAC will simply be called the ADC.

In the block diagram shown in Figure 2.3, the S/H block is the 'sample and hold' function. The input signal is captured and held as an analog voltage on an internal capacitor. This allows the signal to stay fixed while operating the DAC, comparator and clocking out the ADC bits. After all the ADC bits are determined, the capacitor is dumped of its charge to get ready for the next sample. Building sample and hold circuits is a real engineering task given the precision of today's ADCs. The sample and hold circuit goes a long way to determine the ultimate resolution floor of any ADC. Later, I will show that the internal ADC of the Mega and Uno is actually better than the 10bit resolution it is limited to.

2.3 Sigma Delta Converter

The sigma delta converter is the heavy lifters of electronic analog to digital converters. There are sigma delta type converters ranging from 16 bit to 32 bit readings or as 76µV to 1.2nV relative resolution. Although, they offer a lot of bits, a single conversion may not deliver the full bit resolution. Often the manufacturer suggests an effective bit rating for a single conversion which is less than the number of output bits. Through averaging of many conversions the lower bits can be realized for static, low noise DC input voltages.

When it comes to "absolute" ADC accuracy, the ADC cannot do better than the voltage reference. For example, a voltage reference costing ~$100 USD has a maximum +/-500 µV output voltage error while a 24 bit ADC has 1µV resolution. Simply buying a high resolution ADC is not the answer to µV accuracy. User calibration over the systems operating temperature with certified lab equipment is required to maximize system accuracy. It has been my experience, achieving 24 bit ADC resolution and 0.05% accuracy requires significant design effort with control over the circuit board design and layout. In practical terms, most Arduino users should be happy with 19 to 21bit relative measurement conversions and near 0.1% accuracy. No need to be discouraged, tracking a sensor's output down to $1/2^{19}$ will

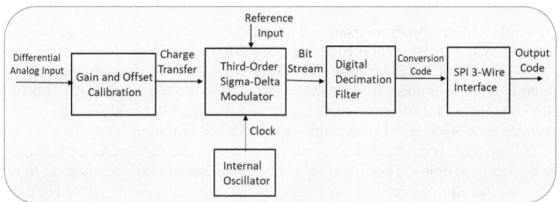

Figure 2.4 Block diagram of a sigma delta converter, based on the 2007 Microchip, MCP3550 data sheet.

open new worlds to most research projects.

The sigma delta converter trades speed for resolution. They are used in most hand held and laboratory instruments. Sigma delta converters normally filter out local wall power 60Hz (50Hz in Europe) noise. Rejecting ac wall power noise is a real benefit for instruments where human hands handle the test leads during the measurement process.

Figure 2.4 is the sigma delta converter block diagram taken from the 2007, Microchip, MCP3550 data sheet. The MCP3550 is a 22 bit sigma delta converter. The 22 bits includes the sign bit as the input signal voltage is differential. Differential inputs will be discussed later under instrumentation amplifiers, section 4.5. Fully explaining the sigma delta converter operation is outside the scope of this publication. However, time will be spent on interfacing and using the MCP3550 device with the Arduino. The MCP3550 will allow the user to see signals ~2000 times smaller than the Arduino internal 10 bit ADC.

Looking at the MCP3550 block diagram, there is a reference input voltage and serial output of ADC bits. All the functions inside the diagram above are transparent to the user including the gain and offset calibration. According to the MCP3550 data sheet, the gain and calibration are performed with each ADC conversion. The differential input signal is sampled and held by an internal sample & hold circuit not shown in Figure 2.4.

An example Arduino program using the MCP3550 inside the AD22B shield can be found in the Chapter 10, section 10.5. The MCP3550 device comes in three flavors, the MCP3550-50, MCP3550-60 and MCP3551. Each has a built in notch filter for removing wall power noise at 50Hz, 60Hz and both 50 & 60Hz respectfully. Each version is rated at 21.9 effective bits out of 22 bits. For the MCP3550-60, the conversion time is ~68mS. The example sketch AD22B program (AD22B_DAC12B_Test, Chapter 10) starts a conversion and then waits for the sigma delta converter to finish. There is a forth version, the MCP3553 which doesn't have any notch filter allowing for faster conversions but only 20.6 effective bits. For most Arduino users, the versions with notch filters will work well inside a noisy lab environment.

Chapter 3: Calibrating the Arduino Uno

More than just starting the engine

Every measurement system for scientific data must be calibrated. Scientific measurements will be recorded and shared with other researchers. I have received calls from people I have never met, just asking me, "How did you validate the measurement?" It's a great feeling to simply start telling them what and how we validated the system. A document providing assurance the system is making valid measurements is required. For measurement systems built in the lab by researchers, this calibration document is critical. In this section, we'll look at calibrating an Arduino Uno. There is a surprise coming for those who have already been powering their Arduino from the USB port of a computer.

3.1 Basic Operation of the Arduino ADC

The Arduino Uno, Mega and Due all have an on chip, easy to use Analog-to-Digital Converter, ADC. The ADC allows the Arduino to measure analog voltages from electronic sensors. The Uno and Mega have 10 bit ADC while the Due has a 12 bit ADC. All Arduino ADCs are successive approximation types. All Arduino ADCs are single-ended which means the ADC only measures positive voltages. For the Uno and Mega the default range is from 0 to 5V and the Due is from 0 to 3.3V. Zero voltage is measured at the Arduino GND pins.

[**Tech Note:** 0V or Ground (GND) must always be defined in any circuit. This seems obvious but when your measurement system is part of a larger system the agreed grounding point is critical. Later in Chapter 9 on reducing electronic noise, I have some suggestions.]

Arduinos have an analog multiplexer (mux for short). The mux allows the user to connect the internal ADC to more than one analog input pin. Multiplexing allows many analog connections but only one analog input to be sampled by the ADC at one time. The Uno has 6 channels labeled A0-A5, the Mega has 16 channels A0-A15 and the Due has 12 channels A0-A11. Figure 3.1 is the basic block diagram of the ADC system on the Arduino.

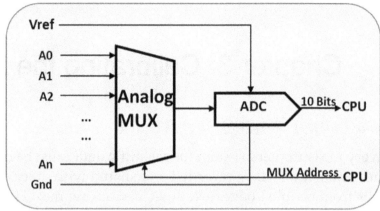

Figure 3.1 Arduino analog ADC system

The CPU must send an address to choose which analog input is chosen prior to any conversion. This addressing activity is invisible to the Arduino programmer. The Arduino programmer simply calls the function "analogRead(An)" where An is the name of an analog input pin. For example:

int SensorValue = analogRead(An);
Where "int" defines the user's variable "SensorValue" as integer type and "An" is the analog pin name needed to address the mux

The function "analogRead(An)" will simply place the ADC reading of the input analog voltage at mux channel number 'n' into the user defined integer variable "SensorValue". The Uno and Mega both have 10bit ADC meaning they resolve the input analog voltage by 2^{10} or 1024 parts. The Due defaults to a 10 bit ADC to be consistent with the Uno. However, it can be programmed to provide 12bits using the function, "analogReadResolution(12);" in the program "setup()" section. The Due can now resolve the input analog voltage by 2^{12} or 4096 parts.

[**Tech Note:** If interested in the details of ADC system inside the Atmel processor used by the Arduino, the Atmel application note, "Atmel-2559E-Characterization-and-Calibration-of-the-ADC-on-an-AVR_AVR120_Application Note-08/2016" is a very good reference.]

The output of the ADC is a binary integer. All integers ('int') inside the Arduino program are 16bits. The Arduino program will automatically take the 10bit or 12bit ADC values and convert them to 16bit integers. Again, this happens invisibly for the programmer. Having these details built in to the Arduino programming makes using the Arduino's very easy to program for reading analog inputs.

The 'nominal' ADC voltage calibration for the Arduino Uno & Mega is:

$$\text{float Vin} = \text{SensorValue} * (\text{Vref}/1024);$$
$$\text{for the Due:}$$
$$\text{float Vin} = \text{SensorValue} * (\text{Vref}/4096);$$

Where "Vin" is a program variable of float type, "SensorValue" as a integer from the ADC, Vref is the upper limit of the ADC (Uno, Mega default is 5V, DUE is 3.3V)

Note, it is common for most authors to use 1024 when it is slightly more accurate to use 1023 ($2^{10} - 1$) because the ADC can actually only output 0 to 1023 (0 to 03FF Hex). This is a slight difference and will be ignored.

I like to generate 'nominal' calibration equations for each system I design. Nominal is NOT the actual calibration but more like the design target. Some engineers call this "calibration as designed". Having an understanding of a nominal calibration aids in finding elements of a circuit which are important for reducing real world measurement error.

3.2 Summing ADC Readings

When calibrating the Arduino ADC, it is useful to sum and average ADC readings. The easiest and fastest means for summing ADC readings is to sum the results as an integer. After summing, calculate the average and perform the conversion to a floating variable (normally voltage). Working with ADC readings as integers speeds up calculations and reduces program working memory. However, there is a limit to a sum of ADC readings based on the type of Arduino integer used for the summation.

ADC bits ranges are:
10 bit ADC – 0000 Hex to 03FF Hex
12 bit ADC – 0000 Hex to 0FFF Hex
Arduino default integer range is:
16 bits – 0000 Hex to 7FFF Hex

Table 3.1 Summing ADC readings with different integers

Int Type	Max Hex	Max Int	10B SUM	12B SUM	22B SUM
int	7FFF	32,767	32	8	N/A
unsigned int	FFFF	65,535	64	16	N/A
long int	7FFFFFFF	2,147,483,647	2,097,152	524,288	512
unsigned long	FFFFFFFF	4,294,967,295	4,194,304	1,048,576	1024

The default 16bit Arduino integer uses the MSB (Most Significant Bit) as the sign bit ('0' for positive values, '1' for negative values). The ADC value is always stored in the Arduino memory with a sign bit even though it's not possible for the ADC to create a negative reading. When summing ADC readings as integers, the 10bit ADC readings will overflow the Arduino integer value after only summing 32 readings. The 12 bit Due ADC can over flow after 8 summations. However, Arduino allows the programmer three other types of integers, 'unsigned', 'long' and 'unsigned long'. The unsigned allows the programmer to use the sign bit as a value bit. The long integer is 32bits long. Table 3.1 specifies how many ADC readings can be summed for each type of integer and ADC resolution. The table includes a summation for the 22bit ADC shield using the MCP3550 ADC.

The code example below is for averaging 100 readings.

```
long int SensorValue;  // SensorValue variable is now a 32 bit
integerSensorValue = 0;
      for (int i=0; i<100; i++)  // perform 100 readings of channel A0 and
sum
      {
      SensorValue := SensorValue + analogRead(A0);  // Reading A0
channel
      }
```

float Sensor100Avg = SensorValue/100.0; //a 100 point average reading of A0

In the last instruction, it is important to use 100.0 with the decimal point to prevent the Arduino from assuming you are dividing two integers since the 100.0 value is a float value.

3.3 Calibration of the Uno

For those wanting accurate calibrations of the Arduino ADC, there is a small problem with powering the Arduino from an USB port. To understand this, remember the Arduino ADC voltage reference,(Vref) is the same Vref used to calculate the nominal conversion from ADC integer to a voltage value. Recall the equation float Vin = SensorValue*(**Vref**/1024). In short, the ADC accuracy is no better than the reference voltage (Vref). Small variations in Vref become variations in the ADC reading.

To make life easy as well as low cost for the Arduino user, Vref = AVcc. AVcc is simply the 5V system voltage for the Uno and Mega and 3.3V on the Due. The Arduino circuit uses a noise reduction RC filter on the 5V supply going to the Vref pin of the ADC. The Arduino developers realized the importance of a good voltage reference. They made the Vref voltage available to the user at the pin labeled, "AREF". The Vref voltage can be directly measured with a standard high impedance voltage meter.

The 5V system voltage on the Uno and Mega comes from either the USB connection (hugely convenient for developing software) or from an onboard 5V regulator. The 5V regulator requires an external DC voltage through the power plug or the "Vin" pin. This means the voltage reference used by the ADC is slightly different depending on the power source. This is a problem. The Arduino supply source changes the calibration!

A limited experiment recording the AREF pin voltage of an Arduino Uno powered from USB ports on from two laptops and once from a 9V battery was performed. The 5V from the two laptops USB ports set the AREF to 4.94V and 4.96V while the 9V battery AREF value was 4.99V. When using the 9V battery on the Vin pin of the Uno, the Uno powers from an onboard voltage regulator. The onboard 5V regulator is a better Vref than the USB ports in my limited test. Looking up the USB 5V supply from one PC manufacturer states the USB 5V power can range from 4.75V to 5.25VDC. I strongly believe, the reader will find the onboard Arduino voltage regulator will offer higher repeatability over USB power. In short, connecting to different USB power sources changes the Uno calibration, which is an error to be avoided.

For fun, let's consider the effects of the 3 measured Vref voltages referenced above against the nominal calibration for the prior section. Assume an ideal 4.0VDC input is at the Arduino Uno analog input. The output is from the Uno ADC is an integer called Cnts (short for counts).

Nominal 5.0Vref Calibration: ADC Cnts = 4.0V/(Vref/1024) = 4.0V/(5.0V/1024) = 819 Cnts
With Vref = 4.94V: ADC Cnts = 4.0V/(4.94V/1024) = 829 Cnts
With Vref = 4.96V; ADC Cnts = 825 Cnts
With Vref = 4.99V; ADC Cnts = 820 Cnts

In the calculation above, I truncated the values to form the integer results.

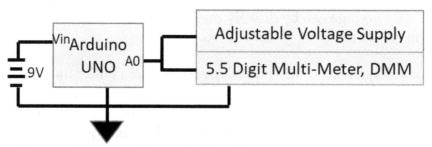

Figure 3.2 Arduino calibration set up

The difference between the Vref = 4.94V from the ideal 5.0V is 10 Cnts or 0.976% error for a 4.0V analog input. This 1% error is easily avoided by knowing the Vref voltage. This just illustrates the value of the Vref in any ADC circuit.

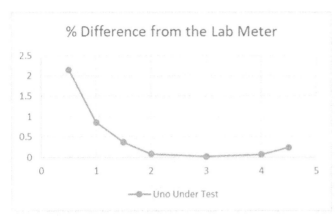

Figure 3.3 UNO vs Lab Meter readings

Now, let's look at running a calibration of a Uno using known input DC voltages. For this calibration, the Uno is operating from a 9V battery. The battery powers the on-board voltage regulator. A battery is a clean, noise free power supply which is a huge benefit to making clean, low noise measurements.

Using the 9V battery, you can still get the ADC readings in real time via the USB port. Simply power the Arduino with the external DC power before connecting the USB cable. Once powered externally, the Arduino will not use the USB for system power. Figure 3.2 is the block diagram for the calibration process I used. I only tested one Uno, so please don't assume this calibration is for any other Arduino Uno or other type of Arduino. A one unit test only represents my Uno and the process I used.

I ran 7 test voltages from 0.5V to 4.5V for a calibration of the Uno. The graph below shows the result of 7 input voltages to my **Arduino Uno compared to my lab DMM, volt meter**. The % difference was calculated using my 5.5 digit, calibrated Digital Multi-Meter (DMM) as the standard. The adjustable power supply was filtered through a large RC filter, not shown. The plotted results of

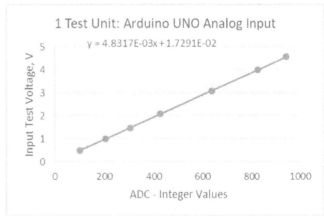

Figure 3.4 Calibration of my UNO

Figure 3.3 were generated using the difference equation below:

$$\% \text{ Difference} = (\text{abs}(\text{DMM-Vin})/(\text{DMM}))/100;$$

Where Vin was calculated as Vin = ADC* (4.99V/1023); DMM is the lab
measurement of the input test voltage at Uno analog channel A0

The percentage difference between the lab meter and the Uno is bell shaped. This is
a normal outcome for most single ended ADCs. Electronic devices have difficulty
operating close to their power rails. Here the Arduino ADC upper and lower power
rails are 5V and 0V respectively.

Imagine if the ADC bit value is ~0.004883V. Now, having a circuit to measure the
difference between 4.9951V and 5.0000V or between 0.004883V and 0.0000V while
also operating on those voltages becomes impossibly challenging.

As measurement system designers, we never want to operate the ADC too near the
supply rails. For maximum resolution and measurement accuracy, I normally aim
for signal input voltages with a max value about 90% of the upper rail. For the Uno,
90% is 4.5V.

The lessons learned from this experiment are:

1. For consistent performance, run your Arduino from an external power source
    (battery) when calibrating or collecting data supporting a scientific test. If
    needed, connect the USB after the Arduino is running off the battery.
2. It is always a good idea to target your input sensor signal to operate in the mid to
    upper midpoint of the ADC range.

Using Microsoft Excel, I curve fitted the 7 calibration points to a straight line (also
called a point-slope) shown in Figure 3.4. The nominal calibration equation
referenced in section 3.1 is also a point slope equation, y = ax + b. Where the slope
'a' is $Vref/2^n$ and the point intercept 'b' is assumed to be 0V. Using the 7 measured
points, the point-slope resulted in: y = 4.8318m*x + 0.01729V. Replacing the y and
the x with the ADC terms we have been working with:

Analog Measured Voltage = 4.8318mV/Cnts*(ADC Cnts) + 0.0179V
Compare this with the nominal calibration from section 3.1 below

$$\text{Analog Measured Voltage} = 4.883\text{mV}/\text{Cnts}*(\text{ADC Cnts}) + 0\text{V}$$

The new point-slope calibrated values and the 'nominal' calibration are compared in the error plot Figure 3.5. Here it is reasonable to say the difference between the 5.5 digit lab meter readings and the Uno calculated values is an error in the measured values. The percent error in the analog voltage shows a clear improvement when using the point slope curve fit equation developed from calibration.

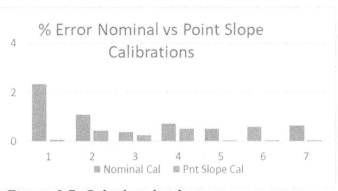

Figure 3.5 Calculated value error

[**Tech Note:** As the difference between the lab meter readings and the uncalibrated Uno readings result in a bell shape, a second order polynomial curve fit should provide better results. I suggest adding more test points in the area of our expected measurements, normally the mid to upper sections of the ADC. For example, 3 additional test points between 3.0V to 4.5V will tighten the mid-range calibration.]

3.4 Other Vref Options

The default voltage reference, Vref, for the Uno and Mega is the 5V supply. However, the Arduino Uno and Mega offer other internal reference voltage options. These options can be set inside your program! For the Uno, "analogReference(INTERNAL)" function call sets the reference voltage to 1.1V using an internal reference voltage. There is no return value when calling this function so it stands alone in your code. I placed it in the "setup()" code so that it only runs once.

The internal 1.1V reference is a true band gap voltage reference. Having an ADC running from 0 to 1.1V offers a higher resolution for low level signals. The nominal calibration is the same equation only replacing the Vref = 5V to Vref = 1.1V. The least ADC bit is now valued at 1.074mV where using the 5V reference the ADC bit is 4.883mV.

However, the Uno offers one more option for a user supplied voltage reference. Using 'analogReference(EXTERNAL)' allows the user to supply a voltage reference at the AREF pin. I successfully used a 3.3V external reference voltage. I connected the 3.3V voltage pin to the AREF pin after the Arduino Uno had booted up. The 'analogReference(EXTERNAL)' function needs to run during the 'setup()' section of your code. This switches the microcontroller to use the external AREF pin input voltage for Vref. CAUTION: I don't recommend this action since the input voltage to the AREF may damage the Arduino if the voltage is not applied in the correct sequence.

Arduino.cc site says the external reference must be less than 5V. They suggest a 5K ohm resistor be used in series with the AREF pin and the external Vref to protect the microcontroller. The 5K resistor will cause a voltage drop as the AREF input has a 32K ohm impedance to ground. In this case, I don't see any real advantage of using an external reference voltage. The Arduino Mega offers another option which makes sense to me.

The Mega has two internal voltage reference options, 1.1V and 2.56V in addition to the Arduino default 5V. Arduino supplies two additional Mega only arguments for the "analogReference()" function: INTERNAL1V1 and INTERNAL2V56. The Mega, therefore, has three ADC reference voltage settings, 5V, 2.56V and 1.1V.

The program "MegaAutoRange" in Chapter 10 illustrates the use of the three internal voltage references. Here, I used the Mega to make an ADC reading using the default Vref = 5V. Based on the result, I adjusted Vref to best fit the input value as: 5.0V, 2.56V or 1.1V. Doing this, allows the Mega to become an auto-scaling ADC, which enables the user to maximize the resolution of the ADC for a given input voltage. The Mega becomes a good voltage meter.

3.5 More Thoughts on System Calibration

3.5.1 To Marry or Not to Marry?

I have worked with the Aerospace Industry and the Oil Industry. Those two industries have a very different expectation about calibration. Let's say we are going to use the newly calibrated Arduino Uno to measure widgets. (Widgets are the universal unit of measurement for anything else.) Our measurement system is shown in Figure 3.5.

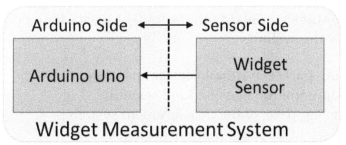

Figure 3.5 The universal widget measurement

This is a very simple measurement system. The Aerospace Industry looks to calibrate the parts of the system. They calibrate the Arduino Uno and the Widget sensor independently. Then combine the two calibrations to get the calibration of the Widget Measurement System. They then validate within some acceptable error the system performance.

This process allows for easy repair and replacement of any one part. It also allows for the qualification and testing of each part. This places pressure on aerospace suppliers live up to their specifications because they will be held accountable for calibration discrepancies.

As an example of combining two calibrations to one system calibration, consider the universal widget measurement system.

The widget sensor calibration supplied by the manufacturers is:
Sensor output voltage = Vo = 21.34widgets/V – 0.3widget
And the Uno calibration: Voltage = 4.8318mV/Cnts*(ADC Cnts) + 0.0179V

The system calibration places the voltage calibration into the sensor widget calibration equation to form an equation from cnts to widgets as below:

$$\text{Widget Measurement} = (4.8318mV/Cnts*(ADC\ Cnts) + 0.0179V)*21.34 widgets/V - 0.3 widgets$$

Or as

$$\text{Widget measurement} = 0.1031 widgets/Cnts*(ADC\ Cnts) + 0.082 widgets$$

The oil industry looks at the system calibration as a whole. They may verify the Arduino Uno and the widget sensor are both working but save the calibration until the widget measurement system is built. This is called 'marrying' the parts. If any part needs to be replaced, the system must be recalibrated. The advantage of this system calibration is normally a better calibration. I say normally because there are exceptions. For one, the widget sensor manufacturer most likely has the best means for calibrating their sensor. The calibration supplied with the widget sensor may not be duplicated once the sensor is inside the system.

The oil industry calibration of marrying parts is normally easier and easier to demonstrate performance when building unique one of a kind scientific measurement systems. In short, marrying parts of the measurement system is commonly done for small production scientific measurement systems.

3.5.2 Closed Loop Calibration

In the perfect world, everyone would close loop calibrate their equipment. Closed loop calibration is running your calibrations before running an experiment and then rerunning calibration after the running the experiment. This aids in validating the data collected from the experiment. If the calibrations before and after repeat (within expected margins), then it is very unlikely something failed during the experiment. The measurement results are strengthened by closed loop calibration.

I only mention the following topic for the reader's consideration. In the real world, before and after calibration is rarely done. It is even less likely to be done if the data from the experiment is viewed as successful. One of my managers once said, "We never question success". He was a person driven to not just to show success but to validate our data by knowing the margin of our successes. For example, if the experiment was repeated 10 times, would we have 10 out of 10 successes or 1 random success and 9 failures? We never had the funding to perform such comprehensive examinations of our measurement systems.

Additional food for thought, on an aircraft telemetry system design, we were asked to stimulate the sensors on power up. The pilot would power the system a few minutes before the test would start. Our project lead called sensor stimulation a "self-test".

We had small heaters to pulse heat on the temperature sensors. We had solenoids to create a small vibration on accelerometers and stuff like that. So, the telemetry would power up, stimulate each sensor and record the result. The actual test would be run and data would be collected. After the test, the telemetry would rerun the 'self-test'. Self-test isn't calibration but our customer at the US Department of Energy was so impressed, our team received some type of certificate of appreciation. I lost my certificate a long time ago.

3.5.1 Accuracy vs Resolution

Going back to the calibration of the Uno. I had 3 power sources, 2 different USB ports from 2 different laptops and a 9 volt battery. The worse error came from the two USB ports. This error was about 1% or 10 Cnts. Now that doesn't sound too bad but it really is. The uncertainty of which power source we are using, degrades the systems accuracy. It takes 3 bits to represent 7Cnts. Using the laptop USB for power reduces the Uno accuracy to only 7bits of the 10bit ADC. However, the resolution of the ADC is still 10 bits.

I define accuracy as the level of certainty of the measurement to provide absolute value measurements in units of measure. Examples of unit of measure are lbs for units of force, degrees Celsius for temperature and Gs of acceleration among others. Where resolution is the value of certainty of the value for ADC bits. Resolution is based on the system measurement noise levels. Noise creates uncertainty in the actual resolution in ADC bits.

We must work hard to achieve accuracy and resolution. This requires removing uncertainty from the system. So, I suggested, using a battery to power the Arduino when calibrating and when collecting measurements supporting your research. The on-board voltage regulator has less uncertainty than the USB ports. Later, I will discuss noise in the measurement circuit.

Some readers will suggest; if we use the same laptop during calibration and when collecting the actual measurements, we have calibrated out the Vref errors. The basic rule of accuracy, you cannot calibrate accuracy. You must design for accuracy. The USB port voltage allowable range is a good example creating uncertainty in your measurements.

One last comment. It is always good idea to use of the one Arduino analog inputs to measure the battery voltage while running an experiment. A simply voltage divider circuit show in section 4.1 will work. Knowing the battery voltage helps insure the system is powered correctly. If battery drops too close to 5 volts, the measurements will be adversely affected while the system may still run and collect bad data.

Measuring the battery voltage might spark the idea of measuring the Vref and/or the 5V from the USB port. There is a problem, the ADC cannot directly measure its own Vref.

For example, we have a Uno powered by the USB cable from a PC. We could use two 50K ohm precision resistors to make a 1/2 voltage divider from the 5V to an analog input. With a perfect $5V_{USB}$ supply, the input to the ADC is 2.5V. As the $5V_{USB}$ is also the Vref to the ADC, the ADC reading in Cnts is:

$$ADC\ Cnts = Vi/(Vref/1024)$$
For our measurement of the USB supply voltage, $Vi = V_{usb}/2$ and $Vref = V_{usb}$
$$ADC = 1024/2 = 512 \textbf{ for all } \mathbf{V_{usb}} \textbf{ values}$$

As seen above, the ADC reading of Vref is independent of the actual value of the USB voltage powering the Arduino. We have no means of directly measuring the actual value of V_{usb}. Your data collection system doesn't have a direct means for knowing its own value of Vref.

Chapter 4: Interfacing Signals to the Arduino

From simple RC circuits to Instrumentation Amplifiers

In this section, I will be interfacing the Arduino analog input pins to the outside world. The first circuits are simply matching the signal to the 0 to 5V input of the Arduino ADC using passive resistors and capacitors. After that, active circuits using operational amplifiers and instrumentation amplifiers, are used to amplify the signal. The back of the book reference sheet "Oh Yea, I was Right" might be useful.

4.1 Simple Voltage Divider for Input Voltages > the Arduino Supply Voltage

The ADC of the Arduino Mega and Uno allow input analog voltage from 0 to 5V. The Arduino Due is only 0 to 3.3V. What if, we want to monitor the battery voltage in our car? The normal battery voltage is 12V and ~13.5-15V when being charged. Can we use a simple voltage divider circuit (two series resistors, see Figure 4.1) for reducing the battery voltage going to the ADC. The voltage divider can reduce the voltages from 0 to 15V to 0 to 5V.

Some ADCs have low input impedances so using two resistors as a voltage divider will introduce measurement error. For the Arduino ADC this is not a problem since it has very high input impedances. To verify the Arduino analog input impedance, I placed 5V through a 500K ohm resistor going into the A0 analog input of an Arduino Uno. No voltage drop was measured across the resistor. This means no current flow was measured going into the Arduino analog input pin. The same is true for the Due only using 3.0V and a 500K ohm resistor.

This very high impedance means the designer can assume the current going into the ADC pin is very near zero and will not significantly alter the measurement.

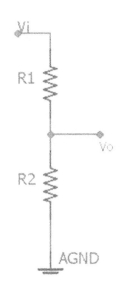

Figure 4.1 Voltage divider circuit

Therefore the measurement system designer can use a simple resistor voltage divider to increase the voltage being measured by the Arduino.

A voltage divider requires two resistors. In Figure 4.1, Vo is the voltage going to the Arduino ADC pin. Vo is a function of the two resistors and the input voltage, Vi as:

$$Vo = Vi*R2/(R1 + R2) = \text{Arduino ADC pin};$$

For example: If R1 = R2, then Vo is ½ * Vi. If you want to measure the battery voltage of our car, we might want to allow Vi to go as high as 20V. We need to pick values for R1 and R2 for a max Vi = 20V. For most voltage divider circuits, I generally use 10K to 100K ohm resistors. Low values waste current while high values invite noise into the signal (more on this in Chapter 9). Our max Vi = 20V, our max Vo = 5V and selecting R2 = 10K we need to solve for R1.

$$R1 = (Vi - Vo)*R2/Vo; R1 = 30K$$
Now knowing R1 and R2
$$Vo = Vi*10K/(10K + 30K) = 0.25*Vi$$

One final design consideration, a designer should always be aware of is the power being developed across each resistor and compare it to its specified power rating found in its data sheet. To complete a look at this simple voltage divider, let's calculate the max current and the resistor heating in watts.

Max current is at max Vi = 20V: Current, I = 20V/(R1 + R2) = 500µA
Power in Watts for each resistor is the max voltage across the resistor times the max current.
Watts R1 = VI = 15V*500µA or 7.5mW
Watts R2 = 5V*500µA or 2.0mW

A standard resistor size used by the author is rated for 1/8 Watts (125mW) or larger. Using 10K and 30K ohm resistors is not a problem. If 10 and 30 ohm resistors were used, the input voltage (Vi) to the Arduino would be exactly the same. However, the current draw on the battery will be high (1/2A) and heating of the resistors could be a problem. For this publication, assume all resistors are rated well above the needed value for use in our measurement circuits.

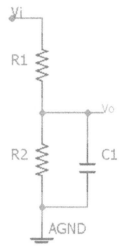

Using the equations above, the voltage divider shown in Figure 2.1 using 220K and 22K resistors can be verified. For the voltage ladder in Figure 2.2. A little more information is needed. Resistors in series add. So, for the max current calculation above, the current was the voltage divided by the sum of two resistors in series. To calculate the voltage ladder in Figure 2.2, we sum the resistors above and below as shown below. In the ladder circuit example, all resistors are the same value.

Voltage for B0: Vi = Vref*R/(R+R+R+R) = 0.25*Vref = 1.25V
Voltage for B1: Vi = Vref*(R+R)/(R+R+R+R) = 0.5*Vref = 2.5V
Voltage for B2: Vi = Vrer*(R+R+R)/(R+R+R+R) = 0.75*Vref = 3.75V

Figure 4.2 Voltage divider w filter

As a measurement designer, the reader may want to take the voltage divider a step further. When working with voltage sources greater than Arduino supply voltage, it is good to make two additional circuit additions, a filter capacitor and over-voltage protection diodes.

Starting with the filter capacitor, a capacitor is placed across R2 to ground in our voltage divider. A capacitance will reduce high frequencies signals and electrical noise passing into the Arduino ADC measurement.

4.1.1 Adding a Capacitor to the Voltage Divider

The capacitor, C1, shown in the voltage divider circuit of Figure 4.2 creates an RC filter with the resistors, R1 and R2. The capacitance impedance is Xc1 at any one frequency. At DC (0 Hz), the capacitance impedance Xc1 = ∞ so there isn't any change in our voltage divider. At high frequencies, the impedance falls where Xc1

<< R2. At frequencies approaching infinity, $Xc1 = 0$ shorting out R2 at those frequencies. So at very high frequencies, the voltage divider has Vo = 0V.

Still working with Figure 4.2, we have a simple RC filter problem. RC circuits are perhaps the most common circuits in all of electronics. So, let's solve it. To start with, it is normal to reference the RC circuit has having a 'pole'. A pole is created by the Xc1 value effecting Vo. In electrical engineering, the frequency point where Vo has dropped to 0.707*Vi is called the frequency cutoff or knee frequency. We will define the frequency cutoff as fc.

$$fc = 1/(2\pi RC)$$
Where R is a resistance value and C is a capacitance value in Farads

Obviously, in the fc equation above, C1 is our C value in the above equation. However, we have two circuit resistors, R1 & R2. For RC filters, the two resistors are seen as being 2 resistors in parallel, having only 1 value. Let R1||R2 stand for the resistance value of two resistors in parallel such that:

$$R1||R2 = (R1*R2)/(R1 + R2)$$

The result R1||R2 is always < either R1 or R2. For measuring up to 20V where R1 = 30K and R2 = 10K, R1||R2 = 7.5K ohms. We now have all the values for calculating fc except C1. Here, we can chose C1 based on the desired fc as:

$$fc = 1/(2\pi 7500 C1)$$
Solving for C1
$$C1 = 1/(2\pi 7500 fc)$$

Being honest, monitoring the battery voltage doesn't take a lot of bandwidth. So, this is a case of, a large value for C1 is good. Looking for a large capacitor with a +20V rating in the capacitor box provides a 47µF. Our fc is:

$$fc = 1/(2\pi(7500)47\mu) = 0.45Hz$$

Figure 4.3 shows the effect of our RC filter on signal frequencies. The 'X' shows the fc point. Now, is this a good fc? That depends on how we are going to use the information. If it is to monitor when the battery is being charged or not charged based on 12V or +13V, sure, I think this works. In fact, the Arduino monitoring the battery should be able to detect when, the vehicle is being started by a drop in battery voltage following by the vehicle charging the battery from the alternator. However, if the goal is to track the alternator's charging pulses in relationship of the engine RPMs, we have a problem. This low value for fc will filter out that part of the signal. Making this type of dynamic signal measurements will be the discussed later in Chapter 5 and 6.

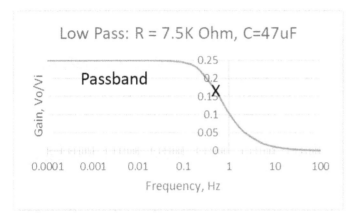

Figure 4.3 Effect of C1 = 47uF. This is a low pass filter called an RC filter.

For now, let's consider one of the principle purposes of the RC filter. One of the largest sources of electronic measurement noise is from the local power grid. In the USA, the power grid is 110 to 120V at a frequency of 60Hz. In Europe the grid is 220 to 240V at a frequency of 50Hz. Let's assume we want to filter out background 50 and 60Hz noise. So, we want fc to be at a fraction of the grid frequency. In the above graph, the fc was at 0.45Hz as marked by the 'X'. The frequencies below fc, are considered to be in the "Band Pass" zone for our RC filter. Those frequencies are passed through with little or no attenuation other than the resistor divider taking 20V down to 5V for our ADC.

However frequencies above fc are attenuated. The local power grid noise at 50Hz or 60Hz will be attenuated going into our Arduino. To calculate the attenuation at 60Hz, use the equation below.

$$Vo = Vi/\sqrt{(1 + (2\pi fRC)^2)}$$

Where f is our frequency, R is R1||R2, and C is C1

For V0/Vi at 60Hz, the attenuation is 0.00753. Assuming Vi = 1Vpp at 60Hz, the output Vo = 7.53mVpp. Vpp, is used to describe the amplitude of a sinewave as the voltage swings from peak to peak.

For illustration, let's ask for the 60Hz attenuation to be less than 1 bit of the 10bit Arduino ADC. We need an attenuation of 0.004883V or lower. For now, assume an fc at 0.05Hz or below will work. Recalculating fc for 0.05Hz while keeping the same capacitor is easier than finding a new capacitor. In general, it's normally easier to choose the capacitor as there are many more resistor options than capacitors.

$$fc = 1/(2\pi RC1)$$
$$\text{Solving for R}$$
$$R = 1/(2\pi fcC1)$$

For fc <= 0.05Hz and C1 = 47μF, R needs to be 65.725K ohms <u>or greater</u>. We also <u>require</u> a circuit gain of Vo/Vi = 0.25 for a 20V input (Vi) to be seen as 5V (Vo) at the ADC. We need to assume either R1 or R2 and solve for the missing resistor. Using R2, we know R2 must be larger than the parallel combination of R1 || R2 = 65.725K ohms and R1 = 3*R2. Assuming R2 equal to 100K ohms then R2 = 300K ohms. Both of these resistors are available as +/-0.1%, 25ppm/C. The parallel resistance is 75K ohms. Our new fc = 0.045Hz.

To complete the evaluation of the RC filter at 60Hz, calculated the RC response to a 1Vpp input gain, Vo/Vi by the equation below.

$$\text{Gain} = Vo/Vi = 1/(\sqrt{1 + (2\pi fRC)^2}) = 1/\sqrt{1 + (2(3.1416)60(75K)47\mu)^2} = 0.000752Vpp$$

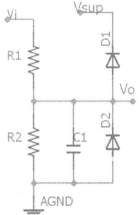

Looks like we over-shot. We wanted Vo/Vi at 60Hz to be less than 0.004883V and we are at 0.000752V. This illustrates a rule of thumb when working with RC filters. Taking the noise frequency and dividing by 100 (2 decades) for the fc value of our RC filter is a good place to start.

Now we have an RC to reduce local 60Hz noise. What if we want to measure voltage up to 20V but those voltages are not fixed by a battery? What if there is a chance the input voltage, Vi, could momentarily exceed 20V.

Figure 4.4 Voltage divider with RC filter and over voltage diodes

4.1.2 Adding Diodes to the Voltage Divider

Protecting the Arduino analog input pins with diodes is also a good idea. The Arduino runs off a low DC voltage, either 5V or 3.3V. If the input voltage to any pin exceeds the operating voltage of the Arduino, the Arduino can be fatally damaged. The analog input pins are more likely to be subjected to an over voltage condition than digital pins. The user is connecting analog pins to sensors or systems operating from power supply sources other than the Arduino supply pins. Some of these supply sources will be greater than the Arduino supply voltage. It is also true when working with more than 1 power supply (we have all done this) it is easy to forget to turn on the Arduino first. Thus placing sensor supply voltage and current on unpowered and defenseless Arduino analog input pins.

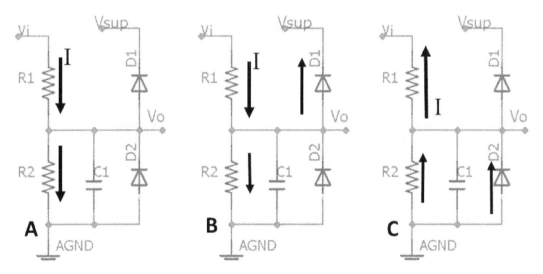

Figure 4.5 Operation of the protection diodes. 'I' is the current path. Case A. Normal operation. Case B. Vi is too large. Case C. Vi is a negative value.

As the reader may already know, diodes only pass current in 1 direction. Figure 4.4 is the same voltage divider shown in Figure 4.2 but now with two protection diodes, D1 and D2. Figure 4.5 has three potential input voltages Vi. For each case, the current created by Vi is shown as an arrow, I. For case A, the input voltage Vi is divided down such that Vo is between Arduino GND and Arduino Vsupply (Vsup). This is the normal operation where D1 and D2 are 'reversed' biased. Reversed biased diodes do not pass current. As such, they are not effecting the output voltage, Vo going to the Arduino input pin. The Arduino ADC will measure the correct Vo voltage.

In case B of Figure 4.5, Vi is too large. Vo is > Vsup. Now, Di diode is passing current, I. The increased current increases the voltage drop on R1. As such, D1 protects the input from an input voltage which is too high. In case C, if Vi is negative, Vo becomes negative, dropping below the Arduino ground. Diode D2 will now start passing current. D2 is protecting the input from voltages too low.

All diode current goes through R1. R1 is a large valued resistor which drops voltage protecting the diodes and the Arduino analog input. Naturally, there are limitations to any protection circuit. If the input voltage is higher than the resistor's wattage capability the protection circuit will be damaged and potentially the Arduino.

[**Tech Note:** All diodes require some voltage to pass current. I normally use "schottky" type diodes with a low voltage drop of 0.3-0.4V.]

In summary, a voltage divider allows our system to measure analog voltage greater than the Arduino supply voltage. Adding a capacitor can reduce noise. Adding protection diodes aid in protecting the Arduino from over or under voltages. This approach works for 0 – 5 volt inputs, but NOT adequate for input signals that swing both positive and negative (AC signals) which is common for many sensors. We have a second type of resistor circuit to deal with these types of signals.

4.2 Coupling ac Voltage Signals to the Arduino

The output voltage on many dynamic measurement sensors as accelerometers, geophones, and transformer coupled sensors among others are ac signals. When no signal is present, the output voltage is 0V. From 0V the sensor output can swing either positive or negative in voltage depending on the stimulus. These ac signals are a problem for the Arduino ADC. The Arduino ADC can only measure positive values. So, we must offset the incoming signal going to the Arduino with a DC voltage.

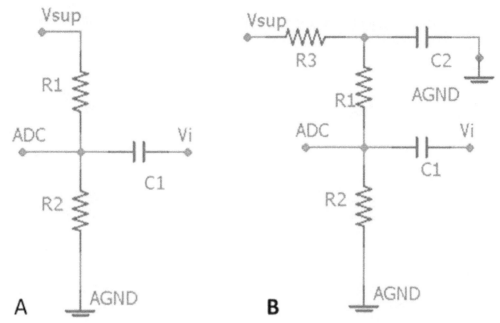

Figure 4.6 Two circuits for coupling ac signals to the Arduino. The input Vi is attached to the circuits through capacitor (C1). Circuit A is simply a voltage divider to center the ac signal on a DC voltage. Circuit B adds an RC filter to the Vsup voltage to reduce power supply noise.

Either of the circuits show in Figure 4.6 can fix this problem. Here, Vi is the sensor output voltage. The input voltage (Vi) to the ADC is shown. Both circuits "A" and "B" are voltage divider circuits using the Arduino supply voltage, Vsup. The DC voltage going to the ADC from circuit "A" is: DC voltage = Vsup*R2/(R1 + R2). In most cases, we will use R1 = R2, where the DC voltage = 0.5*Vsup. This voltage divider circuit can be used with any Arduino.

C1 in both circuits "A" and "B" allow the ac signal to pass through it while blocking the DC voltage from effecting our sensor output. This capacitor should be a non-polarized type such as a ceramic capacitor. The choice of dividing resistors and choice of capacitor affects the point at which the ac signals can easily pass. Just as in the low pass RC filter, this circuit has an fc for the high pass frequency. The fc for circuit "A" is shown in Figure 4.7.

High Pass fc = 1/(2πRC)
Where R = R1 || R2 = (R1*R2)/(R1+R2), if R1=R2 then R = R1/2. C is C1.

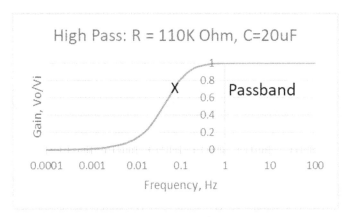

Figure 4.7 The high pass of the RC filter

Usually, we want to pass as much of the sensors ac signal as possible. The ac signal is attenuated at frequencies below fc. Using a large C1 capacitor and large R1, R2 resistors moves fc down in frequency. Lowing fc passes more ac signal to the Arduino analog input. Using R1=R2=220K ohm and C1 =20µF, the fc = 0.072Hz. Looking at the gain graph in Figure 4.7, frequencies below 0.072Hz (shown by the 'X') are greatly attenuated. Frequencies above fc have small to zero attenuation.

There is a slight problem with circuit "A". The supply voltages from the Arduino are naturally noisy, see section 9.2.1. The supply voltage is supplying power to all the digital circuits which are constantly switching logic levels. This noise is hardwired in to our ADC input through R1. Circuit "B", provides a low pass RC filter in series with R1 of our resistor divider. Its sole purpose is to remove power supply noise. So, the value of C2 doesn't need to be precise. We only need a large RC. This capacitor can be a polarized electrolytic type.

If we let (R1 + R3) = R2 we are back to a DC offset voltage equal to ½ the Arduino voltage. For example, let R2 = 220K, R1 = 200K and R3 = 20K ohms. Let C2 = 220uF. The RC low pass filter is a bit more complex to calculate. The R3 is parallel with R1+R2 as R3||(R1+R2) = 19.1K ohms. The RC with C2 is fc = 1/(2*π*19.1K*220µ) or ~0.038 Hz. Most of the time, simply assume R3||(R1+R2) = R3 is close enough for this type of application.

The effect of the large C2 does slightly change the fc for the Vi signal coming from C1. This is true because C2 is shorting out R3 at signal frequencies. However, R1||R2 is still true where R1 is 200K and R2 is still 220K.

$$R1 || R2 = (200K*220K)/(200K+220K) \text{ ohms} = {\sim}105K \text{ ohms}$$
$$fc \text{ for the input is } fc = 1/(2*π*105K*20µ) = 0.076Hz$$

Here the shift from fc =0.072 to 0.076Hz is minor. Most 20µF capacitors are +/-10% or more.

[**Tech Note:** If the fc value is critical, measuring the actual value of C1 is required. Using the known capacitor value allows the designer to choose the resistor values to match the fc needed.]

4.3 Current Loop (Constant Current) Sensor Interface

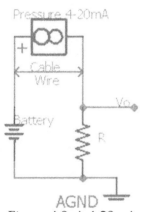

Figure 4.8 A 4-20mA, constant current pressure sensor circuit

There are a lot of sensors with internal active electronics for driving the analog output signal. Many use current flowing in a circuit (loop) to carry the signal. They offer two benefits to the user. Current loop sensors can operate over just two wires, a supply voltage and ground wire. Voltage output sensors normally require at least 3 wires: a supply voltage, a signal and a ground wire. Current loop sensors have yet another advantage, operation over long cables. I once ran a current loop sensor on 6KM (3.7Miles) of logging cable.

The way they transmit their information is very simple and they operate over a wide range of DC supply voltages. The current draw of the device is based on the sensors output. Simply supply enough voltage to operate the device and monitor the current to collect the sensor information. This type of sensor is often referenced as 2-20mA, 4-40mA or 4-20mA sensors. The first number is the nominal current needed for the device to operate. This base current is not a function of the sensor value. The larger number is the maximum current the device will draw. This upper current is the sensor's full scale output.

For example: A commercial pressure transducer is 4-20mA. It requires 10V to 40V DC to operate. Using the Arduino Due, we have a 12bit ADC with 0 to 3.3V input. Looking at the circuit in Figure 4.8, the pressure sensor is in a loop with its cable, a battery and a resistor. The battery has its negative terminal attached to the Arduino

GND. The resistor also has one terminal attached to the Arduino GND. Current flows from the battery through the cable, through the pressure sensor, back through the cable and finally through the resistor.

Current loop sensors have positive and return pins. So the voltage polarity must be correct when connecting the sensor. The Vo connection is attached to the Due analog input. This resistor convert's loop current to a voltage the Due can measure. The analog input voltage to the Due, Vo is calculated below:

$$Vo = I*R$$
Where I = sensor current.

This is the standard IR voltage drop equation. We want the sensor output at full scale to be ~3V. This gives use head room below the ADC upper rail of 3.3V. The maximum current from the sensor is 20mA. R is calculated by:

$$R = 3.0V/20mA = 150 \text{ ohms}$$

Good news, 150 ohms is a standard resistor value. Now, 20mA is a lot of current (a down side of current loop sensors). Once again it is important to consider the power being dissipated across the resistor. The calculated power dissipation for the resistor in watts is:

Power in watts for R = (maximum current)(maximum voltage) = 20mA*3V = 90mW

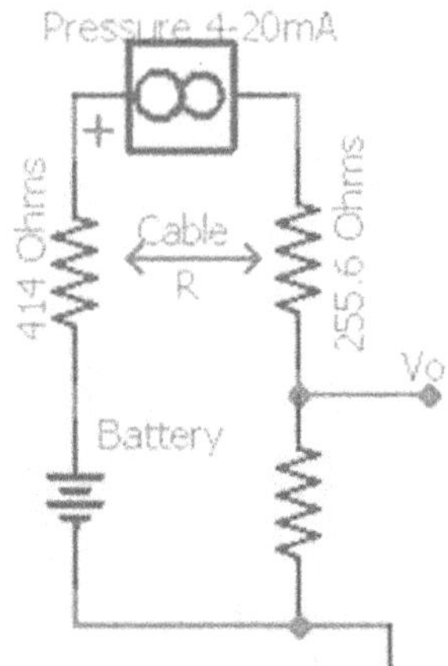

Now, ¼ watt resistors are common and inexpensive. However, I suggest using a ½ watt resistor or larger. At 90mW (max full scale sensor output) the ¼ watt resistor is going to heat up. At 0 pressure, the sensor output is only 12mW, less heating. Heating the resistor is dependent on the IR drop which is our pressure signal which is not desirable because resistor self-heating value will slightly change its resistance value. A drifting resistance will interfere with calibrating the system. Also, temperature cycling of the resistor will shorten its operating life. So, using an oversized resistor will allow for more surface area to reduce self-heating.

Figure 4.9 A 4-20mA, circuit with a very long 6 Km cable

One final and obvious comment, the resistor needs to have a low temperature coefficient (even the ½ watt). The resistor's temperature coefficient is the expected change in resistance due to the resistors temperature. A standard low cost resistor may have a temperature coefficient of +/-500 parts per million ohms (ppm). Low temperature coefficient resistors are +/-25ppm or less.

The only question left to answer is, "What is the battery voltage?" For the example pressure sensor, the minimum required sensor voltage is 10V. Our maximum signal voltage is 3V. Adding the voltages around the loop: we require a minimum 13V. However, this summation is missing the loops wire IR voltage drop. If the wires are only a few feet long and constructed of standard 18-24 AGW wire, we could just use 15V and not worry about the wire resistance.

For fun, let's consider using 6KM logging cable. Standard logging cable is two wires, a copper inner conduct and a large steel outer conductor also used for strength. Looking up a 1/8 inch OD logging cable from a well-known manufacturer, I find the resistance of the copper inner wire is 69 ohms per KM. The return outer steel wire is 42.6 ohms per KM. The total cable resistance is:

$$\text{Total Cable Resistance} = (69.0 + 42.6) * 6KM = 669.6 \text{ ohms}$$

Wow, that's a lot of wire resistance. Figure 4.9 shows the cable resistance as circuit resistors. Now, recalculate the minimum battery voltage at 20mA by summing all the RI voltage drops.

$$\text{Min Battery Voltage} = 669.6\text{ohm} * 20mA + 150*20mA + 10V = 26.4V$$

A minimum voltage of 26.4V means we need a 28-32V battery or bench power supply. This actually points out something nice about most current loop sensors, they are designed for a wide input voltage. In our example, the pressure sensor can handle up to a 40V supply voltage. That's really nice but we live in the real world. If we build this system with a 32V supply, the day will come when someone will connect the sensor directly up to the 32V supply because rolling out the 6KM cable is a pain. With an allowable 40V input, we're OK. This has actually happened with a larger 40mA system and ~100V supply to drive the cable. Yes, failing to connect with 6KM of cable, quickly blew out the sensor's electronics.

[**Tech Note:** When working with logging cables, the nominal resistance values given by cable manufacturers is at the wire standard 20°C. Once inside the well, the well temperatures will heat the cable. The cable resistance values increase with temperature requiring more supply voltage. I have published calculations of logging cable resistance as a function of well temperatures for hot geothermal wells.]

[**Tech Note:** For some reason, many people think the current loop transmitters are better or faster at driving 'electrically long' cables. This is not true. Any time the cable length is approaching ¼ of the shortest wavelength of the signal, there will be attenuation. This attenuation is independent of the type of signal driver.]

Going back to the short cable and the 15V battery. What if we only had a 12V battery? Could the circuit work? Yes, replace the 150 ohm resistor with a 10 ohm resistor. Now the Vo voltage across the resistor is only 0.2V max. Using a 12V battery provides 1.8V of operating room (I'll leave it to the reader to verify this). However, the resolution of the signal is very poor because it's only 6% of the ADC range. The fix is to amplify the signal with an operational amplifier.

4.4 The Operational Amplifier (Op-Amp)

The operational amplifier (Op-Amp) is a major building block of most analog electronics. If you have not used one before, don't be afraid. They are simple to use. Many come in an 8 pin dip IC package for plugging into a proto board. Finding op-amps working from 0V to 5V or 0V to 3.3V is not hard. However, always check the operating voltage range when buying them.

Although this book cannot show every type of op-amp circuit, there are really only a few "cookbook" circuits needed for making scientific measurements. There are a few important additional details on choosing the right op-amp other than the operating voltage. These will be covered later after the non-inverting and inverting op-amp circuits.

4.4.1 Non-Inverting Op-Amp Circuit

Figure 4.10 is a 'non-inverting' op-amp circuit. Our sensor output needing to be amplified is the Vi input to the amplifier's '+' pin. The Vo pin is the output of the amplifier. This would go to the next stage or perhaps directly to the Arduino analog input. All linear op-amp circuits must tie the amplifier Vo back to the '-' input pin. Here R1 is connecting those two pins together. R1 and R2 set the gain of the non-inverting op-amp circuit. The –Vsup and +Vsup pins are the power pins for the device. For most Arduino circuits, the –Vsup pin will be grounded. The +Vsup pin will be tied to the Arduino supply voltage, either 5 or 3.3V.

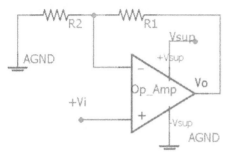

Figure 4.10 Non-inverting amplifier circuit

The gain of the non-inverting op-amp circuit is simply: Vo = +Vi*(1 + R1/R2). In the last section 4.3, we needed an amplifier for the 10 ohm resistor in the current loop circuit. The voltage output of the current loop was only 0.2V (20mA * 10 ohms). To increase the signal voltage to 3V for our Arduino Due requires a gain of 3v/0.2v or 15. Assuming R2 = 1000 ohms, we need an R1 = 14,000 ohms for the non-inverting op-amp circuit. Now, Vo = 0.2*(1 + 14K/1K) = 3.0V. That was easy.

My circuit only shows 5 pins, leaving 3 pins remaining on an 8 pin package. Often, manufacturers simply mark the extra pins NC for 'not connected'. Some manufactures will use these pins for offset voltage adjustment. More on the offset voltage adjustment pins later.

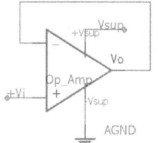

Figure 4.11 Analog buffer circuit

A small change to the non-inverting op-amp circuit is the buffer op-amp circuit, Figure 4.11. If we short out R1 = 0 ohms in Figure 4.10, then the non-inverting op-amp circuit has a gain of 1 where Vo = Vi. The op-amp input pins are very high impedance. The output impedance of the op-amp is very low. So the buffer circuit can take a signal from a high impedance sensor and drive a cable or other low impedance circuit.

4.4.2 The Inverting Op-Amp Circuit

The second op-amp circuit is the 'inverting' amplifier circuit. It is just as simple as the other op-amp circuits. It is not used as often in measurement circuits. The input signal is amplified and inverted. Few sensor signals need to be inverted.

See the inverting op-amp circuit in Figure 4.12. The input Vi is now at R2. The other end of R2 is connected to the '-' pin of the op-amp. The gain (Vo/Vi) is really easy, Vo = - Vi(R1/R2). So we would not use this to amplify the 0.2V current loop signal in the last section. The output of the amplifier would amplify the 0.2V to Vo = -3V. For most Arduino applications, the output of this amplifier will need to drive the ac circuit given in section 4.2. In the inverting op-amp circuit of figure 4.12, the voltage supply is both positive (Arduino voltage) and a negative supply voltage. The Arduino doesn't have a negative supply pin.

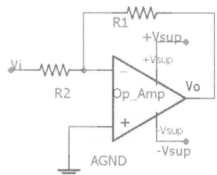

Figure 4.12 Inverting amplifier circuit

A simple example will aid in knowing when to use an inverting op-amp circuit. For example, many (older) accelerometer sensors have a 0V output when there isn't any acceleration. From the 0V level, the acceleration can be either positive for increasing acceleration (speeding up) or negative for deceleration (breaking). If our expected acceleration sensor output is +/- 0.2V, we need an amplifier and circuit to match the signal to our Arduino Mega.

We can use the ac offset circuit from section 4.2 to center our ac signal on a 2.5V DC. This allows the input to the ADC to swing +/- 2.5V. I suggest setting the amplifier's gain to swing the input signal +/-2V (0.5V to 4.5V). This avoids driving the ADC rail voltages.

$$\text{Gain} = -Vo/Vi = -R1/R2 = -2V/0.2V = -10$$
Where gain is the inverting op-amp circuit signal gain

Assuming an R2 value of 2.2K ohms, we can solve for R1.

$$R1 = (Vo/Vi)R2 = 22.0K \text{ ohms}$$
Where R1 and R2 are from Figure 4.6A

Because the gain is -10, we need to remember, our accelerometer signal needs to be inverted in the Arduino during processing or else the data will show deceleration when accelerating.

There is one more detail about the inverting op-amp circuit needs to be considered. The non-inverting op-amp circuit has a very high impedance for the incoming sensor signal. So, the sensor's driving impedance isn't a problem. The inverting op-amp input impedance is equal to R1. Our R1 is only 2.2K ohms. This can load down some sensor output voltages. Obviously, I could have chosen, R2 = 22K or 220K making R1 220K or 2.20M ohms. However, large resistances increase the noise floor of any circuit. Another solution for the low impedance is to use the buffer circuit of Figure 4.11 between the sensor output and the inverting amplifier input.

Time to look at some of the important parameters of the op-amp needed for our measurements.

4.4.3 Input Offset Voltage

The circuit designer will always evaluate the input offset voltage (often shorted to "offset voltage") of any amplifier. Understanding this parameter is critical for low frequency, high resolution sensor measurements such as temperature, strain, inclination and pressure among others. The input offset voltage is defined as the DC input voltage needed to drive the output voltage to zero volts for a unity gain circuit (also called a buffer circuit). See Figure 4.13.

For a low cost, general purpose op-amp the offset voltage can be +/-2mV to +/-5mV. Since the resolution of the Uno ADC is 4.883mV, the offset voltage appears to be is too small to cause a problem. However, the offset voltage is subject to amplification by the amplifier just like any input signal.

In the non-inverting op-amp gain example used a gain of 15 to increase the 0.2V input to 3.0V. If an op-amp with an offset voltage of +/-2mV was used, the offset error would be 15X the input offset voltage. The circuit offset error is +/- 30mV which is ~+/-6 cnts from the Uno ADC. For most scientific measurements this is unacceptable.

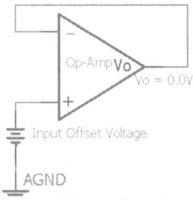

Figure 4.13 Input offset voltage

The cost of a precession (<+/-10µV) input offset voltage op-amp is easily justifiable. Now a gain of 15 is only +/-150µV.

Many op-amp manufacturers provide device pins identified as "offset" adjustment pins. By connecting resistors or a potentiometer to these pins, the user can zero the offset voltage of the amplifier. Sounds good, however I never use this option. My negative bias is for two reasons. First, the offset adjustment resistors can change the linear response of the amplifier. Second, the amplifier's temperature offset voltage drift increases with these additional resistors. My advice: Buy better low offset voltage amplifiers and use the calibration to correct for the DC offset as a function of measurement system. With most op-amps, the offset adjust pins are left unconnected.

4.4.4 Input Bias Current

Like the input offset voltage, input bias currents must drive the Vo = 0.0V. The good news, most modern operational amplifiers are designed with extremely high input impedances requiring input currents in 10pA to 10nA range. The TI LMP2231BM has 'typical' values of 10µV input offset voltage and a max input bias of 0.02pA.

There are some old op-amp designs (1970s) and some very fast (+100MHz) op-amps with input currents requiring matching input resistances to balance the offset voltage recreated by input bias currents. For 99.9% of electronic measurement systems, this issue is avoidable.

4.4.5 Rail-to-Rail

Rail-to-Rail (R-R) is used to describe the range of input voltage and output voltage of an amplifier. The rail references the amplifiers supply voltages. In general, op-amps will be running (single-ended) off the Arduino supply, 5V or 3.3V. We want R-R output amplifiers for driving signals the full range of the Arduino ADC of 0V to 5.0V or 0V to 3.3V for the Due.

To produce R-R output voltages, most amplifiers compromise the output drive current near the rails. The normal output impedance of an op-amp is <20Ω. However for some R-R output amplifiers, the impedance jumps to 10-20K within a few 0.1V of the high rail voltage. This reduces the measurement system performance near the Arduino supply voltage. Also, many R-R output drivers cannot drive a true 0V. The output might be limited to 40mV. So the term R-R output is not always 100% accurate.

As learned in the calibration of the Arduino Uno, it is always good to leave a little head room near the rails of the measurement system.

The R-R input of an op-amp means the input signal can range to either voltage supply rails. R-R input is also important but not always a requirement. Many op-amps lack the ability to respond to an input near their high supply rail, as 5V for the Uno or Mega. So, they don't have an R-R input but most measurement systems don't need to amplify such a large input signal. Many non R-R input op-amps allow for a 0V input without loss of performance.

4.5 Instrumentation Amplifiers

The instrumentation amplifier is a bit more complex than the op-amp. With a little understanding, the instrumentation amplifier can make sensitive electronic measurements look easy. When asked, how did you make that measurement? You can say, "I ran the signal through an *instrumentation amplifier*", the name itself sounds good.

The development of IC instrumentation amplifiers has reduced the effort to design scientific measurement systems. They offer a huge advantage over op-amps by easily removing common mode voltage from a signal before amplification and allowing for a virtual ground. The terms "common mode voltage" and "virtual ground" will be explained a little later.

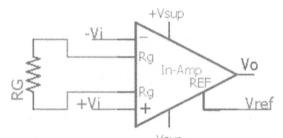

Figure 4.14 Basic instrumentation amplifier with gain resistor

There are two basic instrumentation amplifier designs. This publication will look at the most common one, the 3 amplifier (internal to the device) design with 8 pins. Most instrumentation amplifiers (in-amp) have the basic pin functions (names) as shown in Figure 4.14.

Like the operational amplifier, the instrumentation amplifier has a signal positive (+) and negative input (-) and output (Vo). There are additional Rg input pins and a REF input pin. The reader will need to check the data sheet on any in-amp for voltage supply requirements. However, most instrumentation amplifiers will run on −Vsup = GND and +Vsup = 5V or 3.3V. The AD623 from Analog Devices runs single and dual supply of +/-2.5V to +/-6V or 0-3V to 0-12V respectfully.

The Rg pins allow the circuit designer to set the gain of the in-amp with a simple resistor. The resistor values for setting gain vary for each instrumentation amplifier so check the data sheets. For the AD623 gain is set using the equation below.

$$G = 1 + (100K\Omega/Rg)$$

Where G is the circuit gain, G*(+Vin - -Vin), Rg is the external resistor value between pins R_g

Looking at the gain equation above, if Rg is an open circuit (no resistor) the gain is 1. For a Gain (G) of 20, we must solve for Rg. Solving for Rg in the equation above: Rg = 100KΩ/(G-1), or 5.263KΩ. We want to use a good quality resistor for Rg. My standard Rg resistor is +/-0.1% of its stated value with 25ppm/°C resistance change or better. For this example, there is a choice between two standard 0.1% values: 5.23KΩ and 5.36KΩ. Picking the 5.23KΩ, our nominal circuit gain is 20.12.

[**Tech Note:** the AD623 data sheet lists a max gain error of 0.35%. Although, not algebraically correct, an estimate of max gain error for the circuit sums the resistor error with instrumentation gain error. In this case, the total estimated gain error of ~0.45% or 20.12 +/- 0.09. This small gain error is the nominal room temperature error. Additional error is caused by temperature drift of both the instrumentation amplifier and Rg resistor. So, temperature calibration of the circuit may be needed. Even so, designing with instrumentation amplifiers is very easy.]

Now with a gain of 20.12, assume the –Vi pin is 1.25V and the +Vi pin is 1.3V. The common mode voltage is the common voltage on both pins. In this case, 1.25V. The differential voltage is 0.05V = 1.3V -1.25V. The gain only multiplies the differential voltage not the common mode voltage. So the output signal Vo is 1.006V = 0.05V*20.12. Again, if –Vi pin is 3.45V and +Vi pin is 3.58V, Vo is 20.12*(3.58 – 3.45)V = 2.616V. Removing the common mode voltage allows amplification of the differential voltage. The amplification of the differential voltage could easily lead to negative Vo values. This is where the REF pin of the instrumentation amplifier comes in to action.

The REF input pin allows the circuit designer to create a virtual ground. Vo is actually the sum of the amplified differential voltage and the voltage applied at the REF pin. Here is a good example where the REF pin can be very useful: Some sensor signals have negative input voltages where the –Vi pin has a larger value than the +Vi pin thus making Vo negative as G*(+Vi - -Vi) = -Vo. Since the Arduino ADC cannot work with negative voltage inputs we can use the REF pin on the instrumentation amplifier to give us an easy method to make sure Vo is never negative.

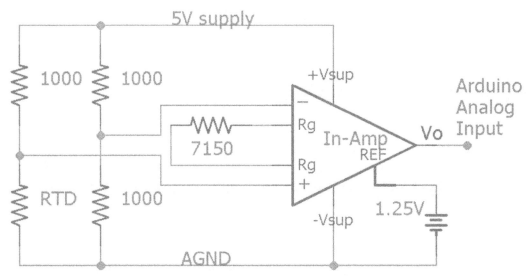

Figure 4.15 In-Amp (AD623) used to measure both positive and negative values of temperature

$$Vo = G*(+Vi - -Vi) + Vref$$
Where Vref is the voltage at the REF input pin

For example, let's assume we want to measure the ambient temperature to correct for temperature drift on a sensor. Ambient temperature is between -10°C and 40°C. Our temperature sensor is a 1000 ohm RTD. RTD stands for Resistive Temperature Device. The RTD is 1000 ohms at 0°C and changes with temperature. The resistance change is 3.85 ohms/°C. Using the AD623 and an Rg of 7.15K ohms, we have a nominal gain of 14.99. The in-amp circuit is shown in Figure 4.15.

The RTD temperature circuit output for 4 temperatures is provided in the RTD column of Table 4.1. If the REF pin is tied to ground, the instrumentation amplifiers output voltage (Vo) is equal to the column under G*(+Vin- -Vin). The -10°C output voltage is not usable with our Arduino. Now driving the REF input pin of the in-amp with a Vref = 1.25V, we have a virtual ground where 0°C from our temperature sensor circuit is now 1.25V. The -10C temperature Vo is a positive 0.514V. Now our software can use ADC readings above 1.25V as positive degrees Celsius and those below 1.25V as negative degrees Celsius.

Table 4.1 Values from RTD temperature circuit

Temp, C	RTD, Ohms	Input +Vi	Input -Vi	G*(+V - -V)	Vo
-10	961.5	2.451	2.5	-0.735	0.515
0	1000	2.5	2.5	0.000	1.25
20	1072	2.593	2.5	1.389	2.639
40	1154	2.679	2.5	2.679	3.929

[**Tech Note:** The inverting amplifier in Figure 4.12 can normally be replaced with an instrumentation amplifier circuit. The inverting op-amp circuit maybe required for faster frequency response as in-amps are generally slow.]

In Figure 4.15, the Vref was an idea 1.25V battery. Those are hard to find. So, we normally have to design a Vref. This bring up the next section.

4.5.1 Reference Voltage, Vref

All electronic measurement systems the ADC is dependent on the voltage reference. In the instrumentation amplifier circuit there is a REF input pin. The voltage reference (Vref) at the REF pin is critical for making valid measurements. Your measurement accuracy is no better than your REF pin input.

The Vref at the in-amp REF pin needs to be a source which can source or sink current without a change in voltage. (Caution: the AREF pin of the Arduino is not a good reference for your instrumentation amplifier.)

In the Figure 4.16, there are three circuits for creating Vref. Circuit A is simply a voltage divider from a regulated voltage. This is the poorest of the three. A small DC current into or out of the REF pin of the in-amp causes a change in Vref. This

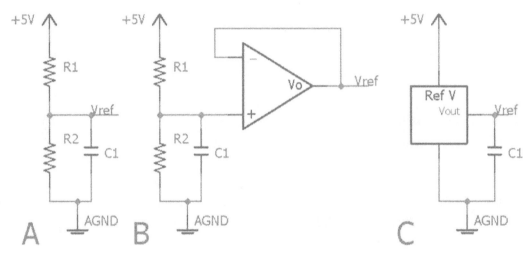

Figure 4.16 Three Vref designs. A is a simple voltage divider. B is improved over A with a buffer amp. C uses a voltage reference IC.

method is NOT recommended.

[**Tech Note:** A word of caution, many measurement systems require multiple instrumentation amplifiers and sharing the Vref from circuit A will cause cross coupling between these sensitive measurements. This form of cross coupling of sensor signals can cause false data correlations between sensors.]

Circuit B is a better choice than circuit A. Circuit B is using an operation amplifier in a buffer circuit (see Figure 4.11) with a very low input offset voltage. If a multi-turn adjustable resistor is placed between R3 and R4, then circuit B can be used to trim out offset voltage error. Many times there are spare op-amps from dual or quad op-amp packaging making this circuit inexpensive. The C1 of this circuit forms an RC filter for the 5V supply noise. The fc for this circuit is the same as the one in section 4.1.

[**Tech Note:** Circuit B shows a +5V DC input to the resistor divider. If this voltage is also the Vref used by the ADC, then any change in the ADC reference voltage also changes the virtual ground of the in-amp. This 'tracking' action is often beneficial.]

Circuit C is the best choice in most cases. The voltage reference IC was designed for this type of application. The addition of capacitance aids in reducing noise and handing fast input signals or noise transients. Check the manufacturer data sheet for good choices of Vref capacitance.

4.6 Measurement Circuit Temperature Drift

The input offset voltage and bias currents like all things in nature have a dependence on temperature. The values used in the previous sections for input offset voltage and bias current are manufacturer 'typical' values at or near room temperature. Good manufacturers also provide a temperature coefficient (V/°C) for input offset voltage and (pA/°C) bias current. Again, buying a low input offset voltage device provides improved performance over temperature.

[**Tech Note:** the manufacturer specified temperature drift is generally not a linear estimation but an envelope estimation of error over the devices operating temperature range. For operational amplifiers and instrumentation amplifiers this value can be in either positive or negative direction from the starting input offset voltage value. Most of the input offset voltage drift is created by a slight mismatch of the + transistor and – transistor input pair. This mismatch can be either + or – in magnitude and direction.]

For example, we want to design a +/-1lb accuracy for a 400lb scale. The scales sensor's output is 0.1V at 400lbs. So we need a gain of 50 to use the full range of our 5V ADC. The nominal signal to the Arduino ADC is: 5V/400lbs = 12.5mV per lb. The Arduino can resolve better than +/-1 lb.

Our amplifier has an input offset temperature dependence of +/- 0.05mV/°C. The user will be operating the scale outdoors with an expected temperature range of 0°C to +40°C. The estimated change in the amplifiers input offset voltage over the expected temperature range (40°C) can result in +/- 2.0mV error. Remember, the input offset voltage of the amplifier is always given at gain = 1. The actual circuit error is the gain times the input offset error. With an amplifier gain of 50, the voltage error is +/-0.1V or +/-8lbs. That's too much. So, we must work to correct for this error or buy a better 'low drift' operational amplifier as a chopper stabilized amplifier.

Chopper amplifiers are promoted as "Zero Drift". Anything manmade suffers changes with changing temperature however, these devices have very low temperature drift rates. The MCP6V31 chopper stabilized operational amplifier specifies an input offset voltage temperature drift rate of +/-50nV/°C. The resulting estimated error is +/- 0.008lbs over the operating temperature range.

[**Tech Note:** in reality, the standard process for measuring stain based weighting systems is to zero the scale just prior to each use, effectively removing temperature drift.]

This simple example looked only at the temperature drift of the operational amplifier. However, temperature drift of any measurement system is a result of all component drift including the sensor. In general, those components prior to signal amplification (including the amplifier itself) will have the greatest impact on measurement drift over temperature. After signal amplification, component drift is less of an issue.

If your sensor output requires a gain of 25 or more, the sensor, any resistors or capacitors and amplifiers need to have low temperature drift specifications. The calibration of the sensor and measurement system must be calibrated over the expected operational temperature range. To use the calibration over temperature, the temperature of the sensor and/or the amplifier needs to be measured as a secondary measurement. So, to correct for temperature of the scale just discussed, requires measuring the scales output but the temperature of the scale and perhaps the temperature of the signal amplifier. So, to make one sensor measurement over a wide temperature range often requires additional measurements.

If the temperature rise or fall of the electronics is too fast, it is not possible to calibrate the system. Individual components in the circuit will heat or cool at different rates with a fast change in ambient temperature. The circuit construction and packaging need to reduce the rate of heat entering or leaving the circuit. This normally means insulation and/or thermal mass. It has been my experience, 1°C/min is slow enough for compensation and 10°C/min is too fast.

Following amplification, the voltage reference and ADC normally have the greatest effect on measurement error created by changes in temperature. Some voltage reference ICs have a temperature pin. By monitoring the voltage at this pin, the designer can develop ADC temperature calibration curves. It is assumed, the voltage reverence is located close to the ADC on the circuit board. For the Arduino, a temperature sensor can be applied to the circuit board close to or on top of the microcontroller IC.

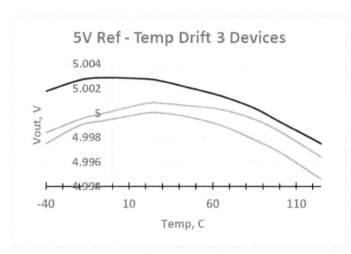

Figure 4.17 Typical output voltage response of a moderately priced voltage reference IC

I cannot show temperature effects for all types of devices. However, the voltage reference IC makes for a good example. The voltage reference is created by the IC designer working with the intrinsic properties of silicon. In short, the voltage reference manufacturer is working to cancel the temperature changes normal to silicon transistors using a bandgap reference circuit. Unfortunately, this cancelation can only be ideal at 1 temperature.

Naturally, most designers target the ideal performance at room temperature. The drift is generally a bell curve with a peak at room temperature. Temperature drift data from 3 test IC voltage references is shown Figure 4.17. This manufacturer specifies the voltage reference at room temp as 5.000V +/-6mV and voltage temperature drift of +/-25ppm/°C. The approximate peak of the bell curves is near room temperature, ~24°C.

[STORY: As a researcher in extreme environment electronics, I have championed two research projects to make a voltage reference from Silicon-Carbide, SiC. SiC is a semiconductor with a bandgap voltage about X2 that of silicon. As such, SiC devices have been proven to work >500°C. The expected temperature sensitivity of SiC is much less than Silicon. Therefore, it seems reasonable for a SiC voltage reference to outperform the silicon voltage references we have today.

There is a large market for voltage references with virtually no temperature drift. However, the design problem is difficult. Small errors in doping and layout along with mechanical stresses from packaging makes the manufacture of any good voltage reference difficult. In short, efforts to make a SiC voltage reference have not worked. I continue to have hope.]

4.7 DC Amplifier Circuit Examples

4.7.1. Example: Op-Amp Thermistor Measurement

To illustrate a near real world application, consider the following: We want to study porous rock fracturing as water inside the rock freezes. We need to track the rock temperature as the water slowly freezes. The temperature sensor will be attached to the rock under test and our Arduino measurement circuit will be an estimated 6 ft away. For small temperature changes thermistors work well, producing a larger signal than RTDs or thermocouples. The cable resistance is estimated to be <2 ohms.

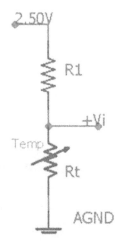

Figure 4.18 A simple thermistor sensor circuit

We want a temperature range of +/-5 °C and have on hand a 1.0K ohm thermistor with +/-0.1 °C accuracy. The 1.0K value is at 25°C. To measure a voltage across the thermistor requires a small current. By design, thermistors are very small. They can fit into small places. So they are sensitive to self-heating. We don't want to cause the thermistor to self-heat so we should keep the thermistor current low (about 50µA). Thermistor data sheets specify a maximum current and 50µA is well below most thermistor's rated maximum current.

For this design, we need a good reference voltage (2.5V) to power the sensor and a precision series resistor, (R1). Figure 4.18 shows R1, the thermistor (Rt) and the 2.5V sensor supply. The sensor's output voltage (+Vi) will go to our amplifier. The amplifier's Vo is going to our Uno ADC input with a 0 to 5V range. Figure 4.19 has the complete non-inverting op-amp circuit needed to increase our digital resolution. The amplifier circuit has a gain = 1 + R2/R3. Finally, as the temperature range is small and we are really focusing on hitting 0°C, it is reasonable to assume a straight line curve fit for the thermistor with a calibrated point at freezing, 0°C.

The manufacturer's data sheet for the 1.0K ohm thermistor sensor provides values for -5°C, 0°C and +5°C as 4,232Ω, 3,265Ω and 2,539Ω respectfully. This is a NTC (negative temperature coefficient) thermistor meaning the resistance increases with dropping temperature. Our amplifier is a non-inverting circuit design but our sensor voltage going to +Vi is increasing with falling temperature, so our Vo will decrease with increasing temperature.

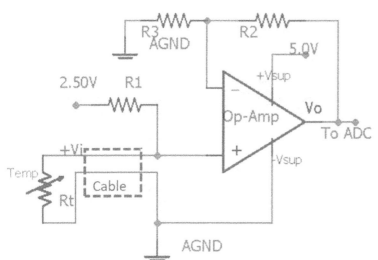

Figure 4.19 Non-inverting amplifier circuit for temperature with a thermistor

To get a sensor current about 50uA we want: 2.5V ÷ (R1+Thermistor) ≈ 50uA. At 0°C, thermistor resistance is 3,265 ohms so R1 is calculated to be 46,450 ohms. There are 46.4Kohm precision 0.1% resistors however a 49.9K ohm 0.1% resistor is much more common and will save on cost. So, the 49.9K value is used. We can calculate the +Vi input voltage using the voltage divider equation from section 4.1.

Our input (+Vi) voltage for the temperature range -5 to +5°C is 0.074403V (0.19545V@-5°C - 0.12105V@+5°C) from the two end point temperatures. Remember the Uno ADC is 0.004883 V/Cnt. Without amplification, the measurement resolution is 0.0074403V/°C ÷ 0.004883V/Cnt or 1.52Cnt/°C. This is poor resolution for a system operating very near 0°C. Let's see if we can do better with amplification.

To choose an amplifier gain assume a max input to the ADC to be 4.75V. This gives us a little head room from the ADC upper voltage rail. The amplifier needs to amplify the largest input voltage (0.19545V) to ~4.75V. Our needed gain (G) is 4.75V ÷ 0.19545 = 24.3 gain. This means, the Uno ADC reading will be maxed out at temperatures below -5°C.

The gain of a non-Inverting op-amp circuit is G = 1 + R2/R3 so we want R2/R3 = 23.3. Starting with R3 = 1.0KΩ using +/-0.1% resistors, we have a 23.2KΩ option for a nominal gain = 24.2. Our temperature range go into the Uno ADC:

$$\text{Max Vi at -5°C} = 0.19545V * 24.2 = 4.7298V$$
$$\text{Min Vi at 5°C} = 0.12105V * 24.2 = 2.9292V$$
$$\text{At 0C, Vi} = 0.1535 * 24.2 = 3.7155V$$
$$\text{The Vi range over +5 to -5°C} = 2.9292V - 4.7298V = -1.80V \text{ or } -0.180V/°C$$

The Uno ADC nominal calibration is 1 count = 0.004883V. Converting ADC counts to degrees Celsius we have:

$$\text{Each ADC count} = (0.004883V/Cnts)/(-0.1800V/°C) = -0.0271°C/Cnts$$
$$\text{At 0C the ADC reading} = 0.3.7155V/0.004883V/Cnts = 761Cnts$$
$$\text{Where the unit 'Cnts' is an ADC integer reading}$$

We can now convert ADC readings (Cnts) directly to degrees Celsius. We need to remove the 0°C integer value, 761 from the ADC reading and multiply the result by the slope -0.0271C/Cnts as below.

$$\text{Nominal Calibration for ADC to Temp, °C} = (ADC – 761) * -0.0271°C/Cnts$$

It's time to consider filtering the thermistor signal. The thermistor is a moderately high impedance sensor. The thermistor signal is going in to a high impedance Arduino analog input. Long wires and high impedances are a good combination for coupling electronic noise. We should place a simple RC filter close to the amplifiers input to filter out electronic noise. Figure 4-20 shows the placement of an RC filter in our circuit.

For this type of slow changing measurement, I normally look to filter out local outlet power noise, either 60Hz or 50Hz. I also want to have an fc for the RC at least 2 decades below the Nyquist frequency. More on Nyquist in section 5.3. If our Uno sample frequency is 10Hz, the Nyquist frequency is 5Hz. My suggested cutoff frequency for our RC is fc = 0.05Hz.

$$RC \text{ filter } fc = 1/(2\pi RC1)$$

Where R is the equivalent resistance looking back from C1 to the sensor with power supplies and capacitors shorted to AGRD. Remember, +Vi of the op-amp is an open circuit. The equivalent resistance is R4 + R1 || Rt. Realistically, R1>>Rt so assuming the equivalent resistance of R4 + Rt is good. Looking in our capacitor inventory, we find 100µF capacitors. Solving for R is now:

$$R = 1/(2\pi fcC1) = 1/(2\pi(0.05)100\mu) = 31.830K \text{ ohms}$$

The Rt value at 0°C is 3.265K ohms. The desired R4 is 28.6K ohms (31.83K-3.265K). Large value capacitors are normally polarized and must be placed in the circuit with that in mind. Large capacitors generally have a wide tolerance, for example: -10% and +50%. For most near DC temperature measurements this is not a problem.

However, if we needed a low pass RC filter with tighter tolerances, we could use a 10µ or smaller capacitor and adjust the R4 value accordingly. Remember, the input pin of the op-amp is near infinite so having R4 = 285K ohms is not a problem.

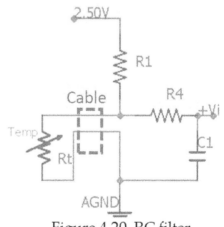

Figure 4.20 RC filter

[**Tech Note:** Our slow changing temperature signal is assumed to be <0.05Hz. This assumption and others in this example are valid for this application but are not true for all thermistor applications. The exponential response of NTC thermistors require greater effort when used over a wider temperature range. I would consider an RTD for wider temperature ranges.]

4.7.2 Example: In-Amp Thermistor Measurement

The op-amp example in section 4.7.1 can also be done using an instrumentation amplifier. There is a benefit with using an in-amp over an op-amp. The output of the op-amp circuit and the in-amp circuits are show Figure 4.21. The in-amp circuit will provide a better match to the 0 to 5V ADC. The op-amp circuit has to amplify both the signal and the common mode voltage. The common mode voltage is the Vi voltage at 5°C,

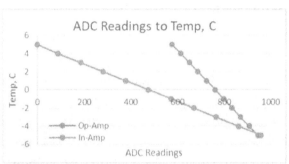

Figure 4.21 Comparing Op-Amp vs In-Amp circuits for ADC resolution

0.121V. As will be shown, the in-amp circuit removes the common mode voltage and then amplifies only the signal. The instrumentation amplifier circuit is shown in Figure 4.22.

Here the RC filter (R4 & C1) are shown. For this example, we will start with the same R1, thermistor (Rt), R4 and C1 values as used before in section 4.7.1. The temperature signal (Vi) is still going to the '+' input. Vo is still going to the Uno analog input pin. The only real difference is the '-' input of the instrumentation amplifier has 0.121V on it. This is the common mode value to remove from our temperature signal. The gain equation for the AD623 in-amp is as given below.

$$Vo = G*(+Vi - -Vi) + Vref$$
Where Vref is the voltage at the REF input pin

$$And\ G = 1 + 100K/R2$$

The instrumentation circuit has the REF pin grounded to AGND. Now, Vo = G*(+Vi – 0.121V). We need to solve for G. The maximum input signal is at -5°C. Assuming a maximum Vo = 4.75V keeps the signal from hitting the upper rail of the ADC. I also fudged the common mode voltage at –Vi slightly below the ideal of 0.121V to 0.117V. This provides some room near the lower rail of the ADC for the +5°C readings.

$$G = Vo/(\text{max signal} - \text{common mode}) = 4.75V/(0.19545V - 0.117V) = 63.8$$

Now solve for R2 as R2 = 100K/(G-1) = 1.592K ohms. A +/- 0.1% resistor value closest is 1.60K ohms. Now, using R2 = 1.60K ohms, the full Vo equation is:

$$Vo = 63.5*(+Vi - 0.117V) + 0V$$

The nominal equation for transforming ADC readings to degree Celsius can be

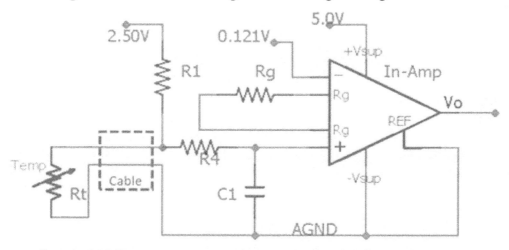

Figure 4.22 In-Amp measurement circuit for the thermistor circuit

calculated by working backwards from the Vo equation above. However, working backwards is a bit messy. Let's assume a two point curve fit to a straight line. The nominal Vo value at 0°C is 2.319V. At 0°C, the resulting ADC reading is 475 Cnts. The ADC reading very near 0 cnts is at +5°C. So, the slope is 5°C/457Cnt and the intercept is 5°C.

$$\text{Nominal Temp, °C} = ADC* -0.01053°C/Cnts + 5°C$$

The above equation is the nominal calibration, meaning, calibration by design. In the real world, this system, just like the op-amp version, needs to be calibrated with real known temperature inputs. For the proposed experiment, we really only need to calibrate the system to 0°C and validate the range. We could place the thermistor in a 0°C environment and adjust the common mode voltage at –Vi until the ADC was reading 475 Cnts. An example of an adjustable common mode voltage circuit is shown in Figure 4.23.

The Trim R should be a multi-turn potentiometer (remember to select a trim potentiometer with a low temperature coefficient). The combination R1 and trim resistor should cover a range of voltages near the 0.120V value at +5°C. With the thermistor at 0°C, adjust the Trim R until the Uno ADC consistently reads 475 Cnts. The C1 capacitor is a good idea assuming the 2.50V is clean. A nominal low cost capacitor of 0.22µF to 1.0µF should work.

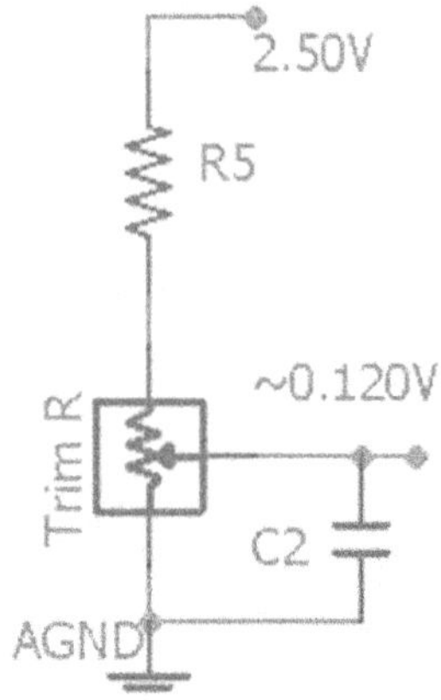

Figure 4.23

The common mode voltage applied to the negative pin of the in-amp, directly affects the measurement just as a Vref voltage applied to the in-amp REF pin. The real difference here is the negative input pin is only an input voltage, an open circuit. There is no need to sink or source current from the negative input pin. Remember, the Vref of the REF pin must sink and source current from the in-amp.

4.7.3 Wheatstone Bridge and In-Amp

The Wheatstone bridge has 4 resistive elements where one is a sensing element, see Figure 4.24. These bridge circuits are known for high resolution measurements and the in-amp is the ideal amplifier. No in-amp discussion would be complete without a discussion on the Wheatstone bridge.

Consider the benefits of the Wheatstone bridge for making scientific measurements. Looking at Figure 4.24, each resistor has a fix value while the sensor has known value across its sensor range. In the case of the 1000 ohm RTD temperature sensor, the RTD is 1000 ohms at 0°C. By choosing R1 = R2 and

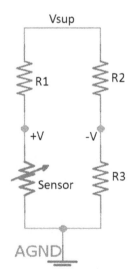

Figure 4.24
Bridge sensor
circuit

R3 = 1000 ohms, then the differential voltage from +V to –V is 0V at 0°C. This result is independent of Vsup. At 0°C, if Vsup is 2.50V or 2.54V or even 4.00V, the differential voltage across the bridge is 0V. This self-cancelling of supply voltage (noise) is great news.

Now consider all four elements are of the same construction and located together. Such that all four resistive elements are exposed to the same environmental conditions as temperature and humidity. They will all react in a similar fashion maintaining the Wheatstone bridge sensor performance over time. The self-cancelling of external environmental factors more great news.

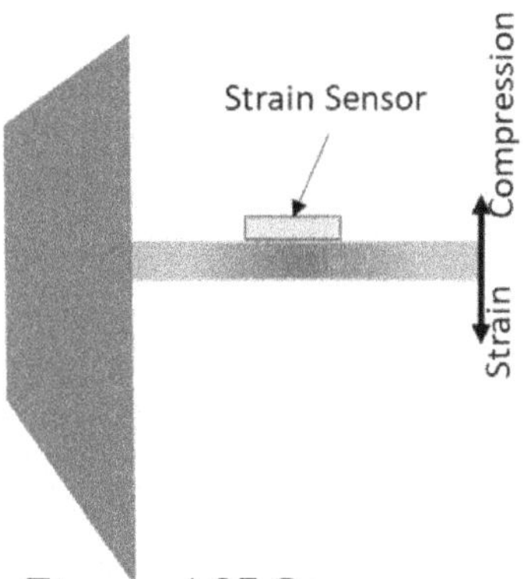

The in-amp is ideal because it only amplifies the differential voltage and the two analog inputs are very high impedance. The in-amp inputs don't load down the resistive bridge circuit. The in-amp doesn't affect the bridge's performance. This is more good news.

Bridge circuits and instrumentation amplifiers are used in 99.99% of all strain measurements. Most strain sensors are foil or silicon resistive sensors which change their resistance value based on strain or compression of the sensor. In turn, the strain sensor is tightly bonded to the surface of the material under test. Strain in the material results in strain in the sensor.

Caution, knowing how to bond strain sensors takes research and practice. Start with foil types and give yourself time to learn. Silicon strain sensor are more sensitive but they are difficult to work with. In either case, there are companies specializing in bonding strain sensors available for hire.

Let's look at how the strain sensor works inside the Wheatstone bridge. Consider, a strain sensor bonded to a metal rod as shown in Figure 4.25. Based on the bending of the rod, the strain sensor will increase resistance for strain and decrease

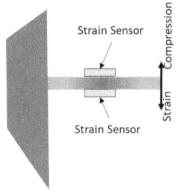

Figure 4.25 Sensor bonded to a metal rod

Figure 4.26 Half bridge circuit

in resistance with compression. This change is very small. Placing the strain gage in the bridge shown in Figure 4.24 will produce a very small differential signal in µVs. This configuration is called a quarter bridge strain gauge circuit.

Now, place a second strain sensor on the opposite side of the metal rod. When the first strain sensor sees strain or compression, the other one see compression or stain respectfully. Replacing R1 of Figure 4.24 with the second strain sensor doubles the bridge differential voltage. This is called a half-bridge strain circuit.

This concept can be extended with a second pair of stain sensors replacing R2 and R3 now called a full bridge circuit. Each side of the bridge (-V and +V) is driven in opposite directions when the rod is bending.

Strain sensor signals are small. They require significant amplification (G =100s) for use with the Arduino. The small signal is subject to both electronical noise and mechanical noise requiring filtering. Mechanical noise as room vibrations from a passing truck can be picked up as small unwanted vibrations in the signal. Figure 4.27 shows an in-amp circuit with an input RC filter.

The RC input filter is actually 2 resistors (R1 & R2) and 1 capacitor (C3). The circuit requires two resistors. In fact, we want the two wires coming from the bridge circuit to be the same length, normally twisted and shielded as discussed in section 9.2.2.1. Any difference in the signal

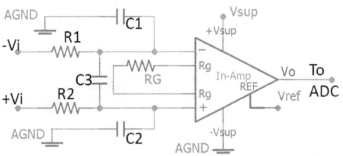

Figure 4.27 In-amp with full differential inputs

path of the differential signal can create error in the measurement. For example, electrical noise picked up by one signal wire and not the other is seen by the amplifier as a differential signal to be amplified.

So, keeping signal paths the same, R1 must equal R2 and C1 must equal C2 in Figure 4.27. C3 is part of the differential filter. Normally, C3 is much larger than C1 or C2. With a large C3, the differential RC filter is calculated as (R1+R2)*C3. The capacitors

C1 and C2 are used as common mode filters for high frequencies, as RF. (See section 9.3.3)

[**Tech Note:** Sensitive strain measurements have an offset voltage drift issue. This is not simply a problem with the electronics. As little as one degree of temperature change will create thermal expansion in the material. Thermal expansion is strain. You will need a means to correct for this offset voltage. I normally program the Arduino to take an average of readings before starting a test. This value is the zero strain value.]

4.8. Choosing Passive Components

When building interface circuits or analog filters, there is a need to use good passive components. Passive components are the resistors, capacitors and inductors. It's normal to start by first choosing the needed capacitors. The range of available capacitor values is much smaller than resistor values.

Most capacitors passing analog signals to the Arduino need to be non-polarized. This means they can have either a positive or negative voltage across the capacitor without any ill effects. Polarized capacitors can actually change their capacitance value based on the voltage polarity. They can also start leaking current and start destructive self-heating.

Multi-layer ceramic capacitors are normally non-polarized and inexpensive, making them a good choice for your Arduino interface circuits and filters. Of the ceramic types, look to use the NPO or COG types. They have the tightest temperature tolerance and they are commonly found in +/-1% to +/-5% capacitance ratings. Unfortunately, they are normally only found in values < 0.2µF. If needed, the ceramic XR7 types can be used with values up to 10µF. The XR7 types have less temperature stability and normally wider tolerances. The Y5U or Z5U types buy a lot of capacitance for the money but have poor temperature stability and +/-20% ratings (or higher) make them a poor choice if you're using them for sensor interface circuits.

Looking at the circuit in Figure 4.22, C1 has one end tied to ground. It is reasonable to use a polarized capacitor for C1 because the circuit is always a positive voltage. Large electrolytic capacitors are inexpensive and they offer a large range of values.

If large value capacitors are required for a filter, they are difficult to find with a reasonable tolerance. For small volume circuit builds, I suggest measuring the actual capacitance of a large capacitor and adjusting the circuit resistors as needed. Many hand held DMMs can measure capacitance.

Avoid tantalum capacitors in filter circuits. They offer a lot capacitance per volume. However, they are always polarized and sensitive to failure if exposed to even small over voltage conditions. If pushed by limited circuit area, use the tantalum with a voltage rating well above any potential voltage exposure. Also before powering up the system, double check that the tantalum capacitors are installed correctly. Tantalum capacitors can fail with an explosive detonation. (Technically, any energy storage device including batteries, inductors and capacitors can potentially explode. I personally have seen/heard more than one tantalum capacitor go bang.)

The resistors are normally 1% or better in measurement systems. The metal film and thin film resistors all work well. For voltage divider circuits or gain setting resistors used with amplifiers, I always use 0.1% with a 25ppm/C or better resistor. A resistor with 200 to 100ppm/C drift will drift enough to alter calibration even at typical room temperatures. My advice is to stay away from wire-wound resistors and potentiometers. Wire-wound resistors have an inductance component which will shift your filters response. Potentiometers are hugely convenient. With convenience comes three disadvantages; they are subject to temperature drift they are subject to vibration and they age poorly.

Finally, it is a good practice to place the any signal filter or interface circuit as close to the ADC as possible. For must Arduino users, this means keeping the wire running from the anti-aliasing filter output to the Arduino analog input pin, short.

4.9 Running On Batteries

One of the many benefit of the Arduinos are their multiple means for powering the circuit. For many readers working on measurement system designs, the power source of choice is a battery. Some discussion on using batteries is in order.

Unlike power converters or USB ports, batteries don't create electric noise to interfere with sensitive sensor measurements. However, batteries can have a higher internal resistance than electrical power devices. It is always best to keep battery wires short and to have a large valued capacitor (>22µF) near the circuits being powered from the battery. The large capacitor, helps source current to meet the demand of electronic devices.

Table 4.2 Nominal battery mAHr ratings

Alkaline Battery Size	Nominal mAHr Rating
D	13000
C	6000
AA	2400
AAA	1000
9V	500

The Arduino pin labeled "Vin" requires at least 7V and maximum of 12V. Batteries have a finite operating time based on current draw. Current consumption of the Arduino based measurement system is dependent on the program being run and any additional power needed by shields and sensors. I searched Arduino.cc for current consumption numbers but I did not find any answers. So, I conducted an unscientific, uncalibrated test to measure Arduino supply current. I used an amp meter and a 9V battery (constructed from 6 AA batteries). Running whatever program was last installed in each Arduino, here are my current measurements (rounded up). Uno measured at 40mA. The Mega was at 90mA. The Due was 100mA. With a current draw of 40 mA for the Uno, a set of 'AA' alkaline batteries (see Table 4.2) at 9 to 12V will run the system for an estimated 2.4AH/0.04A = 60 hrs.

The operating time is also dependent on the current draw with respect to the size of the cell. Although, the 9V (transistor radio battery) lists 500mAHr, this is true for current draws <15mA. The Uno will run from a 9V battery but the battery life will be significantly shorter than calculated.

In practice, I found building battery packs of 9V to 12V from "AA" batteries or larger works well.

[STORY: To emphasis the use of running instrumentation off of batteries, here is one of my favorite battery stories. Once, I was asked to measure the power pulse (V* I) of a manmade lightning bolt. The lightning bolt was needed to validate safety equipment protecting storage sites. In this case, the manmade lightning strike could carry several 1KA from a high voltage capacitor bank. We built a small portable battery operated system similar to the Arduino. It had an 8 bit microcontroller. We added fast flash ADCs and an external fast digital counter circuit to measure the pulse width and amplitude. To verify our measurements before going to the field, we had $250K worth of lab equipment with extremely fast oscilloscopes and timers in an equipment rack.

During the test to verify our electronics were working, the entire rack of lab equipment was wiped out by the lightning bolt EM pulse. Our little Arduino-like circuit made some measurements but were they correct? We worked at getting the lab equipment to work without success only to blow out a couple of $50K oscilloscopes.

I had an idea. I purchased a very large UPS (Uninterruptable Power Supply) which is basically a large battery backing up the wall power in case of a power outage. We powered on the lab equipment through the UPS. Just prior to firing the lightning bolt, we unplugged the UPS from the wall. The UPS started beeping its warning but the lab equipment continued to run from the UPS backup battery. As the reader has guessed, we validated our measurements. Lessons learned: even high end laboratory equipment can benefit from running under battery power and don't under estimate what you can do with an Arduino and a few additional circuits. Our low cost, little system was displacing $250K worth of lab test equipment.]

Chapter 5: Recording Dynamic Signals

Making the Arduino work for you

Up to this point, most of the focus has been on making measurements very near DC. Now, the focus will be on more active signals such as accelerometers for measuring vibration.

5.1 Digital Sampling with the Arduino

In order to understand using a digital sampling system for dynamic measurements, some basic ground rules and author nomenclature need to be defined. The basic Arduino sampling system is shown in Figure 5.1.

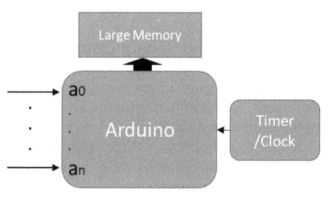

Here, dynamic measurements are being made too fast for human interpretation. So, all

Figure 5.1 Diagram of a basic digital sample system

sensor input is being saved to a large memory (as an SD card) in real time for later processing. All data collected must be associated with either time or position or both. Saved data must synchronized with other elements of the scientific test. Position is the location where the measurement was physically taken. Position examples are sensor readings based on an engine's throttle position or a logging tool's location deep inside an oil well. For our discussion, our dynamic measurements will be made based on time as suggested in Figure 5.1.

The easiest timer/clock to use is the Arduino internal timer. The Arduino has a counter running at 1.0 KHz tracking the number of milliseconds since the Arduino was turned on. This is a 32 bit counter or "unsigned long" integer. It can run for

~49 days before cycling back to 0mS. For recording long term tests (days, weeks, months), a real time clock (RTC) may be needed for greater accuracy. There are several RTC Arduino shields available at low costs and with example software. For this publication and most applications, the Arduino internal clock works well.

All sensor readings should be stored in their rawest form of information. Rawest form is the ADC value along with the time stamp. By convention, an ADC sensor reading is 'X(n)'. The 10th ADC value is X(9) as we started with X(0). A series of ADC sensor readings is: X(0), X(1), X(2).... X(n). For every 'n' measurement a time value is assigned. The time is a function of the sample frequency or fs.   If the sample frequency is 100Hz, the sample period is 1/fs or 0.01s. X(0) is defined as the ADC sample at time = 0s. X(1) is defined as the ADC sample at time = 0.01s and so on. X(n) is the ADC sample at n times 1/fs seconds.

5.1.1 Recording Sensor Data

The two tables in Figure 5.2 are using the saved data from an Arduino ADC measurement. The first two columns in each table was the actual Arduino ADC saved readings with a time stamp. Ten ADC readings were made at a sample rate of 10Hz or sample period 1/fs = 0.1S. Using the information saved in the first two columns the next two columns were created. These columns have a time stamp and calibrated voltage measurement.

Table A

n	ADC	Time, S	Output,V
0	512	0	2.500
1	632	0.1	3.088
2	707	0.2	3.451
3	707	0.3	3.451
4	632	0.4	3.088
5	512	0.5	2.500
6	392	0.6	1.912
7	317	0.7	1.549
8	317	0.8	1.549
9	392	0.9	1.912

=

Table B

Time, mS	ADC	Time, S	Output,V
205	512	0	2.500
305	632	0.1	3.088
405	707	0.2	3.451
505	707	0.3	3.451
605	632	0.4	3.088
705	512	0.5	2.500
805	392	0.6	1.912
905	317	0.7	1.549
1005	317	0.8	1.549
1105	392	0.9	1.912

Figure 5.2 Examples for saving measured values with a time stamp

To create the "Output, V" column, the ADC reading were processed using the system calibration which is the same for both tables, however, the "Time, S" columns were generated differently for each table shown below:

Table A: Time, S = $n*1/fs$;
Where $1/fs = 0.1s$
Table B: Time, S = (Time, mS – Start Time) / 100mS;
Where Start Time = 205 (time of the first reading) and 100mS = 0.1s = T

Although both tables of ADC readings are the same, Table B is generally the better way of saving your information because it is recording the actual time, 't' in milliseconds using the Arduino "millis()" function. It is also better because small errors in the sample period, '1/fs' can create large timing drift error given 1000s of readings being stored. However, writing the full "millis()" time value to memory for each set of readings takes more processor time than writing the 'n' sample counter.

Just a comment, it is easy to simply store only the ADC readings without any time stamp. The assumption is the time value can be added after the fact. However, this is dangerous, as data files can be corrupted omitting a section of readings. Another type of failure can occur when the recording system skips a reading periodically due to an interrupt or failed memory write. An expensive test run to collect scientific data with corrupted measurement data can be far worse than not running the experiment at all! Having the actual time tag is a small price to pay and provides a set (column) of expected values in our measurement system. In short, if the recorded timing information is correct, there is hope all the readings are also correct.

5.1.2 Sampling Data at a Constant Rate

In most cases, we want to sample our sensors at a constant sample rate. This is really critical when timing signal events or when using digital signal processing routines as provided in Chapter 7.

Microcontroller processors generally have a number of internal counter/timers useful for interfacing the controller to the outside world. The same is true for the Arduino microcontrollers. However, it appears to me the Arduino IDE has limited access to these functions. I assume it's because the Arduino IDE must work across a number of microcontrollers in the Arduino family. There are user generated libraries for handling internally generated timers/interrupts which can be added to the Arduino IDE and linked into your sketch program. These functions can optimize your data collection timing and optimize the use of limited processing time by running in the background of your program.

However, I have used user generate libraries in the past for different systems. They tend to lack continued support and become unusable over time. My suggestion, learn the methods used by these third parties well enough to create your own. For now, I will provide some constant (or close to constant) sample rates using three easy to understand methods supported in the general Arduino IDE. The methods are:

1. Loop timing using the millis() function
2. Loop timing using the delayMicroseconds() function
3. External clock generated IO input pin

5.1.2.1 Loop Timing Using the millis() Function

Time to look at an example of Arduino code with a fixed sample rate below 1KHz. I used a loop for collecting three analog inputs and saving the ADC measurements along with a time stamp to as SD card. The complete example sketch using an Arduino Mega called SD_Logger can be found in the appendix of Example Programs. For now, only a few key timing program sections will be discussed here.

First, global variables and constants are defined in the program.

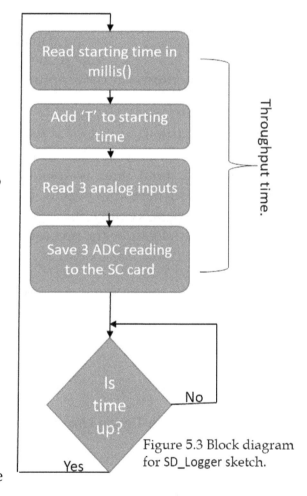

```
const int chipSelect = 53;  // for
the SD card on a Arduino Mega
unsigned int T = 30;        //
Sets the sample period T in milli-
seconds
unsigned long TimeS;        //
Recording the sample time stamp
unsigned long TimeP;        //
Add T to TimeS  sets TimeP time
to next sample
```

The 'unsigned long' variable is a 32 bit integer used to capture the Arduino 32 bit, millisecond timer in "TimeS". The Arduino millisecond timer starts at 0 counts when the Arduino boots up. It run continuously counting the milliseconds since power up. The counter can run for 2^{32} milliseconds, counting milliseconds for ~1200 hrs. The "T" variable is used to define the sample period. The sample period is the desired time between sets of ADC

Figure 5.3 Block diagram for SD_Logger sketch.

readings. The throughput is the time required making ADC readings and saving those readings. To take and save data at a constant rate, we want the throughput to be < the sample period. Figure 5.3 shows the block diagram for the SD_Logger sketch.

In the SD_Logger sketch, the period is set by adding 'T' to the starting time 'TimeS' just before reading and saving the ADC readings. Along with the ADC readings, the TimeS value is saved as the time stamp for that set of ADC readings. After reading the analog values and saving them, the microcontroller is delayed until the millis() timer is equal to the "TimeS + T". Below is the basic code for these functions.

TimeS = millis();
TimeP = TimeS + T;
[--- perform our data capture and save to the SD card ----]
while (millis()<TimeP){ };

In my SD_Logger sketch example, T = 30. So, after the set of 3 analog readings are made and saved to the SD card, the "while (millis()<TimeP)" statement holds up the Arduino until the internal timer is equal to TimeP. This is done by the Arduino continuously reading the millis() value. During this period the Arduino is doing nothing else and this processing time is lost. In more advanced programs, using the 'while' statement could allow the processor to be looking for an input from the user or an interrupt.

Under this structure, the program needs to perform the ADC readings, perform any calculations and save the readings with a time stamp before the time T is up. If the required data collection operation (called Throughput) takes too long, the T value needs to be increased.

5.1.2.2 Loop Timing Using the micros() Function

In the prior section a timing loop using the milli-second timer was limited to sample frequencies below 1KHz. So, I wanted to try the "micros()" function. The micros() is the µS counter inside the Arduino. This will allow for higher timing resolution and much shorter sample periods. Using the Arduino Due, I was able to get sample rates over 50KHz.

On the Arduino.cc web site, it states that the micros() counter has only a 4 count resolution. All counter values are in multiples of 4µS. I think this is true accept for the Due. The Due runs at 84MHz, ~5X faster than the Uno or Mega. The micros() function for the Due returns any integer value suggesting it has true micro-second resolution.

In the SRAM_LP sketch in Chapter 10, I used the same type of timing loop as in section 5.1.2.1 only now with "micros()" replacing "millis()". I also used the faster Due for this sketch. It worked very well. However, for some reason, over 1000s of data samples, the micro-second counter started returning a corrupt result while in fact, the micro second counter was still running correctly.

This issue may simply be operator error. However, it gave me a reason to try a different method.

I created a simple 'for' loop to count the number of samples to be stored in an SRAM, Static Random Access Memory. Like the SD card, the SRAM uses the SPI interface. The big difference is faster than the SD card. A block diagram of the timing loop is shown in Figure 5.4.

A full programming example is provided in Chapter 10 called the SRAM_Scope2. I will discuss some of the details here.

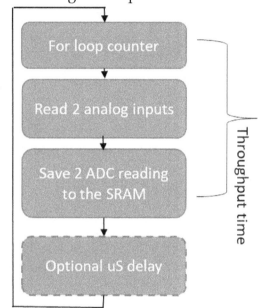

Figure 5.4 Block diagram for SRAM_Scope2 sketch

First, the main "void loop()" starts with declaring the variables used in the throughput loop. The throughput loop runs faster if the variables are local.

```
int Chan1 = 0;   //analog input A0
int Chan2 = 0;   //analog input A1
int samp = 125; //Max samp=32K
```

The SRAM memory can only hold ~65,000 16bit integers. For the program to store two analog ADC readings takes 2 integers so the number of samples is limited to samp = 32,500. The actual data collection code is below.

```
timeS = micros(); //read the starting time
for (int i = 1; i <= samp; i++) {
  Chan1 = analogRead(A0);
  Chan2 = analogRead(A1);
  SPI.transfer16(Chan1);
  SPI.transfer16(Chan2);
  delayMicroseconds(22);// optional delay
  } // end 'for' statement
// record time spent
timeF = micros();
unsigned long  timeT = timeF - timeS;
```

Looking at the code above, the variables timeS and timeF are all "unsigned long" meaning they are 32bit integers. The micros() counter is a unsigned long integer. The Arduino.cc web site reports some issues with using the micros() and delayMicroseconds() for periods longer than 16383µS. So, if you need longer periods use the millis() function.

Table 5.1 Due sample rates

The difference between the timeS and timeF is timeT and is the time required to perform the statements within the 'for' loop. The 'for' loop counts out the number of samples (samp). The two analog channels are read and saved to the SRAM. As shown within the code above, the optional delay is set to 22µS. With a 22µS delay, the estimated sample frequency is 25KHz. This value and others are shown in Table 5.1. These sample

fs in KHz	Delay
55.64	None
49.99	2
25	22
10	82
0.999	982

frequencies were estimated. Two timings were made for samp = 5,000 and 10,000. I then estimated period between samples as below.

$$\text{Sample Period} = (\text{timeT}(10000) - \text{timeT}(5000))/5000$$
Where timeT(n) is the total time in µS for taking and sampling n samples

The estimated, fs is simply 1/(sample period). The reason for taking the difference between 5000 and 10000 reading is to remove the small fixed delay in setting up the timing loop. I would not use this as a means for precision timing of events. I believe it works well enough for most digital sampling and signal processing routines.

This routine was used to make many of the Arduino high sample rate plots shown in this book. I used my scope to verify the timing measured by timeT. In truth, I believe the timing measured using timeT is comparable to the timing resolution than my scope.

This timing process was also used for the SRAM_Scope4 (can be downloaded from Onmeasurement.com) which measures and saves 4 analog inputs.

5.1.2.3 Loop Timing Using an External Clock

The most accurate means for a constant sample period is to use an external real time clock designed for high timing accuracy. Using the internal Arduino mS and µS counter/timers is really good for short timing durations. However, to clock for periods of hours, months and years, the go-to technology is the real time clock, RTC.

There are a number of RTC shields available and for very little cost. Most of them are based on the Maxim family of RTCs using the I²C interface. The I²C (also I2C) interface is a serial bit interface. It is slower than the SPI serial interface but it also requires only 2 wires for interfacing to a number of I²C devices on one bus. The I²C requires the Arduino to send out an address for the device being talked to. This addressing requires time. Also the I²C clock speed is slower than the SPI. The speed for the Maxim RTCs is 400KHz.

Once the RTC is set up, it can be used to externally trigger the Arduino measurement system to take a set of data readings. Most of the RTC shields offer a programmable clock pulse from the Maxim chip. The pin is normally labeled as "SQW" for square wave. The setting options for this pin are 1Hz, 1024Hz, 4096Hz and 8192Hz. Many RTC shields also have a 32.768KHz output. This square wave can be used to interrupt or to trigger the Arduino to record analog inputs.

Chapter 10 has a demonstration sketch program called "RTC_Rev5". The program includes a couple of features from the DS3232/DS3231 Maxim RTC. These RTCs allow reading the temperature of the RTC chip and turning on/off the output frequency (SQW pin). The sketch sets the SQW frequency to 4096 Hz using the "RTC.squareWave(4096)" statement.

Another common RTC shield is based on the Maxim DS1307. Like the DS3232 and DS3231, all track time from seconds, minutes, hours, days, months and years including leap year. They all offer a battery backup terminal to run the RTC from a backup battery should power fail. RTCs can provide system time for years to support field testing.

The advantage of the DS3232 and DS3231 devices is a temperature compensated crystal for greater long term accuracy. Just like to voltage drift of the voltage references shown in Figure 4.17 timing accuracy has a temperature sensitivity.

[STORY: Joe Henfling and I had a project to monitor an underground geothermal fluid reservoir over the course of a year. We tracked any change down to 0.1inch in the fluid table. The system was inside a California well. By chance, our system was in the well Dec 2004 when the magnitude 9.2 earthquake occurred in the Indian Ocean creating a huge tsunami. Sometime later, the Indian Ocean quake hit California after traveling around the world. The fluid reservoir peaked and fell as California rock formations vibrated. During that moment, the fluid level in the reservoir fell and did not recover. Meaning, an earthquake on the other side of the world had widened the fracture holding the geothermal fluid reservoir. Using our RTC timing, the USGS was able to say exactly, our reservoir was reacting to the Indian Ocean quake. This may have been the first time a reservoir fluid measurement captured evidence of a secondary earthquake as a result of a quake on the other side of the global.

Our 8 bit microcontroller running at ~0.1 the speed of today's Uno made the measurement. The news release on this work was publish in the world press over 30,000 times.]

5.2 Saving to an External Memory

The Arduino has very limited memory space for saving captured data. An external data storage device is needed. The most common Arduino external memory for data storage is the SD card. There are a large number of micro and full size SD card shields on the market. These shields work with the SPI interface. There are very good Arduino sketch program examples at www.arduino.cc and as part of the Arduino IDE.

In most electronic systems I have worked with, we used electronic memories soldered in place. These are more mechanically sound. Reliability is always an issue supporting expensive testing. Electronic memory as static RAM can record data at microcontroller speeds. However, RAM is expensive. An example using the Microchip, 23LC1024 SRAM (static random access memory) is provided. This example used the Due running at 84MHz.

5.2.1 Saving Data to the SD Card

I have tried a number of different SD card shields. They all worked when they were the sole connection to the SPI interface of my Arduino. There seems to be a problem with the SPI interface on the SD shields I tried. The SD cards run on 3.3V, while they must interface to 5V Arduino. For a device to share the SPI bus, the device input and output pins must go to high impedance when their select chip (SC) pin is high. The low cost SD shields I have tried, failed to go to high impedance when the SD card is not selected because of the 3.3V to 5V interface. For the discussion below, the SD card was the only device on the SPI bus. In example sketch program AD22B_DAC12B_Test in Chapter 10, I used the SD card on the normal SPI bus and created a separate SPI interface for the AD22B and DAC12B shields.

The Arduino SD library functions are good at creating and saving files in standard text format. As a text file, any number of fellow researchers can read in your test data. It is easy to send text data files out for review. The Microsoft Excel text file format is popular since it can be read directly into Excel.

To create a text file compatible with Excel starts with creating a file name *.csv. Each ADC reading or timer reading is saved as text and separated with commas and each set of readings must be terminated with a line return. The Arduino code sends a line return with each "filename.println()" command. The recorded values separated by commas will load into the Excel spread sheet as columns.

Table 5.2 Excel data file

Chan 0	Chan 1	Chan 2	Sample t
541	1023	850	28
541	1023	942	57
541	1023	982	87
541	1023	998	117
541	1023	1004	147
541	1023	1008	177
541	1023	1009	207
541	1023	1009	237
541	1023	1009	267
541	1023	1009	297
541	1023	1009	327

I created a file named "simlog.csv" and the data loaded into Microsoft Excel without a problem. Table 5.2 was a cut and paste from Excel. Here, the data from each analog reading is placed in the correct column. The column labels are created in the Arduino setup() section of the "SD_Logger" sketch in Chapter 10. Excel does a good job of converting text between the commas as either ASCII letters or Arduino values either integers or floating point values. The forth column is the 32 bit "long int" from the Arduino timer. Excel accepts these values also.

This is a versatile means for saving data.

Caution: It is common to ignore the first ADC readings after the Arduino powers up. In fact, the Arduino only powered up 28mS before saving the first set of readings shown in Table 5.2. Alternatively, a startup delay could be implemented to ensure the system is stable before making the first ADC readings. Life is not perfect and neither is the "SD_Logger" sketch. The standard Arduino interface to the SD card lacks a large enough buffer to write large amounts of continuous data to the SD card. As such, the standard Arduino SD code requires the SD card file to be opened and closed often. Opening and closing files causes delays. For our example with a sample period of 30mS, the measured time between each reading is plotted in Figure 5.5. Here, there are ~900 data readings with 8 taking longer than 30mS. One of which is 80ms. Now, for many applications, this is a minor 1% problem. For others, timing errors are

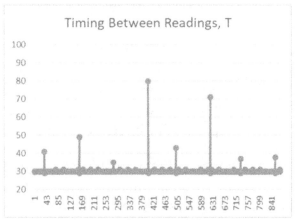

Figure 5.5 Plot of SD card throughput

unacceptable. For example, if using the digital filters presented in Chapter 7, the step change in voltage per sample period is a measure of frequency. The filter results depend on constant sample period to correctly filter your digital data.

Here are three potential solutions.

One is to increase the sample period to 100mS resulting in a sample frequency to 10 sps (down from 33.3 sps). This solution doesn't guarantee all samples taken will be exact to T = 0.1s but those cases in excess would be rare <<1%.

A second solution is to adjust for timing errors by interpolation between points, assuming a straight line curve fit between two points. This is a poor solution requiring writing a special purpose program to perform this function. This type of solution has been used to correct for noisy wireless data transmission problems.

The best solution used by hardware designers is to use SRAM ICs (Static Random Access Memory) for really fast data collection. Unlike flash memory technology, SRAM runs at Arduino speeds and with fixed write and read timings. However, large RAM memories are expensive when compared to SD cards. The next section is looking at an SRAM for fast ADC storage.

5.2.2 Saving to SRAM (Building an Arduino Scope)

SRAM memory is as fast as the Arduino. SRAM is electronic, volatile memory. Volatile means if the device losses power, the memory is lost. So, the storage is only temporary. Once the data is captured, it needs to be downloaded to a non-volatile memory as a SD card or computer hard drive.

I connected a 23LC1024 SRAM from Microchip to the SPI bus of a Due. This SRAM sells for <$3 USD. The device can be connected directly to the Arduino SPI bus. The SPI bus is available to the user by a 6 pin

Figure 5.6 Pinout and connections for the SRAM

header connection called the ICSP. The ICSP connector is located in the mid-section of the board. Pin 1 has a small white dot or the number 1 next to it. The connections to the 23LC1024 are shown in Figure 5.6.

This SRAM is a 1Mbit device. It's rated up to 20MHz SPI clock speed. The default SPI clock configuration for the Arduino Due is 4MHz. The program stores each ADC reading as a 16bit integer. At the 4MHz clock the time to store one ADC reading is ~4µS. I used the statement below to increase the Due SPI clock to 14MHz for a ~1.15µS storage time. The Due and Uno/Mega use different instructions.

```
SPI.setClockDivider(6); //Speed up Due SPI to 14MHz
SPI.setClockDivider(SPI_CLOCK-DIV2)//For UNO/Mega 8MHz
```

The SRAM can store up to ~65K, 16bit readings. In the example program SRAM_Scope2 sketch, I recorded two analog inputs for 125 samples each. The SRAM chip can hold 32,500K readings for each of the two analog inputs. However,

by collecting only 125 samples with each trigger, I could record 4 sets of readings using the Serial Plotter option under "Tools" in the Arduino IDE. The serial plotter in Arduino IDE (version 1.8.4) only plots a total of 500 sample points. By triggering and recording 125 each time, I create unique traces to illustrate circuit performance at 4 different input frequencies. I don't think you can do that on a standard oscilloscope.

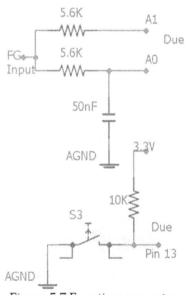

A function generator (FG in Figure 5.7) generated sinewaves of known frequency and constant peak to peak voltage. The Due A0 analog input had a low pass, RC filter in front of it. The Due A1 analog input had the straight FG signal. By paralleling the two signals, we can monitor the effect of the RC filter while testing the SRAM to store data at 25K samples per second.

Figure 5.7 Function generator (FG) interface to the Due with a switch to signal the start high speed capture.

I used the "micros()" function to track the Arduino's internal microsecond timer. I used the 'delayMicroseconds(2)' to delay the next ADC reads so that I could have consistent sample periods between readings. In the program example, the sample rate, fs is 25KHz. I also connected a push button for triggering a digital input to the Due. I used this to allow manual control when sampling should start.

I used the serial plotter option to display the 125 captured ADC readings on A0 and A1 inputs. For each set of 125, I changed the function generator frequency but not the amplitude. The serial plotter added each data set in series. This is an interesting option not found on standard oscilloscopes.

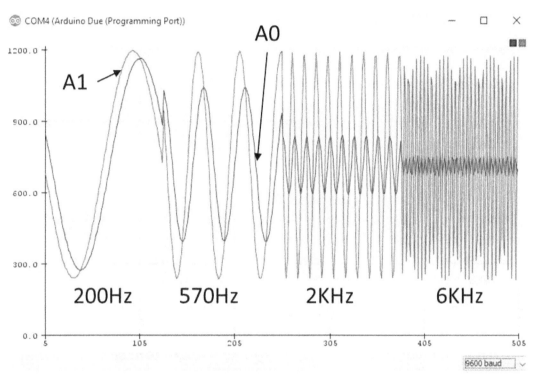

Figure 5.7 Due with SRAM demonstration of an RC filter

The first frequency was 200Hz and the final was 6KHz. The results are shown in Figure 5.7. The RC filter has it's -3dB pole near 570Hz. The second frequency was at 570Hz. The start of each data set of 125 was done by pushing a button so the starting points of each set are random.

 Looking at the results shown in Figure 5.7, it is clear that the A0 readings are subject to a low pass filter. At 200Hz there is little attenuation. There is a shift (delay) between A0 and A1 readings. This shift is normal for an RC filter approaching its cutoff frequency (fc). At 570Hz, A0 looks to be well attenuated from the A1 readings. Nearing 6KHz, the A0 readings are highly attenuated.

Later, in the digital filtering section, I used this same set up to demonstrate a 2 pole digital Butterworth low pass filter. The digital filter was also designed for -3dB at 570Hz.

5.2.3 Saving Your Data to the PC

To save data to the PC requires software on the PC. For this task, Joe Henfling (one of the reviewers of this publication) wrote a small program to communicate with the Arduino Uno. The PC program is called, "RTC_Software_Rev2.exe". It should work with Mega, Due and other Arduinos but it has not been tested. There are other more featured software programs out there for capturing Arduino data. However, Joe's is currently available at www.onmeasurement.com.

Everything said about saving data to the SD card file applies here. The measurement data should be saved with a time stamp. The saved file should have the name and version of the Arduino sketch along with the column headers. The data is saved in a text file named, "myData.csv". So following the text file outlined as in section 5.2.1, the file can be directly read by Microsoft Excel.

The PC software allows the Arduino to sync its RTC to the PC without reprogramming the Arduino. This means any PC can set the time because the Arduino IDE is not required. In fact, the Arduino IDE needs to be off so that the PC software can connect to the Arduino via the USB port.

Chapter 10, has a demonstration program using the Arduino Uno, DS3232 RTC and the PC software for capturing 4 Arduino analog inputs.

5.3 Nyquist Frequency and Aliasing

The Nyquist-Shannon sampling theorem tells us, a digital sampling system can represent the frequency information in an analog signal if the digital sampling is at least twice the highest frequency of the analog signal. The sampling theorem is often indirectly referenced by engineers as the Nyquist frequency, fn. Where fn is ½ of the sampling frequency, fs. The Nyquist frequency is a design requirement to prevent signal aliasing. Aliasing is a **major problem** of any sampling system and it's avoidable. To avoid aliasing, limit the bandwidth of the analog signal to frequencies below, fn.

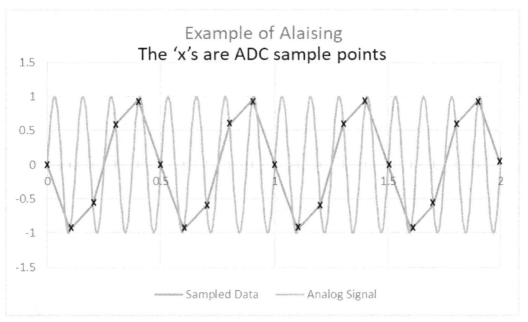

Figure 7.8 An example of aliasing

The Arduino ADC, like any electronic sampling system, is capable of signal aliasing. Most Arduino sketch examples of sensor measurements written in the public domain are susceptible to aliasing. As will be explained later, aliasing includes false measurements even at DC or 0Hz.

Aliasing occurs when there are frequencies in the continuous analog signal above the Nyquist frequency. An example aids in explaining aliasing: Let's consider a measurement system with fs = 10Hz or as 10sps. Our Nyquist frequency, fn = 5Hz. Assume our analog input signal is an 8Hz sinewave. Our sample system can only represent frequency information between 0Hz and 5Hz. The sample system will fold (or map) the 8Hz analog input into an aliased 2Hz signal. The erroneous 2Hz signal is an aliased signal. In Figure 7.8 "Example of Aliasing", the sample system makes an ADC reading every 0.1s of a continuous analog 8Hz sinewave. Each 0.1s measurement is indicated by the tick mark shown on the 8Hz sinewave. The ADC captures a signal voltage level but fails to capture the signal changes occurring between the 0.1s intervals. The sample system plots its captured points as a 2Hz sinewave connecting the tick marks.

In truth, a sample system will map an infinite number of frequencies into 2Hz. In the frequency folding diagram in Figure 5.9, we see how 8Hz maps into 2Hz but so does 12Hz, 18Hz and so on forever.

Note: 10Hz maps into 0Hz to create an alias DC voltage! The reader might feel this event is unlikely. However, in practice, this is a real occurrence. The sample frequency is a function of the Arduino internal clock. There could be other circuit functions tied to the Arduino clock which generate a small amount of noise on the ADC input signal. This correlated noise can create a DC error voltage.

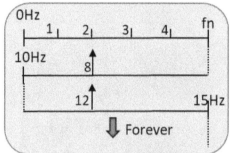

Figure 5.9 Frequencies above Nyquist fold into lower frequencies

The general solution to aliasing in a digital sampling system is to have an analog filter between the sensor and the ADC input. This analog filter is called the anti-aliasing filter (sometimes called the AA filter). The anti-aliasing filter must be an analog circuit since only an analog filter can bandwidth limit a continuous incoming signal.

[**Tech Note:** we cannot remove false aliased digital values with a digital filter or other digital process once they are sampled by the digital sampling system. Aliased frequencies simply become part of the measurement.]

[**Tech Note:** the Nyquist-Shannon sampling theorem is applied exactly the same for 2-D (images) or 3-D data. For each axis, the Nyquist frequency is calculated the same.]

In Figure 5.10, an Arduino Due was used to sample two incoming analog channels at 25KHz each. The Nyquist frequency is 12.5KHz. The Arduino IDE (version 1.6 and newer) option for the serial plotter was used to capture 166 samples per trigger. I used a function generator to drive the two inputs. I could change the frequency of the test signal before triggering the Due to take the next set of 166 samples.

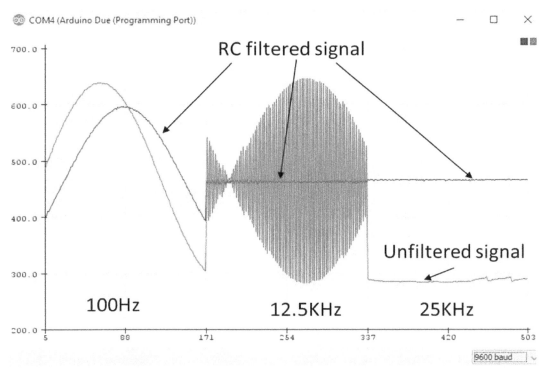

Figure 5.10 Example of aliasing DC voltage and using an AA filter

For the first 166 points, the input frequency was 100Hz. The unfiltered trace is directly from the function generator and the filtered trace is passing through an RC with an fc = 100Hz. The loss of signal amplitude through the RC filter can be seen in the 166 samples with an input at fc, 100Hz. The next input was at 12.5KHz, the Nyquist frequency. We are only getting 2 measurement points for each sinewave, the frequency is there but we lack fidelity in seeing the true signal amplitude. More on this topic when discussing "oversampling".

Armed with the above information, the third section of Figure 5.10 is the one I was wanting to show. With an input of 25KHz, the sampled output has a huge DC value! The RC filtered trace shows us the true DC value going through the RC filter. The unfiltered is a DC aliased reading! Also note, the little RC filter is a reasonable anti-aliasing filter. The signals from the RC are very close to zero at the Nyquist frequency and reject all higher frequencies. This illustrates the Nyquist theory and the value of a simple RC filter.

[**Tech Note:** The sample system requires the elimination of the Nyquist frequency (fn) and above from the incoming analog signal. This has a deeper meaning. Any sensor response to events faster than fn will also be eliminated, resulting in real world considerations. For example, the speed of a logging tool moving down a well measuring rock formations is limited by the digital sample rate. The logging tool's ability to detect a change in rock formation is the result of the digital sample rate AND the 'speed' of the tool moving down the well. The same is true for a rocket guidance system. The controllable speed of a rocket is a function of the sample rate of the navigation system.]

Conclusion for Nyquist Frequency and Aliasing

1. All digital sample systems are limited by the frequency content they can represent.
2. The Nyquist frequency is ½ the sample frequency and is the point at which high frequencies start aliasing as lower frequencies including DC.
3. Once aliasing has occurred, those frequencies appear as real data to the system.
4. The Nyquist frequency is NOT the rated bandwidth of the sample system. It is the minimum frequency for which the sample system needs protection from aliasing. We want zero Nyquist frequency content in the signal sampled by the ADC. If the measurement requires signal content "close to" or higher than the Nyquist frequency, the sample rate must be increased.
5. Having a measurement system meeting the requirements of the Nyquist Theory, may not meet the users expectations. We may need to consider oversampling.

[**Tech Note:** Some will notice the beat frequency in the 12.5KHz measurement in Figure 5.10. This is caused by a slight difference in the function generator's 12.5KHz and the Due's sampling frequency resulting in an beat frequency in the amplitude.]

5.3.1 Oversampling and Nyquist

Oversampling is a term often used as a marketing adjective. I believe it is often miss used. So, I wanted to reference a credible definition for oversampling. I opened my copy of the 1993 "The Electrical Engineering Handbook" by Editor-in-Chief Richard C. Dorf published by CRC Press. On page 782 (this *handbook* is over 2600 pages long) I found the following definition.

"Oversampling converters: A/D converters that sample frequencies at a rate much higher than the Nyquist frequency. Typical oversampling rates are 32 and 64 times the sampling rate that would be required with the Nyquist converters."

Here A/D converter is what I call the ADC. Also, another way to specify a Nyquist frequency is from the point of view of the analog signal. If the highest frequency in the analog signal is 100Hz, it can be said the signal's Nyquist frequency is 100Hz. So, our minimum sample frequency must be 200Hz. To have an oversampling rate of 32 requires a sample rate of 100Hz * 32 = 3200 samples per second (fs).

Let me provide my thinking on oversampling. First, "The Electrical Engineering Handbook" is defining oversampling correctly. However, their typical 32 and 64 times are optimistic for most systems and suggests a binary value. I don't know of any hardware or software reason for binary oversampling value. Oversampling can be any value greater than 1. They are looking at Nyquist as the highest frequency in the signal, not the ½ the sampling rate normally used in signal processing terms.

To me, it's a question of signal measurement fidelity. In Figure 5.10, the sinewave input at 12.5KHz was sampled at the Nyquist sample frequency value with unacceptable amplitude resolution. At frequencies approaching ½ the sample rate, no system has enough measurement fidelity to visually show what the signal really looks like. Let's assume we have a near perfect anti-aliasing filter where the input to the ADC at 12.5KHz is zero while leaving signals un-attenuated below 12.49KHz. We have satisfied the Nyquist sampling theory but the end user is unhappy with the measurement results approaching 12KHz.

In Figure 5.11, I have a function generator suppling a signal of 1 frequency. My Arduino has a sample rate of 25KHz with a Nyquist sample frequency of fn = 12.5KHz. The unfiltered input can be considered to have the perfect anti-aliasing filter. As Figure 5.10 has already shown the results of an input frequency of 12.5KHz (oversampling of 1) does not provide useful fidelity. In Figure 5.11, I have lower input frequencies with oversamples listed in the Table 5.4.

Table 5.4 Oversampling values

Sampling rate of 25KHz		
Input Freq.	Oversample	Samp/Cyc
625Hz	20X	40
1.25KHz	10X	20
2.5KHz	5X	10
4.17KHz	3X	6

In this case of the nearly perfect anti-aliasing filter and a customer needing to see signals with a frequency content approaching fn, my minimum suggested sample frequency is 10X the customers expectation or a minimum oversample of 5X. It is my impression, most people when looking at a sinewave sampled 10 times per cycle readily see a reasonable representation of that sinewave. In Figure 5.11, the 4.17KHz input is oversampled 3X and the sinewave looks like a triangle wave. As can be seen, an oversample of 10X is much better. An oversample of 20X is even better. The value of oversampling is subject to the law of diminishing returns on your sample speed investment.

Now, look at the RC filtered trace in Figure 5.11. Note, the signal coming through the RC filter is being attenuated at higher frequencies. It is fair to say, the poor RC anti-aliasing filter is reducing the input signal's content of low oversampled frequencies in our measurement.   (We have an under-oversample filter?) This slow frequency roll-off is the weakness of an RC filter as an anti-aliasing filter.   More on anti-aliasing filters will be discussed later.

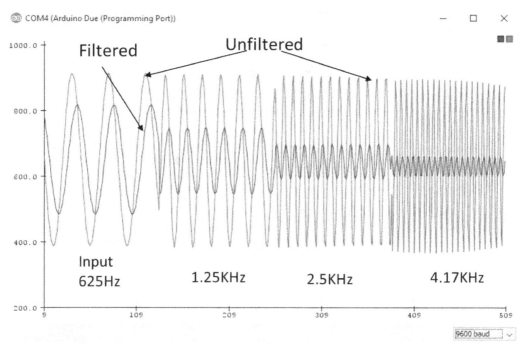

Figure 5.11 Examples of oversampling a sinewave of 1 frequency. The sample rate of the Arduino was 25KHz.

There is clearly an engineering trade-off to be considered here. If we have a high order (multi-pole) expensive anti-aliasing filter there is a greater need for higher oversampling. On the other hand, if a poor RC filter will work well enough as an anti-aliasing filter, why create a system with high oversampling?

When designing a digital sample system, there are several engineering trade-offs. With faster sampling comes a loss of ADC resolution. We have to trade ADC resolution (# bits) for speed if cost is considered. And cost is always considered. Also, faster sample rates requires more memory for storing the data. Faster sample rates requires faster measurement throughput. Throughput is the rate the system can make the measurements and store and/or display them. Faster throughput can greatly drive up system costs with faster processors and memory.

Hopefully, I have explained oversampling in a way easy to understand. In the real world, oversampling is a measure of "goodness". Marketing people may offer a more favorable sounding oversampling values.

5.4 Understanding Analog Signals

Any new project in electronic measurement starts with, "What does the signal look like?" Below is a list of questions an engineer should answer about any signal before beginning the design of the data collection system.

1. What is the expected peak to peak amplitude?
2. What bandwidth is needed to capture information?
3. What portion of the incoming signal contains the desired information?
4. What is the driving impedance of the sensor?

Often scientific experiments are a team effort. It is very likely no one person knows all the answers to those 4 questions. As the person responsible for capturing the electronic measurement data, you have to represent what is easy to do and what is not. Easy is using the Arduino (for example) and anything not easy requires more effort (i.e. project costs). Many researchers see instrumentation as an overhead expense to the project.

[STORY: I was asked to be a technical consultant on a $10 million dollar experiment to collect data in an environment so harsh it was expected to operate over the next 20 years unmanned. The system was asked to take about a dozen high resolution scientific measurements. This was a great project to advance science. However, the instrumentation budget was only allocated ~1.6% of the total project funding. That was an extreme case, however, knowing how to do a lot with a little in this business is always appreciated and normally a requirement. Hopefully, this book will aid the reader in that ambition.]

Going back to those 4 questions, normally a good instrumentation system starts with finding the correct sensors. Finding the best sensors is typically something the researchers already have a good handle on. Carefully looking over the specification sheets for those sensors is a good start toward answering those 4 questions. Remember, the data collection system doesn't add information to the sensor output, it can only make it easier to see the information. Good sensors are normally worth the expense.

Finally, time for the universal truth: if we can correctly predict the outcome, then we have little reason for doing the experiment. The true information in our data is in seeing what wasn't expected. Armed with this knowledge, the answers to the 4 questions can never truly be given. Let's look at questions 1 through 4 as engineers with calculators.

5.4.1 Signal Peak to Peak Amplitude?

Here, we estimate the maximum and minimum expected sensor response normally in terms of a voltage going to our Arduino ADC or other ADC shield attached to the Arduino. Some pressure sensors have low output voltage of 2mV per 1000psi and 0V for 0psi. So, if the experiment is expecting to see a maximum of 4000 psi, we expect to see only 8mVpp output. An amplifier will be needed to make this measurement. That amplifier need to have a low offset voltage as discussed in section 4.4.1. Or perhaps, the signal is as much as 80V, then the voltage divider discussed in section 4.1.

[**Tech Note:** if the amplitude of the sensor is higher than the maximum voltage the Arduino can measure, signal conditioning to reduce this voltage will be required. More on this later.]

5.4.2 Bandwidth?

Bandwidth is often the signal component least known. The researchers may only have a ballpark guess of the expected rate of expected change in the sensor and the length of an event pulse. For example, they might have an estimate of signal change and estimate of sensor output pulse width as shown in Figure 5.11.

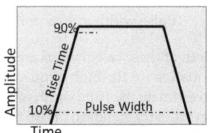

Figure 5.11 Estimating frequency content of an event pulse

There is a correlation between the fastest rise (or fall) time of a signal with the bandwidth of the signal. We can estimate the signals frequency content by measuring or estimating the fastest change in the signal. The bandwidth is important as it sets the minimum system sample frequency and Nyquist frequency of the anti-aliasing filter.

An example pulse in Figure 5.11 is an illustration to work with. To estimate the highest frequency of the signal start by measuring or estimating the rise time for the signal to move from 10% to 90% of the peak level. The rise time is in seconds. To estimate the highest frequency needed to be captured, use the following equation:

$$\text{High Freq} \approx 0.35/(\text{rise time between 10\% and 90\%})$$
The rise time between 10% and 90% in seconds results in frequency in Hz

I'm don't know who first developed the equation used to estimate high frequency content of a pulse. Many years ago when it was taught to me, the professor justified the 0.35 constant value using the rise time of a sinewave. The points at 10 and 90% are used because it is generally difficult to measure signal at 0 and 100%.

In some cases, the Arduino data collection system is not able to capture DC values as the DC value is a negative voltage or a high voltage. A few sensors as a Geiger Muller tube operate from +400C DC. We may need to estimate the lowest frequency needed for the high pass circuit. Start by estimating the pulse width at the 10% levels. My estimate of the lower frequency is roughly $1/(2.2*\text{pulse width})$, as shown in the equation below. Unlike the high frequency estimate, this one is my own. In the past, I would use the base width of a pulse as ½ of a sinewave. I found this to block too much of the pulse amplitude. Going to a multiple of 2.2 seems to help by including some of the pulse width lost at the 10% points. Both the estimates of high and low frequencies of a signal provide a place to start.

$$\text{Lower frequency} \approx 1/(2.2*\text{pulse width})$$
Pulse width at 10% points measured in seconds results in frequency in Hz

Both of these calculations are based on a sinewave approximations. The first equation for the high frequency is an industry standard. I have used it many times to estimate the bandwidth of a long transmission cable. The lower frequency is not an industry standard. I use these equations as a starting point if no better information exist.

To clarify, consider the following scenario: we are asked to digitally capture the shock pulse received by a skydiver opening a new type of parachute using bungee cords. (To be honest, I have no idea what the real shock pulse looks like. I like staying inside the plane.) Let's say the pulse is positive as the skydiver decelerates.

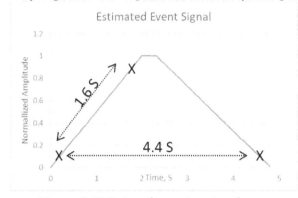

Figure 5.12 Points for estimating freq.

Accelerometers can be mounted on any of 3 axis and 2 polarities. Always keep good notes when assembling these things and everybody on the team should agree on axis labels.

Looking at Figure 5.12, the front edge of the shock is the fastest rise taking 2 seconds to reach the peak. Once at the peak acceleration, there is a flat spot or rounded peak as the system starts to reduce acceleration. The acceleration is starting to slow so I determined it had a slightly reduced slope taking 2.5s to return to zero. The faster rise time is the front edge so it will be used to set the highest frequency. The front edge rise time is 1.8s – 0.2s = 1.6s between 10% to 90% points. The estimated bandwidth to pass this signal is fc = 0.35/(rise time) = 0.219Hz. It might help to note, this calculation doesn't use signal amplitude. We are working with the rise time NOT the slope (V/s).

To capture event data (a pulse), we want a sample frequency at least 10X oversampling the estimated bandwidth frequency to provide reasonable fidelity. For this project, fs = 2.2Hz is a minimum.

The signal output of many accelerometers are bi-polar going both positive and negative voltages. To interface to the Arduino, requires passing the signal through a high pass filter section 4.2. We need to estimate a low frequency requirement to design the high pass filter. To calculate the lower frequency, I estimate the pulse width at the 10% points.

The lower end frequency is approximated = 1/(2.2* pulse width) = 1/(2.2*(4.6-0.2)) = 0.103 Hz. Our estimated system measurement minimum bandpass is from 0.103 to 0.219Hz. Our needed sample rate is 2.2Hz or faster. In the real world, there is no need to have a tight high pass tolerance. I would design for 0.02Hz or so. In the end, the team needs to discuss the bandwidth requirements and sampling rates to get buy-in.

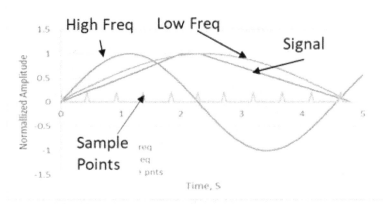

Figure 5.13 Over lay of estimated sinewaves.

So the reader can visually gage validity of the two frequency estimates, I created Figure 5.13. The figure shows the original signal used for estimation along with two sinewaves. The high frequency sinewave is more than one cycle in the plot. The low frequency is only ½ of a sinewave. The base line trace has a spike at each

point a 2.2Hz sample would be taken.

In truth, we have an estimate of an estimate. Nature rarely produces such uniform signals. Our Arduino could easily sample the acceleration sensor at 5Hz or higher for better fidelity. We could use an instrumentation amplifier for sampling down to DC to avoid the high pass filter. The goal of the above exercise was to help define a place to start.

5.4.3 What portion of the incoming signal contains the information?

There are several means for sensors to transmit information other than voltage or current amplitudes. Many high precision piezoelectric based sensors provide a changing frequency as their output signal. The Quartzdyne pressure transducer is one of the best in the oil industry. The output range is 10K-100KHz depending on the well pressure. This requires the Arduino to measure the frequency and convert frequency to pressure.

In actual practice using the Quartzdyne pressure transducer, we counted the number of pulses over a full second using a simple comparator circuit. This provides a high resolution measurement but at very slow sample rate. This is the same trade-off found with ADC resolution vs sample rate. Note: Quartzdyne does sell a digital version with a SPI interface.

Other sensor applications require timing of events or the phase relationship between signals to capture information. For example, earthquake seismic signals are captured with sensors positioned at different locations. Finding where the earthquake epicenter requires knowing the arrival times and the phase of the incoming seismic signals for each sensor location. In this case, the analog and digital filters need to be well known and calibrated.

Another type of phase problem is the sampling phase of our system. The Arduino internal ADC can only measure one input at a time. Sometimes this is simply not acceptable. For example, all 3 axis orientation sensors are sampled simultaneously when measuring the heading of a rocket. The calculation of orientation is dependent on the position of each axis with respect to the other two axis. In a case like this, there are ADCs with simultaneous conversions for 3 to 8 channels. Many of these have SPI interfaces which are easy to interface with using the Arduino. Another means for simultaneous ADC conversions is by tying the "start" conversion lines together of three ADCs. The AD22B ADC shield discussed in this book could be used this way. After the conversions are completed, each AD22B shield is then read independently using the SPI interface.

5.4.4 What is the driving impedance?

Most Arduino users will not worry about the driving impedance. The Arduino's analog inputs are much higher impedance than most sensors output impedance. The amplifier circuits and anti-aliasing circuits presented in this book also have very high input impedances. You will remember, there is one exception: the inverting amplifier circuit has a low impedance.

There are cases when the sensor's driving impedance must be factored into the measurement. For example, assume we have a sensor with an output voltage up to 15V. Of the sensor's output impedance of 960 ohms, and is located 200ft away on a cable whose resistance is 15 ohms for each wire (signal and return) we have the circuit shown in Figure 5.14. We will use the voltage divider circuit from section 4.1.

The R1 = 30K and R2 = 10K are the same resistors from section 4.1. The maximum signal out of the sensor is 15V. The maximum current in the loop is the sum of the resistances divided by the maximum signal voltage.

Max Current = 15V/(Rs+2Rc+R1+R2) = 15V/(960+30+30K+10K) = 365.94µA
Where Rc is wire resistance, Rs is sensor internal resistance

Max V0 to the Arduino analog input is Max current * R2

Max Vo = (Max current)*R2 = 3.6594V

If we had not included the sensor internal impedance and the cable resistance, we would have calculated Vo with Vi = 15V since Vo = 15R2/(R1 + R2) = 3.75V. That's a difference of 3.75 – 3.66 = 90mV from the real value. In terms of the Uno ADC, 90mV is 18 counts of error.

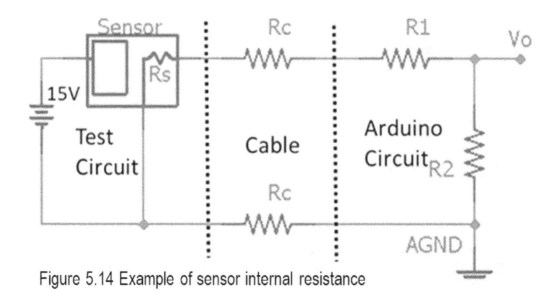

Figure 5.14 Example of sensor internal resistance

Chapter 6 Analog Anti-Aliasing Filters

Making professional measurements

Anyone conducting scientific measurements will benefit from a basic understanding of analog filters. The anti-aliasing filter is an analog filter needed to professionally capture dynamic signals. This section takes the reader from being good at making measurements with the Arduino to a professional data collection designer using the Arduino.

6.1 Active Analog Filters

Active analog filters are op-amp based analog signal filters. These filters remove unwanted frequencies contained within the analog signal. The use of op-amps allows for the easy construction of multi-pole filter circuits. The more poles, the higher the filter order and the more effective the filter. The RC filter discussed in prior sections is only 1 pole. The benefit of a 3 pole filter over a 1 pole filter is well worth understanding and will be outlined later.

Computer Aided Design (CAD) programs are used to design active analog filters. These programs are easy to use and can be found on the web often for free. I will suggest how to best use CAD tools and where to find some for free or a very low cost. I will show how to modify the CAD designs for your purposes. I will also show how to design your own simple active filters using only a calculator.

The nice thing about CAD filter tools, they allow the user to play around and design all types of complex analog filters. Playing around is the easiest form of self-education. Below is a partial list of some CAD Filter Design sites:

Analog Filter Wizard by Analog Devices at:
http://www.analog.com/designtools/en/filterwizard/
WEBENCH® Design Center by Texas Instruments at:
http://www.ti.com/design-tools/overview.html
eDesignSuite STMicroelectronics at:
http://www.st.com/content/st_com/en/support/resources/edesign.html
eSketch or Filter Wiz by SchematicA at:
http://www.schematica.com/index.html

SchematicA has two downloadable programs, Filter Wiz and eSketch. Filter Wiz lite is free and it will design your analog active filter with a number of options. I found one good option I really liked. Filter Wiz lite can transfer the filter design to eSketch. The eSketch software was $22 at the time I purchased it. eSketch is a general purpose circuit design tool for calculating the frequency response of your circuit. The benefit of this program, is you can design an active multi-pole filter and add the other interface circuits from Chapter 4. This allows the reader to simulate the circuit from the sensor to your Arduino. I did find a few simulation problems with inductors (not commonly used) but for what I paid, I found this is a fun tool.

Working with CAD programs is a bit difficult at first. The CAD programs start by asking for what type of filter do you want, low pass, high pass, band pass or other. It will also ask for the desired filter circuit topology as Butterworth, Chebyshev, Elliptic or Bessel. Hopefully, I can remove some of the terminology blindness created by CAD filter design programs for first time users.

There are two basic design paths used by CAD programs depending on user inputs. Consider a low pass filter design. The user can supply the order (same as # of poles) of the filter and the frequency cutoff, fc, as path "A" of Figure 6.1. **OR** the user can enter the frequency cutoff along with the required stopband frequency (fs) with required attenuation, as path "B" of Figure 6.1.

With path "B", the program will calculate the required "order" of the filter to achieve the required attenuation from fc to fs. The closer fs is to fc or the higher the attenuation (normally in dB), the higher the number of required poles (order).

I normally ignore the attenuation entries and go with the # of poles and my desired fc. I do this because I generally have a good idea of how many poles I want (or can afford). The more poles the more circuit complexity. For a Butterworth low pass active analog filter: 2 poles takes 1 op-amp, 2 resistors and 2 capacitors, 3 poles takes 1 op-amp, 3 resistors and 3 capacitors, 4 poles takes 2 op-amps, 4 resistors and 4 capacitors and so on. For most Arduino user working from a proto-type board and limited budgets a 4 pole active filter is a lot of work. So, I normally stop at 3 poles. In the following sections, I will provide a means to approximate the attenuation for the Butterworth filters given the number of poles.

Working with the CAD program using path B, requires passband and stop band attenuation values is good if you know your required attenuation. Section 5.4.2 can give you some ideas toward knowing these numbers. In this case, the CAD program will generate the circuit with a high enough order whether 1 pole (RC) or 10 poles (5 op-amps, 10 resistors and 10 capacitors) to achieve your required attenuation.

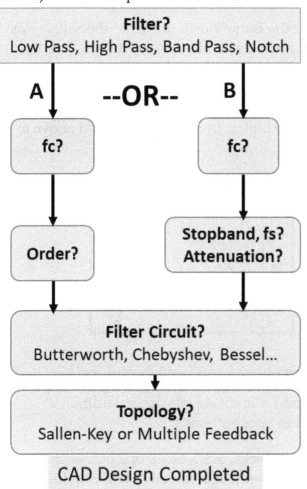

Figure 6.1 CAD analog filter design

Attenuation is normally in dB. If you're not familiar with dB, I cover that in an upcoming section.

The most popular active analog filter is the Butterworth. The Butterworth filter has a flat pass band and a reasonable roll-off for frequencies above the filters cutoff frequency, fc. Perhaps the second most popular is the Bessel filter. The Bessel lacks the high roll-off of other filters but for applications where signal phase or group delay is critical (as seismic monitoring, vibration of an aircraft wing or audio equipment) the Bessel filter is the only acceptable solution. More on Bessel filters in section 6.4.

I predict, ~90% of Arduino users will want the Butterworth filter and the Sallen-Key circuit topology. The Sallen-Key circuit is a non-inverting op-amp design. The multiple feedback option is an inverting op-amp design. With the right op-amp, Sallen-Key filters can be powered directly from the Arduino voltage supply. The Sallen-Key input impedance is very high so no worries about loading down the sensor. At DC, 1 volt in is 1 volt out, only the higher frequencies near and above fc are attenuated.

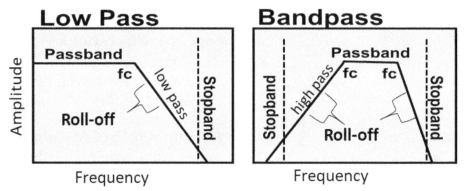

Figure 6.2 Diagrams for referencing filter terms used the author

[**Tech Note:** The Sallen-Key topology can add a small signal gain in addition to filtering the signal. Gain will be discussed in later sections.]

The CAD programs build up active filters as blocks. Each block of 2 poles has an op-amp. Each block can drive the next block without loss of signal. I will provide some notes on these circuits followed by some basic filter circuits anyone can build <u>without</u> a CAD program.

Referring to Figure 6.2, passband refers to input signal frequencies being pass through the filter. For these frequencies, the filter gain is ~1. Gain is the filters output signal divided by the input signal, Vo/Vi. The fc is the frequency cutoff (sometimes called the critical frequency or the frequency knee) is defined as when the filter gain falls to 0.707. After that point, the frequency roll-off dominates the gain of the filter.

[**Tech Note:** Why use G(ain) = Vo/Vi ≈ 0.707 as the fc point? The 0.707 value is the approximation of $1/\sqrt{2}$. This is the simplest mathematical expression for the effect of a pole creating the knee in the frequency plots of Vo/Vi. The reader may want to research how $1/\sqrt{2}$ is derived. Also, $1/\sqrt{2}$ is the -3dB point of the filter also known as the half power point.]

Along with passband there is a "stopband". Stopband is a <u>user</u> defined requirement for the filter's attenuation at a desired frequency. There will be much more on this topic later.

Looking at the bandpass plot of Figure 6.2, there are 2 frequency cutoff points. One cutoff for removing low frequencies and another for removing high frequencies. The fc for cutting off low frequencies is the high pass part of the filter. Naturally, the fc for cutting off high frequencies is the low pass part of the filter. (Some CAD programs call these fh and fl, I will stay with fc as fc1 and fc2). The roll-off slopes for the high pass and low pass of a band pass filter can be same but they are <u>not</u> <u>required</u> to be the same. Most CAD filter design programs assume an equal number of poles for both sides of a band pass filter. In general, I have found a 1 pole (RC) filter high pass works well enough while a multi-pole low pass filter is needed. This saves on filter components. In cases like this, use the CAD program for the low pass filter circuits and simply add a high pass RC (section 4.2) to the output of the final low pass circuit. In the next few sections, I will show how to place your input signal filters in series to build complex electronic filters from simple circuits.

As it is common to serial connect filter blocks, we need to understand filter gain in dB (decibel). CAD programs will provide filter frequency response in either gain (Vo/Vi) or dB.

[**Tech Note:** Another reason for understanding the decibel unit, it is often associated with power (loudness of speakers for example). A loss of 3dB in acoustic power is another way of saying the acoustic intensity is down 50%. Basically, human ears are acoustic sensors rated in dB.]

6.1.1 Working in dB

It is common to reference filtering circuits in dB, log base 10. The benefit of using dB is that we can add filter responses when connecting filter blocks in series. To demonstrate cascading filters, assume we have 3 filter blocks A, B and C as in Figure 6.3. Remember, the CAD design has each block with a high input impedance and low output impedance so that each is independent of the other block.

Figure 6.3 Example of a series of analog filters

Let's say, Filter A is a bandpass filter with fc1 = 0.25Hz and fc2 = 100Hz where Filters B and C are both low pass filters with fc = 100Hz. We want to calculate Vo if Vi is a 0.1Hz, 1Vpp sinewave. Knowing the response for Filter A at 0.1Hz is Vo/Vi = 0.2 while the response for Filter B and C is Vo/Vi = 1, we can calculate the response in both gain and in dB as shown in the equations below.

System voltage gain is the product of the filters as: 0.2 * 1 * 1 = 0.2
Now in dB; Gain in dB = 20*log10(Vo/Vi)
System gain in dB is the sum of the filters as: -13.98dB + 0dB + 0dB = -13.98dB
Solving for Vout/Vin argument in the dB equation, Gain = $10^{-13.98/20}$ = 0.2

Now, taking on a more realistic problem, assume Vin is at 300Hz with the Vo/Vi of each filter as: 0.32, 0.12 and 0.12 for filters A, B and C respectfully.

System voltage gain is 0.32 * 0.12 * 0.12 = 0.00461
System gain in dB is -9.90dB + -18.41dB + -18.41dB = -46.73dB
Working backwards, Gain = $10^{-2.336}$ = 0.00461

OK, the dB allows adding filter response but so far, either way a calculator was need. So, what's the big deal?

The higher the number of poles a filter has is often referenced as the filter's order. The more poles, the higher the order, the faster the roll-off after fc. With Butterworth filters, the amplitude roll-off is -20dB per frequency decade per pole. An ideal 1 pole low pass Butterworth filter has a roll-off of -20dB per decade while a 3 pole low pass is -60dB per decade. For example, if we have a 1 pole Butterworth filter with fc = 10Hz the attenuation at 100Hz is -20dB and -40dB at 1000Hz. Where a 3 pole Butterworth with fc = 10Hz will have -60dB attenuation at 100Hz and -120dB at 1000Hz. This is why filter designers normally talk in dB.

Just to help clarify, let me repeat that last 1 and 3 pole Butterworth example using slightly different terms. We have two Butterworth filters each with frequency cutoffs (fc) of 10Hz. If we input 1Vpp noise at 10Hz, what is the attenuation at 100Hz?

$$\text{The 1 pole Butterworth response} \approx \text{-20dB.}$$
$$\text{In terms of Vo/Vi, Vo} = (10^{-20/20})Vi = 0.1Vi$$
$$\text{The 3 pole Butterworth response} \approx \text{-60dB.}$$
$$\text{In terms of Vo/Vi, Vo} = (10^{-3})Vi = 0.001Vi$$

This really shows the filtering power of a 3 pole over a 1 pole filter. Even more interesting, the resolution of the 10bit ADC Arduino is 0.004883V/Cnt. At 100Hz, the 3 pole fc = 10Hz, Butterworth filter reduces 1Vpp noise to a point below the resolution of the Uno or Mega Arduino. That noise is now invisible to our Uno or Mega measurement.

Other notes on dB usage

The unit dB is a ratio of two voltages, two currents or two of anything. As such, the unit dB is open to user defined interpretation. Different groups use dB slightly different and this can (will) become confusing. Here are some of the other electronic uses of dB.

First, referring to filter attenuation in simply dB (not negative dB). People working with analog and digital filters assume the listener/reader understands there is a negative sign in front of the dB value when discussing filter results.

Second, amplifier people sometimes use dBm. This is the same thing as discussed above. In signal processing, we assume an input of 1Vpp (or as 1Vp-p). Amplifier people sometimes like to assume an input of 1mVpp or 1mV watt.

6.2 A CAD Designed AA Filter

The Sallen-Key Butterworth filter is commonly used for anti-aliasing analog filters. Using Filter Wiz lite, I asked for a low pass Butterworth filter with a 1Hz cutoff frequency. I asked for a 3rd order using the Sallen-Key topology. The result in shown in Figure 6.4.

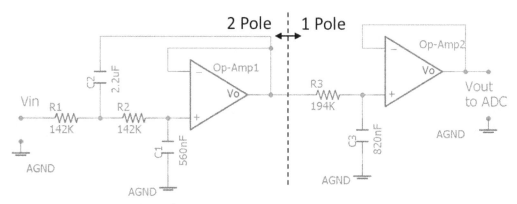

Figure 6.4 A CAD, 3rd order, low pass, Sallen-Key, Butterworth filter

The active low pass filter in Figure 6.4 is composed of a 2 pole and a 1 pole block. In this circuit, the amplifiers don't provide gain, they are simply buffers to isolate the input from the output of each block. If signal gain is wanted, the Op-Amp2 circuit can be modified by adding two resistors in the negative feedback of Op-Amp2 for a

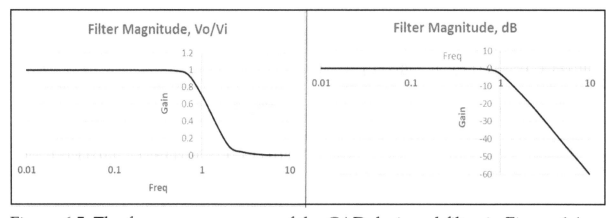

Figure 6.5 The frequency response of the CAD designed filter in Figure 6.4

non-inverting amplifier as show in section 4.4.1.

The Sallan-Key provides a near infinite input impedance at DC for both filter blocks. To calculate the input impedance at DC, assume the capacitors are open circuits. Now, R1 and R2 are in series with the positive input of the operational amplifier which we already know is nearly infinite. At high frequencies, the input impedance is estimated by assuming the capacitors are shorted. Now, we have R1 followed by a short to ground. So, at high frequencies the input impedance is equal to R1, 142K ohms.

The frequency response of the 1Hz CAD designed filter is shown in Figure 6.5 in both Vo/Vi gain and dB. It is common to display the dB plots as log-log. The -60dB from 1Hz to 10Hz is easier to see in the dB plot.

Assuming our measurement system had a sample frequency of 10sps, the Nyquist frequency (fn) is 5Hz. At 5Hz the filter's response is ≈ -42dB or 0.008V at 1Vpp input. This would make a reasonable anti-aliasing filter as it is unlikely we have a 1Vpp noise level.

6.2.1 CAD Active Analog Filters and Arduino

All the Arduino ADCs have virtually infinite analog input impedances. This high impedance means we can eliminate the Op-Amp2 in the Figure 6.4 example circuit. Only the R3 and C3 passive components are needed. When building filters for the Arduino, consider using 3 or 5 pole CAD filters and saving the last amplifier.

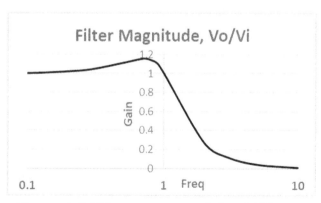

Figure 6.6 Filter response of the CAD filter shown in Figure 6.4 if the 1 pole section is removed.

Warning, in the 3 pole CAD example, there might be a desire to have only a 2 pole filter by removing the 1 pole side, (R3, C3 and Op_Amp2). This may not result in the filter hoped for. To illustrate, I implemented the first 2 pole circuit without any following RC.

The magnitude of the filters output after removing the second 1 pole block is shown in Figure 6.6. Note, the magnitude of the filter's output near fc, 1Hz is NOT flat while the 3 pole filter was flat. The CAD program is actually increasing the Butterworth filters 'Q' knowing a 1 pole filter is the next stage. A higher Q improves the filter. However, for most applications, the flat passband is preferred. So, when designing a 2 pole active filter, it is best to start the CAD program with a 2 pole target filter for a flat passband.

6.3 Simple Anti-Aliasing Filters Using only a Calculator

As promised, this book will aid any Arduino user wanting to use their Arduino for scientific measurements without a lot of cost. The CAD anti-aliasing filters are great however, they require a lot of parts which also means a lot of assembly time. In this section, we will look at the simple RC filter and how to use RC filters with amplifiers to make active analog filters. These amplifiers can also improve the sensor interface to the Arduino. In this section, all you need is a scientific calculator to get the job done.

6.3.1 The Mighty RC Filter

Let's be honest, the simple RC filter is used 100X more often than any other electronic filter. The RC is used to smooth the power supply voltage and the voltage reference for the ADC on the Arduino. RC filters are good for smoothing the power supply of any sensor and sensor signal amplifiers. These types of power smoothing applications are called: bypass capacitors,

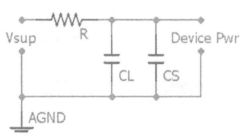

Figure 6.7 RC filter with parallel capacitors

decoupling capacitors or bypass circuits.

Figure 6.7 shows a typical RC filter used as a bypass circuit for the power of some electronic device or sensor. The Arduino DC supply pin is a noisy supply because there are many digital circuits drawing power from the DC supply. These digital circuits do not draw power in a well behaved DC manner. Digital circuits pull power as current pulses synchronized with the system digital clock. These current pulses create ripple voltage on the DC supply coming from the Arduino. All sensors and circuit amplifiers will benefit from simply using a RC bypass circuit between the Arduino supply and the sensor or signal amplifiers. Let's look at the bypass circuit and then the RC anti-aliasing filter.

For most RC bypass power pin filters, the R in the circuit might not actually exist as a discrete resistor. It's simply the resistance (impedance) of the circuit board trace or wire. The capacitor is placed very near the power pin of the device. For low noise analog circuits, I use actual resistors. The filter will benefit from a discrete resistor of 5 to 51 ohms to improve the bypass circuit filtering. Naturally, the tradeoff is a loss of some supply voltage to the analog circuit or sensor. In most cases, the currents required by the circuit or sensor are small, only a few mA, so the voltage drop will be negligent.

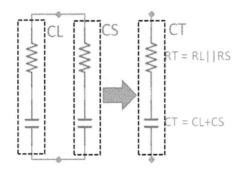

Figure 6.8 Parallel capacitors make for a better capacitor

[**Tech Note:** Using a discrete resistor has a side benefit of troubleshooting if things are not going well. By having a discrete resistor, the current of the circuit in question can be calculated by measuring the voltage drop across the resistor. Also, the circuit can be somewhat isolated (depending on the IC) by removing the resistor during troubleshooting.]

For the high resolution AD22B shield I used in this book, the R is actually a small 100μH inductor supplying power to the AD3550. The 22bit ADC circuit also uses two bypass capacitors, CL = 2.2μF and CS = 0.22μF. The reason for the 2 parallel capacitors?

Capacitance in parallel add while the internal impedances of those capacitors don't. In fact, the effective total capacitor internal resistance is reduced.

No capacitor is perfect. Each capacitor has a small internal resistance to current flow. In the Figure 6.8, the non-ideal capacitors CL and CS from the bypass filter circuit are shown with their internal resistors. The total capacitance remains the sum of capacitors. However, the ability to respond to transient noise is improved. The new RT is less than either RL or RS. The reasoning for using a large value and a smaller value capacitor is because the smaller capacitor generally has a smaller internal resistance. Paralleling gives us the best of both capacitors.

[**Tech Note:** As paralleling capacitors improves performance, a similar situation exists with placing inductors (chokes) in series. Inductors in series reduce the apparent inductor's internal capacitance allowing the inductors to work at higher frequencies.]

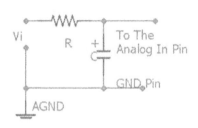

Figure 6.9 RC filter for analog input signals

Now is a good time to consider an RC anti-aliasing filter. Figure 6.9 is the same RC filter discussed earlier. The only difference is the application. The obvious issue with a simple RC anti-aliasing filter is the poor roll off. Let's say, we have a sample system running at fs=10Hz or as 10sps. We want a -40dB anti-aliasing filter at 5 Hz as our band stop frequency. Using an RC, we have only 1 pole for a roll-off of 20dB per decade for every decade, 10X in Hz. So, to get -40dB we need to back our RC frequency cutoff two decades, fc = 5/100 or 0.05Hz. We need an fc of 0.05Hz for our RC anti-aliasing filter.

Two Useful Equations for RC Filters: Frequency, $fc = 1/(2\pi RC)$ and $R = 1/(2\pi fcC)$

Starting with a 0.22µF capacitor and fc = 0.05Hz then R = 14.5M ohms. That's too large a resistance for most measurement systems. We need a larger capacitor. Remember the Arduino analog input pins can only accept positive voltage inputs and the RC anti-aliasing filter in the circuit is grounded at one end to the Arduino ground. We can use polarized electrolytic capacitors in this application. Assuming a 22µF capacitor, the required R is 145K ohms. This is a much better resistor value.

We could also measure 220µF rated capacitor and calculate the required resistance value.

The problem with RC anti-aliasing filter is the wide transition zone. The transition zone is the area around the cutoff frequency, fc where the filter response is not ideal. In Figure 6.10, the RC filter is compared with higher order Butterworth filters. As can be seen in Figure 6.10, there is attenuation of the frequencies in the passband as the frequency approaches the knee at fc. For the simple RC filter, the attenuation is >1% going back to ~0.1Hz with an fc = 1Hz. Following fc, the poor roll-off of the RC filter allows passing of unwanted frequencies. The RC filter has a wide transition zone.

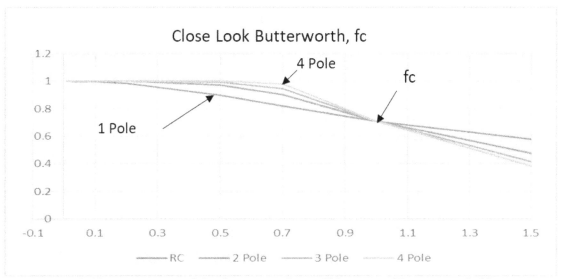

Figure 6.10 Close-up view of the frequency knee (fc) point of Butterworth filters based on the # of poles

To illustrate the transition zone in another way, I created Table 6.1 showing the filter gain around fc = 1Hz. There are 1 to 4 pole filter results shown. I define useable bandwidth of our bandpass as a gain response of 1 to 0.99. The 1 pole filter has a usable bandwidth up to ~0.1Hz. The 2 pole filter has a usable bandwidth of 0.2Hz. This doesn't seem like much of an improvement but it's a 2X gain in bandwidth. The 3 and 4 pole circuit are good to ~0.5Hz.

If we define our band stop frequency as the point where attenuation is greater than the bit value of our Arduino Uno ADC (0.00488V) then the 1 pole band stop is ~110Hz. For the 2 pole, band stop frequency is ~20Hz and ~7 Hz for the 3 pole Butterworth filter. In Table 6.1, the white area is the transition band. The obvious point to be made here is that higher pole filters reduce the transition band and increase the useable band pass of the filter. Not as noticeable but also true, the law of diminishing returns is at play here. Going from a 1 pole to a 2 pole filter reduces the transition band more than going from 3 poles to 4 poles and so on.

[**Tech Note:** Nature is a cruel engineer. Nature doesn't allow for a perfect filter to exist. It is possible to achieve near ideal gain response in the filter but doing so creates error in the phase part of the signal. A perfect phase response filter, results in poor amplitude response filter. Perhaps, Nature is good at keeping engineers employed.]

Table 6.1 Illustration of the filters transition zone, shown in white

Freq, Hz	1 Pole	2 Pole	3 Pole	4 Pole
0.01	1	1	1	1
0.02	1	1	1	1
0.03	0.995	1	1	1
0.05	0.998	1	1	1
0.07	0.997	1	1	1
0.1	0.995	1	1	1
0.2	0.982	0.999	1	1
0.5	0.897	0.97	0.992	1
0.7	0.82	0.8998	0.945	0.979
1	0.707	0.707	0.707	0.707
2	0.448	0.247	0.125	0.0598
7	0.143	0.02	0.003	0.0004
10	0.101	0.01	0.001	0.0001
20	0.05	0.0026	0.00012	0.000006
70	0.014	0.0002	3.00E-07	4.00E-08
100	0.01	0.0001	1.00E-07	9.00E-09

6.3.2 Building Anti-Aliasing Filters into Signal Conditioning Amplifiers

Most sensors will require some signal conditioning to best match the 0 to +V input range of the Arduino ADC. Normally, we are taking about using an operational amplifier or an instrumentation amplifier for signal amplification. So, why not use those devices as part of an anti-aliasing filter?

I have developed simple means of doing just that. The reader is unlikely to find these tools inside any normal text book. These circuits are not as good as a Sallan-Key Butterworth filter but close enough for many applications.

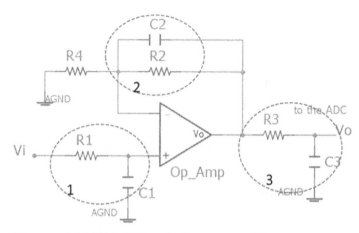

Figure 6.11 The 2.5 pole, low pass filter

For example, a high gain op-amp circuit with analog RC filters is shown in Figure 6.11. This is almost a 3 pole low pass filter, note the 3 RC combinations. This is also a non-inverting amplifier stable at any gain. Not all Sallan-Key circuits are stable with gain over 4. With this circuit, you only need a calculator to calculate the RC components and circuit gain. I'll call this the 2.5 pole filter. OK, there is no such thing as a ½ pole. I'll explain later.

In the 2.5 pole filter, there are 3 RC poles. Each RC pair is circled and numbered. Each of the poles are independent of each other thanks to the operational amplifier. RC poles 1 and 3 are standard RC poles which have the standard response to ac signals. Pole 2 is sometimes called the Miller Capacitance or Miller Effect. Here R2C2 pole attenuates the circuit's gain at fc. This is a non-inverting operational amplifier circuit with a gain = 1 + R2/R4 at DC. As the input signal frequency increases, the R2 resistor becomes increasingly bypassed by C2. At very high frequencies, C2 looks like a short circuit. This drops the gain to 1. This pole doesn't continue to attenuate output frequencies past the gain of 1 so I call this the ½ pole of the 2.5 pole filter.

Pole 2 has the same knee point frequency, fc = $1/(2*\pi*R2*C2)$. All three RC poles are at the same fc. Since they are all independent, they can all use the same RC combination of capacitors and resistors.

There is a small problem. Calculating the same fc for each RC pole results in a system response which is at a much lower frequency.

The pole of an RC filter is defined as when $\left|\dfrac{VO}{Vi}\right| = \dfrac{1}{\sqrt{1+(2\pi fcRC)2}} = \dfrac{1}{\sqrt{2}}$.

For our system, we have 3 equal and independent poles. However, we can't use the same RC equation for calculating fc. The frequency knee for our 2.5 pole circuit is as below.

$$\left|\dfrac{VO}{Vi}\right| = \dfrac{1}{\sqrt{1+(2\pi fcRC)2}} * \dfrac{1}{\sqrt{1+(2\pi fcRC)2}} * \dfrac{1}{\sqrt{1+(2\pi fcRC)2}}$$

We need to shift the frequency cutoff, fc in the above equation results such that:

$$\left|\dfrac{VO}{Vi}\right| = \left(\dfrac{1}{\sqrt[3]{2}}\right) * \left(\dfrac{1}{\sqrt[3]{2}}\right) * \left(\dfrac{1}{\sqrt[3]{2}}\right) = \dfrac{1}{\sqrt{2}}$$

If interested, the algebraic solution can be downloaded from the web site: OnMeasurement.com. For this publication, I want to offer cookbook solutions where only a calculator is needed.

Table 6.2 provides the results from a series of independent and equal RC poles. The shift factor is the X value for 2 to 5 RC poles. Here, we need to use the X value to shift calculation of fc for each RC.

Table 6.2 Factors for shifting independent RC poles in a signal path

Factor/# Poles	2	3	4	5
X =	1.554	1.961	2.299	2.593

Consider the following for an example using the shift factor X= 1.961 for the 3 independent RC poles as in Figure 6.11. We want a circuit fc of 100Hz and a gain of 20. To calculate the needed RC values, shift the RC calculation by 1.961 as:

The fc for the RCs is 196.1Hz = 100Hz * 1.961 = 100Hz * X
Where 100Hz is the desired system fc and 1.961 is the shift factor for 3 RC independent poles

Using 0.47µF capacitors:

$$R = 1/(2*\pi*196.1Hz*0.47\mu F) = 1727 \text{ ohms}$$

If we design the 2.5 low pass filter with RC's comprised of 0.47µF and 1727 ohm resistors, we will have an amplifier circuit with an fc =100Hz. For the gain, the amplifier is a non-inverting op-amp circuit. This circuit was discussed in section 4.4.1. Knowing R2 is 1727 ohms and we want a gain of 20:

$$\text{Gain} = R2/R4 + 1 \text{ so } R4 = R2/(\text{Gain}-1) = 91 \text{ohms}$$

With these few calculations, we solved all the circuit elements needed for the 2.5 pole, AA filter in Figure 6.11. No CAD programming needed.

6.3.3 Simulated Real World AA Filter Example with an In-Amp

Let's work an anti-aliasing filter problem using an instrumentation amplifier and independent RC filters. In truth, this is close to a real world problem. It's also true that most CAD active filter design programs don't work with instrumentation amplifiers. Hopefully, many of the readers will find this example very useful.

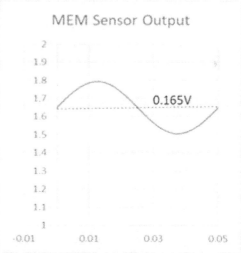

Figure 6.12 Estimated output from the off axis MEM accelerometer

We are asked to instrument the battery assembly of an electric car for vibration. The car drives a test track designed to provide a year's worth of speed bumps and pot holes. By monitoring the shock and vibration, we hope to learn the best way of mounting large battery packs in electric cars. All accelerometers are the same type of devices. We are told to expect 30G-25mS peak signals on the axis of impact and 20G-25mS on the two off axis.

The team chose a low cost MEM accelerometer with a maximum sensitivity of 7.2mV/G and drive impedance of 32K ohms. Acceleration is normally in units of 'G's for gravity. The largest required amplifier gain is on the off axis accelerometers. They see the lowest level of acceleration at only 20Gs. The expected peak output is only +/-0.144V on the off impact axis accelerometers. Figure 6.12 is an illustration of the expected MEM accelerometer output signal. The MEM supply voltage is 3.3V and the output at 0 G's is 1/2Vsup or 1.65V DC.

We need to sample really fast, so we chose to Arduino Due. With a DC bias of 1.65V at 0 Gs, the maximum signal allowed by the Due is 0 to 3.3V DC. Our circuit gain needs to be 1.65V/0.144V or Gain = ~ 11.45. This amplification will allow the highest resolution of the Due ADC. We round the gain down to 11 to provide some headroom for our measurement.

The required signal bandwidth for this test is 120Hz. We decided to sample at fs = 8KHz with an anti-alias filter fc = 400Hz and a stop band at -40dB above 4KHz. The fc to stop band is a decade. We need 2 RC poles for a -40dB roll-off per decade.

The instrumentation amplifier circuit to be used is shown in Figure 6.13. This is a non-inverting in-amp circuit with a fixed gain using Rg. There is an RC filter coming in to the in-amp and one between the in-amp and our Adruino Due analog input. The only circuit twist here is that R1 is actually the output resistance of the accelerometer sensor. So, R1 is fixed. We can add a second resistance is series to increase the resistance of our RC if needed.

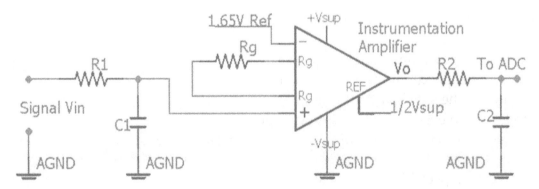

Figure 6.13 A 2 pole low pass in-amp with gain and DC offset voltage

The accelerometer has an internal impedance of 32K ohms. Calculating RC for a shifted fc (for 2 RC poles) is xfc = 1.554*fc = 1.554*400 Hz or 622Hz. Now, C1 = 1/(2* π*R1*xfc) = 8.0nF. We're in luck, 8.0nF is available. Using R1=R2=32.0K and C1=C2=8.0nF for a circuit fc = 400Hz.

Picking an instrumentation amplifier requires checking the amplifiers bandwidth. Instrumentation amplifiers are complex, high precision devices. Not all will support our ~10KHz BW requirement. The AD623 data sheet reports 100KHz bandwidth at a gain of 10. Looks like it will work. However, if our gain was 100, the specified bandwidth is only 10KHz. Bandwidth of amplifiers fall with increasing gain. So, check the data sheets for gain vs bandwidth of op-amps and in-amps.

Using the AD623 and we want a gain of 11. Now Rg = 100K/(Gain-1) = 10.0K ohms.

Another word of caution. Rg is NOT in the same circuit location as R2 from the 2.5 pole filter of Figure 6.11. We can NOT create an RC pole using Rg. In fact, Rg is similar to R4 in the 2.5 pole filter. Never place a capacitor across either of these resistors as this will actually amplify noise or even cause the circuit to oscillate out of control.

In the instrumentation amplifier circuit in Figure 6.12, there are two reference voltages, 1.65V and 1/2Vsup. If the ADC is the Arduino Uno or Mega, Vsup = 5V, for the Due Vsup = 3.3V. MEM accelerometers are low cost and come in a wide range of G ratings. They normally operate from a 3.3V DC power supply. The 0G output voltage of the MEM accelerometer is equal to ½ the supply voltage, 1.65V. The MEM sensor provides an analog voltage where below 1.65V are negative G values and above are positive G values. By connecting the 1.65V to the negative Vin input pin, the instrumentation amplifier will amplify only the difference.

The Vo of the instrumentation seeks a negative voltage to amplify the –V/G signal. The REF input pin provides the answer. If we are using the Uno or Mega; placing a 2.5V (1/2Vsup) reference voltage on the REF pin of the instrumentation amplifier, Vo = 2.5V when Vi = 1.65V at 0Gs. No capacitors are needed. No high pass filter issues. In this example, we are using the Due, the same 1.65V reference can be used on both the negative Vin and REF input pins. In the Arduino software, subtract 1/2Vsup from the ADC reading will capture the amplified +/- G signal.

Remember the voltage on the REF pin should be same as discussed in the instrumentation reference section 4.5.1. The 1.65V reference on the "-" pin can be a simple voltage divider using two resistors. Using a ½ voltage divider circuit with the Due 3.3V supply is how the MEM accelerometer works. Using a voltage divider from the Due 3.3V supply to create the 1.65V input reference allows the system to be self-correcting for small errors in the 3.3V supply voltage. Self-correcting bias circuits are always welcome.

6.4 The Bessel Filter and IC Filters

Up until now, all the filter discussion has been on the Butterworth filter. As I mentioned at the start, the Butterworth is a good choice for most applications. However, the Bessel filter is an analog filter with a unique ability. The Bessel filter has a linear phase and a near constant group delay. This means, the Bessel filter maintains the signals shape better than any other filter while attenuating high frequencies.

The topic of phase and group error is complex. I will provide the 'standard' illustration of this type of error. I mathematically simulated a digital 10Hz Butterworth filter and subjected it to a 5V pulse with near infinite rise and fall times. As we know, fast rise times mean high frequencies. The input pulse and Butterworth response are shown in Figure 6.14A and B.

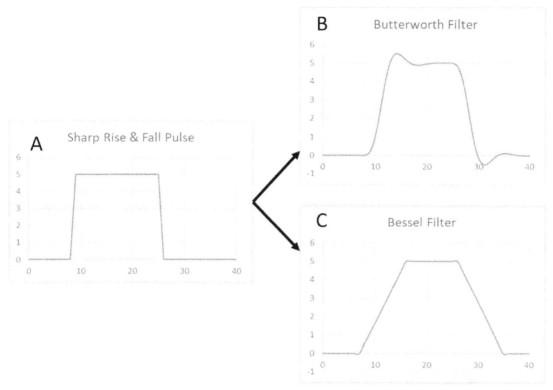

Figure 6.14 A. Fast rise times mean high frequencies B. Butterworth filter response C. Bessel filter response

In The Butterworth filter is ringing caused by both the input fast rise and fall. However, the simulated Bessel filter doesn't ring, Figure 6.14C. The Bessel's response better represents the pulse input.

Even though Figure 6.14 is showing a potential real world problem, I have a bit of an issue. Why would we ever use a low frequency, multi-pole Butterworth filter to capture digital pulses? In a well-designed system with dominate input signal frequencies well below the fc value of the Butterworth filter, this is not a major problem. This is my opinion. However, there are times (and industry convention) when Bessel filters are required.

The trade off in uniform phase filtering is a slow roll-off. In fact, the attenuation of the Bessel filter is so poor, I suggest NOT designing one even with a CAD filter design program. You will need 5 or more poles to get a reasonable roll-off. I suggest buying an integrated circuit filter, like the MAX7401 (5V) or MAX7405 (3V).

These are high order, 8 pole switch capacitor Bessel filters. They are small 8 pin devices. These devices are rated for frequency cutoffs (fc) from 1Hz to 5KHz. However, they require a user supplied clock. They also require at least an analog RC filter for anti-aliasing the signal input.

The switched capacitor Bessel filter IC's require a digital clock to determine the filter's fc. If you want an fc at 2KHz, simply supply a clock of 100X or 200KHz. If you want an fc = 120Hz, the clock is 12KHz. The clock can come from your Arduino. Most likely, it would be easier to use a second clock circuit (555 or better) or a function generator. As the switched capacitor circuit is actually a digital sampling process, there needs to be a simple RC filter on the input to prevent aliasing at 50% of the clock frequency.

It should be said, there are switched capacitor Butterworth filter ICs also. So, if you want an 8 pole Butterworth filter, consider a filtering switch capacitor IC.

Conclusion to Bessel Filters

1. The Bessel filter is a better filter for maintaining the quality of the signal while removing high frequency content. There are applications and industries where Bessel filter are the standard. I suggest using them.
2. If a Bessel filter is needed, consider using an integrated circuit filter. They are easy to set the fc frequency and offer a multi-pole solution.
3. Remember, the integrated circuit, switch capacitor filter is still a sampling system which requires an RC AA filter.

6.5 ADC Quantization Levels and Nyquist Frequency

Every ADC has a noise floor based solely on the level of quantization of the incoming signal. Assuming the incoming signal is a sinewave the signal-to-quantization noise floor is:

$$\text{Signal-to-Quantization-Noise-Ratio (SQNR)} = \sim(6.02 * Q + 1.76) \text{ dB}$$
$$\text{Where Q is the number of ADC bits}$$

For the 10bit Arduino ADCs, the SQNR = ~62dB. What does this mean to measurement system designers? The SQNR value is used to fix the required anti-aliasing filter attenuation. The goal is to reduce the noise floor of the signal below the SQNR value following the anti-aliasing filter. This forces the designer to create an anti-aliasing filter of -62dB at the Nyquist frequency (fn) for all 10bit Arduino input signals.

However, the SQNR value is a ratio (dB) not an absolute input or output voltage level. For most sensor based inputs to the ADC, the sensor signal is larger than the background noise level. For example, if we have an input sensor signal of 1V and a noise level of 50mV, we have a signal-to-noise ration of -26dB before any anti-aliasing filtering is performed. In this case, we only need a stop band attenuation for our anti-aliasing filter of -36dB, (62dB - 26dB) at fn. In rare cases, the converse can be true, the input signal noise can be larger than the sensor signal in which we are interested. In that case, the anti-aliasing filter requires higher attenuation at fn than -62dB.

For high resolution ADCs like the AD22B shield or even a 32bit ADC, the SQNR value is 134dB and 194dB respectfully. The level of anti-aliasing filtering at these values is easily achievable on paper but difficult to achieve in the real world. In the real world, anti-aliasing filters create a noise floor even with the input shorted to ground.

In short, electronic engineers spending a life-time building laboratory grade calibration quality meters might never achieve a measurement better than 24-28 bits of absolute accuracy. They often have the advantage of working inside a fully electrically shielded enclosure. Even the manufacturers of 32 bit ADC devices don't promise anyone 32 bit resolution when making a single measurement. The lower bits are there only to support averaging of a DC voltage for maximum resolution not accuracy. If the input voltage to the ADC is static, then to gain an estimated 1 additional bit (as going from 10bit to 11bit ADC) requires averaging 4 readings. For 2 additional bits requires averaging 16 readings and 64 readings for 3 additional bits. The lower bits of a 32 bit ADC are noisy so averaging could increase resolution. More on this topic is covered in section 6.6.

The Arduino is a functionally powerful little processor but it was built for low cost. The noise generated by a digital signals running on a 2 layer circuit board is enough to make very high resolution measurements difficult. For the majority of readers interested with working with the Arduino in the real world should temper their expectations. Achieving 20 to 22 bit relative resolution and 15 to 18 bits of absolute accuracy is doing very well.

Conclusion? Engineering is the art of compromise. Engineering is knowing the tradeoffs. My best advice, look at what others have done in your field of study. Consider how you can build on their work. In the end, budgets and time maybe the largest obstacles to building the ideal measurement system. I'm writing this book to aid the reader in maximizing their time, their budget to get the best possible measurement outcome.

6.6 Converting Arduino 10Bit ADC to 13Bit ADC

A very slow sloping input voltage was applied to both the AD22B shield and Arduino Uno channel A0. The output of both ADCs is shown Figure 6.15. Clearly, the limited quantizing resolution of the 10 bit ADC internal to the Arduino is showing. (The small offset of the two traces was done to ease seeing the two different traces following the input ramp voltage.)

Figure 6.15 A slow increasing slope signal is applied to the AD22B and Uno A0. The difference in bit resolution is clear

Interestingly, by adding a small noise to our input signal, the effective resolution of the Arduino ADC is actually improved! Figure 6.16 is a repeat of the test in Figure 6.15 but now with 'Dithering' in input signal and averaging the 10 bit Uno readings.

Here is how you can increase the effective resolution of the Arduino. First, the Arduino

ADC is really good. The clear stair step seen Figure 6.15 is because the Arduino ADC has a lower noise floor than the resolution of the ADC. In short, averaging these readings as they stair step with the input ramp does little to improve the reading resolution.

Dithering is adding a small ac noise to our signal with a voltage peak-to-peak (Vpp) near an ADC step size. For the Arduino with a 5V reference voltage and 10 bits, that small noise voltage is 2.44mV-4.88mV. Now, most authors suggest a "white" noise signal for dithering. Which is good for the general case of dithering. However, developing a white noise generator at the correct Vpp is a project in itself. This example is using a triangle wave at 1 frequency, 120Hz and averaging 149 ADC readings over a period of 1/60sec. Triangle waves are easily created using a very low cost 555 timer chip.

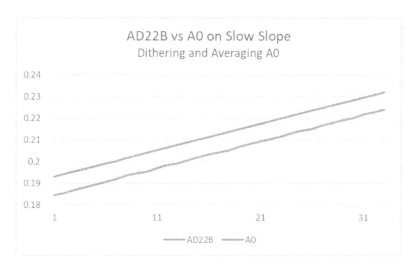

Figure 6.16 The Uno A0 input signal is dithered and averaged. This increases the measurement resolution.

The frequency of 120Hz was chosen because it's an integer multiple of our common lab noise 60Hz found in the US. By averaging over 1/60 or 16.67mS, the Arduino ADC crushes both common 60 Hz noise and the 120 Hz dither signal. The average of an ac coupled noise signal over 1 period (or integer multiples of a period) is zero volts as shown in the digital filtering section 7.1. So, not only is our injected dither noise level below 1 ADC step voltage but we are crushing it by averaging over 2 periods.

There is an obvious trade off of this process, the ADC sample rate is reduced. Slower ADCs for higher resolution is a normal engineering trade off. The AD22B uses the MCP3550-60, 22bit ADC with a sample time of 66mS. The Uno ADC with dithering is not higher resolution than the AD22B but for many scientific applications, the dithered ADC is a significant improvement in resolution. So, how does dithering work?

In words, the small dither signal is adding a triangle wave with a +peak voltage and a −peak voltage to the DC signal voltage. This noise causes some readings to read 1 bit high and some 1 bit low. By averaging readings the DC value is now based on the percentage of high and low readings providing summations between the ADC steps. The triangle wave is the best wave for dithering. To get an estimated 1 additional bit requires averaging 4 samples. For 2 additional bits requires 16 reading average and 64 for 3 additional bits and 256 for 4 bits. In the example given, a 149 average was taken to cover the period of one 60Hz cycle. The estimated effective ADC resolution is now 13 bits or 8X the basic Arduino Uno or Mega resolution.

To avoid confusion, it needs to be said, "Sample averaging to gain increase ADC resolution is NOT the same as a moving average". Taking 149 ADC readings as fast as the Arduino Uno can run and then averaging to generate 1 X(n) value every 16.67mS is invisible to our measurement system. The measurement system has a maximum fs = 1/16.67mS or 60 samples per second. Our Nyquist frequency is only 30Hz. We need an anti-aliasing filter of -60dB or more. System calibration needs to demonstrate 13 bits resolution. As a Department of Energy and NASA technical reviewer, I would ask for evidence of improved ADC resolution when averaging was used and I never allowed more than 2 bits without a clear demonstration. Technically, you can take a million point average and claim an additional 10bits of resolution but can you prove it?

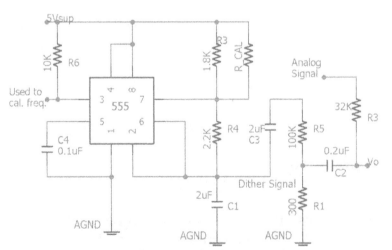

Figure 6.17 Circuit used to create the dither signal.

The circuit used for dithering is shown in Figure 6.17. This is a 555 timer circuit. The normal output pin of the 555 is pin 3. I used pin 3 as a means to calibrate the circuit's output frequency. There are tons of internet descriptions and books on creating a frequency output using the 555 IC. So I will not detail the calculated values for the timing resistors (R3 and R4) and capacitor (c1).

The 555 develops a near triangle wave across C1. The amplitude of this triangle wave is 1/3Vsup, 1.67Vpp. R1 and R5 create a voltage divider reducing the 1.67Vpp to ~5mVpp which is slightly more than desired but at 120Hz, it will work nicely. Now, C3 and R3 are used to mix the incoming analog signal with the dither signal at Vo going to the Uno input. Looking at Vo, C3 and R3 create a high pass for the 120Hz dither signal and a low pass for the analog incoming signal. This RC has an fc of ~24Hz.

To aid the reader in repeating this work for their own purposes and for different frequencies, as 50Hz in Europe, the code below was used to measure the time needed to average ADC readings. To measure time taken for averaging, I used the Arduino function "micros()". The micros() was read before running the code below and it was read following the code. The difference is the number of micro-seconds needed for the "for(int i=0;i<149;++)" statement to read and sum 149 readings and the Arduino to calculate the average value.

```
long tTaken = micros(); // start time
long sensorI = 0; //sets our starting value
for (int i=0;i<149;i++)
  { sensorI = sensorI + analogRead(A0);} // repeated 149 times
float sensorV = (sensoI/149.0)*0.004883 ; //Our sensorI was a 32 bit
//summation integer, we reduced it to the floating value average and
//multiplied by the basic Arduino calibration.
tTaken = micros() - tTaken ; // tTaken is the time taken averaging
```

Will dithering benefit higher resolution Sigma Delta Converters. The act of dithering the AD22B shield requires a dither ac voltage of ~1.2µVpp. In truth, dithering at this level is rarely needed as the signal noise is going to be close if not in excess of the required dithering voltage.

Also, even in the case of the Arduino ADCs, if the input signal change is faster than an ADC step voltage at the sample rate, dithering is of less value. For making precision measurements of near static sensor signals as strain on a weight measurement system or many temperature measurements dithering offers an advantage to the Arduino user. The cost of a dithering circuit is small and allows the Arduino user an option for increased precision using existing hardware.

[**Tech Note:** Some 555 circuit experts will point out that the voltage across C1 is not a true 50% duty cycle triangle wave. The choice of R3 and R4 can reduce this error. This error will shift the ADC bit thresholds. This error is minor should be repeatable in calibration which I have not proven. However, this is a low cost means to improve the conversion results as demonstrated in Figure 6.16.]

6.7 The Arduino AD22B High Resolution Shield

The Arduino can be used to make amazing measurements. The AD22B shield uses the MCP3550 from Microchip. The MCP3550 is a 22 bit ADC with a SPI interface. Originally, I purchased a MCP3550 shield for little cost. It was built on a 2 layer circuit board without any power filtering or its own voltage reference. In chapter 10, I throw a number of reasons why these factors lean to noisy measurements. I built my own shield to see if I could push the accuracy and resolution of the Arduino system for scientific measurements.

I built the shield using a 4 layer circuit board. The 4 layer board has a ground plane. The ground plane reduces noise coupling in from the environment. In truth, I always use ground planes in my measurement circuits.

The AD22B shield has its own 2.50V voltage reference with capacitor filtering. Again, the normal internet ADC shields often use the 5V Arduino supply at the voltage reference. The AD22B input can be either 0 to 2.5V for maximum resolution and accuracy or 0 to 5V used by the Arduino. The input options are header pin selectable.

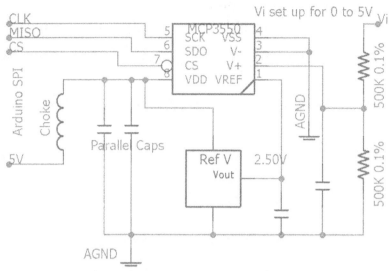

To achieve the 0 to 5V input option, I used a voltage divider of two 0.1% low drift 500K ohm resistors. This is a 1M ohm impedance to the input signal therefore loading of the sensor signal is minimal. I used all 805 surface mount resistors and capacitors because they are easily hand soldered. By changing the lower 500K ohm to a 100K ohm resistor, the

Figure 6.18 The AD22B circuit set up for 5V inputs

input voltage range is increased to 15V.

The MCP3550 IC has a two pole low pass circuit for filtering the Arduino supply voltage going its power pins. The MCP3550 can operate on either Arduino voltage supply, 5V or 3.3V used by the Arduino Due.

The sketch AD22B_DAC12B_Test working with the MCP3550 shield is provided in Chapter 10. In this sketch, the circuit connection to the MCP3550 are shown in Figure 6.18. The data plotted below was taken using the AD22B, the programmable DAC12B shield and a 5.5 digit lab voltmeter are shown in Figure 6.19. The AD22B and the lab meter were in agreement at 19-20bit resolution using an Arduino Uno.

6.8 The Arduino DAC12B Shield

With the AD22B shield, I created a low noise programmable power supply for powering sensors called the DAC12B. The DAC12B shield is based on the MCP4921 from Microchip. The MCP4921 is a 12 bit Digital-to-Analog Converter (DAC). The DAC has SPI interface making it easy to program using Arduinos. I built the

AD22B and the DAC12B shield at the same time using a layer circuit board with a ground plane. The output circuit of the DAC shield has a small power transistor to deliver up 50mA from 0 to 10V. The DAC shield can be used as a small programmable power supply for powering sensors.

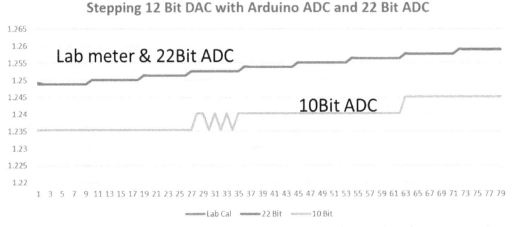

Figure 6.19 Stepping up the 12 bit DAC with a 10 bit and 22 bit ADC. The stair step resolution of the 10bit ADC is easy to see. The lab volt meter and AD22B are virtually the same.

The data plot in Figure 6.19 is from the AD22B and DAC12B shields using an Arduino, Uno. The 12bit DAC was stepped up 1 bit at a time. The DAC12B shield output voltage is measured three times. One measurement was by the 10bit Uno ADC. Another measurement was the AD22B shield via the SPI to the Uno. Finally, the DAC shield output was measured by a 5.5 digit laboratory voltage meter. The simple block diagram of the test circuit is shown in Figure 6.20.

Looking back at the plotted data of Figure 6.19, there are 4 steps from the 12Bit DAC for each level of the 10bit Uno ADC. One of the DAC steps shown is located very close to a transition point of the 10bit Arduino. This causes the bouncing between 1.235 and 1.240V or as in binary between 0011111101 and 0011111110. This is normal.

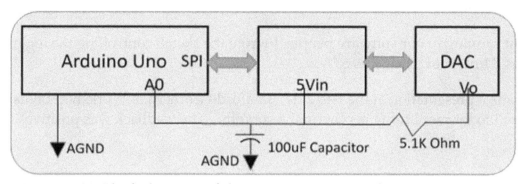

Figure 6.20 Block diagram of the test circuit used in figure 6.16

The laboratory voltage meter and the 22Bit MCP3550 inside the AD22B are virtually the same reading. The AD22B is within the accuracy of the laboratory meter with the DC voltage output from the DAC12B. ALL readings, both the 10Bit and 22Bit ADC are plotted without averaging! These are single ADC conversions. The sketch used by the Uno is called, "AD22B_DAC12B_Test" and is provided in Chapter 10.

The actual photo of the test circuit is shown in Figure 6.21. The Arduino is powered via the USB cable from a laptop not shown in the image. USB power is the reason for the 10Bit ADC voltage readings are so low. A conventional prototype plug in board was used to mount the AD22B and the DAC12B along with the filtering RC used on the input. It is amazing to see DC voltage resolution this good using a prototype build sitting on an open lab bench.

I should admit, the reason I decided to write this book was because of this test. I had created the AD22B and DAC12B to support a research project. I connect the Uno to the shields and I simulated taking measurements over 12,000ft of logging cable to an analog tool running at a cool 250°C inside a

Figure 6.21 The Uno with the DAC12B and AD22B shields

geothermal well.

Without running to our software people, I wrote the sketch controlling the logging tool in < 8 hrs. Wow, that was easy.

So, I made a presentation at the Feb 2017, Stanford Geothermal Workshop on using the Arduino for monitoring geothermal reservoirs. The feedback was positive.

Chapter 7 Digital Filters

Making your measurements stand out

It is a rare case when a set of raw data measurements are the end result of a scientific experiment. Normally, some type of digital signal processing is used to improve the user's ability to see the information collected within the measurements. In general, digital signal processing (DSP) does not add information to the data set but rather removes unwanted information or interfering noise.

7.1 Digital Filters

Most authors talk about the two most common linear digital filters, the FIR (Finite Impulse Response) and the IIR (Infinite Impulse Response) digital filters as being roughly equivalent. I suggest they are not equal. This section will outline simple and practical digital filters I feel will work well with the Arduino.

There are several powerful digital non-linear filters which offer unique solutions for signal processing to remove unwanted interference. This book looks at the easiest non-linear filter to implement on any Arduino: the Median filter.

7.1.1 Is it real?

Digital filters are used after the ADC has done its job and the raw data is recorded. The digital filter makes seeing the desired data easier by changing the actual ADC values. As measurement system designers, we need to improve the visibility of sensor data while exercising care not to create false interpretations. We don't want digital processing creating false correlations between data points or between two sensors. False correlations can alter the experiment's outcome. So before processing the measured values, we need to ask, "How do we validate our data is real?" The best time to ask this question is before conducting an experiment.

The reader needs to know how to judge your measurements for validity. How can the measurement system be tested before running the experiment? What proof of performance is expected? How can different sensors be used to validate each other? When developing a measurement system, consider secondary measurements to aid in validating the required measurements. How are sensors readings used in calculations of the final result? This might sound like a lot of questions. Trust me, once a test has been run, any results being questioned will fall first on the person taking the data.

If there is one golden rule for collecting scientific data it is; always keep the rawest form of your measured data as possible. This means applying no algorithm (no digital filter) to the ADC measurements without saving those **raw measurements first**. If that is not possible, save as close to raw readings as possible. Digital filters may not be backward recoverable. Processing doesn't add information to your measurements it removes "unwanted" information/noise.

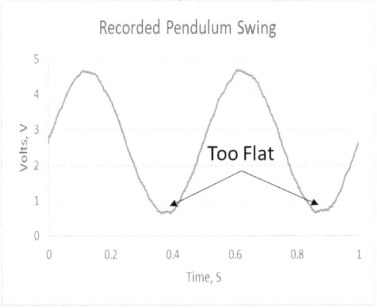

Worse case, at the time of the experiment, something unexpected/unwanted might happen. The data collected may have a critical role in understanding what really

Figure 7.1 Smoothed Pendulum Swing Measurement

happened. I have been on two "tiger" teams digging into what went wrong in an expensive experiment. I have learned, <u>trust your measurements</u>. The only means to trust your measurements is to have them tested for validity before the actual experiment. The memories of the experimenters are weak and subjective to outside influence. Your well-made measurements can record the real story.

Once, an experiment has been run, bad measurement data can create more problems than ever expected. There are cases where research has been retracted. Having the raw data might allow for correction over retraction.

For example: let's say, we want to measure the swing of a clock pendulum in a vacuum to show the swing is ideal without air resistance. The distance measurement used to track the pendulum swing is subject to some small noise in the measurement.

The pendulum displacement swing is a simple sinusoid wave at one fundamental frequency. Looking at our 'digitally filtered' data, (Figure 7.1) there appears some "mechanical instability" of our pendulum at the lower peaks. What could be causing this? Some defect in the pendulum bushing?

Now looking at the raw measurements plotted in Figure 7.2. There is a lot of measurement noise at all the peaks. In truth, there isn't any more noise at the peaks than found anywhere else in the signal. Physics tells us the pendulum must slow down to zero displacement as it changes directions. So, the small errors in the measurement can dominate at the peaks. The measurement noise here is 'white' noise, meaning it contains all frequencies.

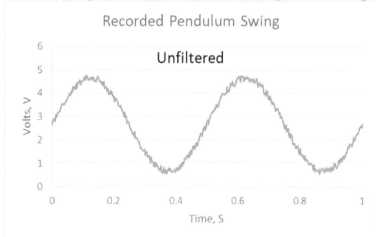

Figure 7.2 Unfiltered Pendulum Swing Measurements

The digital filter reduces the amplitude of the noise while also limiting the bandwidth. Following the filter, we now have "colored" noise. Colored is random noise which fell within the passband of the digital filter. The colored noise visually correlates with the swing of the pendulum. In truth, fixing the pendulum's bushing will not fix this problem. However, a better sensor might. If the first rule is to save the raw data then the second rule of signal processing is: if you want better data get a better sensor.

I realize this is no way to start a section on digital filtering. The first two rules of DSP are telling the reader don't do it. What I hope to get across is this: digital signal processing is like the icing on the cake. It makes the cake look really good but it still has to taste good. First, get the best measurement you can and then look at how to add the icing on top.

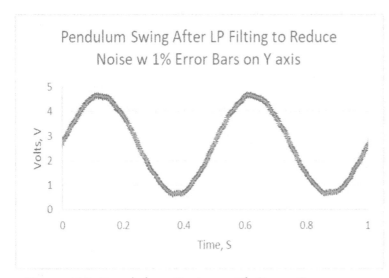

Figure 7.3 Pendulum Swing with Error Bars

Getting back to the pendulum example, this is a basic "linear" digital filtering problem without a good solution.

Placing error bars on your measurement data is good practice but is rarely done. Error bars of 1% were placed on the digitally filtered data, see Figure 7.3. Now, the small noise fluctuations in the measurement are less likely to cause concerns. These plots were made using Microsoft Excel which has several error bar options.

Conclusions to "Is it Real?"

1. Digital Signal Processing alone doesn't add information to the signal. It only works to remove unwanted information or interfering noise.
2. If you truly want better measurement data look for a better sensor.
3. Save the rawest form of your measurements as possible. Digital processing may not be backward recoverable.
4. At the start of a project, ask some basic questions as, "How can I validate the measurements?" You and your team need confidence before pushing the plunger.

5. Always look for secondary measurements to aid in supporting your primary required measurements.
6. Any successful experiment uncovers the unknown. When questions are raised, trust your measurements.

7.3 The Dreaded Moving Average

My experience tells me, the vast majority of people making electronic measurements use the moving average as a digital filter for removing noise. It is easy to use and it does 'smooth' ADC measurement noise. However, after reading this section, the reader might never use a moving average again. At least not use it when capturing dynamic signals.

The moving average is technically classified as a finite impulse response (FIR) filter. Below is a 5 point moving average FIR filter similar to the "Smoother" sketch example provided at the Arduino.cc website.

Smoother Equ: $Y(n) = a_0X(n) + a_1X(n-1) + a_2X(n-2) + a_3X(n-3) + a_4X(n-4)$;
Where $Y(n)$ is the result, $X(n)$ is the current ADC reading, $X(n-1)$ is the prior ADC reading(s), and a_n are the coefficients for the FIR filter. For the moving average of 5:
$$a_0 = a_1 = a_2 = a_3 = a_4 = 0.20 = 1/5$$

OK, this looks complex. I need to define how to read and write digital filter equations. By convention the ADC samples are taken one at a time and they are indexed by an integer value, 'n'. The first reading is at n=0, the second at n=1 and so on. The 'X(n)' values are ADC readings made by the Arduino. Here $X(n)$ is the nth ADC reading with n starting at 0. So, if we have taken 20 readings (0 to 19), the 21st reading just taken is $X(20)$. So, in the smoothing equation above, if we use $X(20)$ as $X(n)$ then the four preceding readings are $X(n-1)$, $X(n-2)$, $X(n-3)$ and $X(n-4)$ OR AS $X(19)$, $X(18)$, $X(17)$ and $X(16)$.

The coefficients of our digital filter equation are listed as 'a'. Each coefficient of a FIR filter can be unique. The coefficients determine the properties of the filter. For the moving average FIR filter all coefficients 'a' are the same, $a_n = 1/$(number of X readings averaged). $Y(n)$ is the result of the filter equation. $Y(n)$ is the filter output at X(n). Y(n) is the digital filter result. There is one Y(n) for every X(n). The smoothing moving average FIR filter looks like this:

5 Point Smoother: $Y(n) = 0.2*X(n) + 0.2*X(n-1) + 0.2*X(n-2) + 0.2*X(n-3) + 0.2*X(n-4)$;

Please realize, I understand this has been a long process to explain taking an average of 5 numbers! However, when we get in to more complex digital filters understanding digital filter equations will be helpful.

For this book all 'Xn' values are integer values from the ADC. Converting ADC integer values to 'floating' point voltage values doesn't add ANY information to our measurement. We either have the needed information in our integer ADC readings or we don't. There is plenty of time to convert ADC integers to floating voltages or Gs (for accelerometers) or degree F or C (for temperature) or other unit after we have completed our digital filter calculations. Also, the Arduino program works faster with 16 bit integers than with 32 bit floating point numbers.

To illustrate the smoother 5 point moving average, see Table 7.1. The raw ADC

Table 7.1 Five point one sided average

Sample	Reading	Result
n	X	Y
239	0	0
240	0	0
241	1	0.2
242	1	0.4
243	1	0.6
244	1	0.8
245	1	1
246	1	1
247	0	0.8
248	0	0.6
249	0	0.4
250	0	0.2
251	0	0
252	0	0

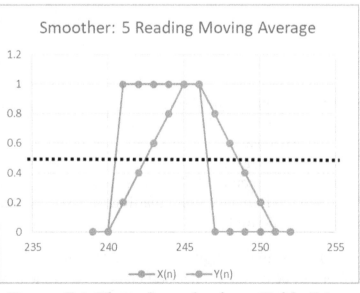

Figure 7.4 Plotted results from Table 7.1

readings are provided in column 'X'. For simplicity, assume all ADC readings up to n = 240 have been 0. At reading n = 241 a 1.0V pulse is captured by our measurement system in the X column. This 1V pulse last through sample n= 246. For every X(n) there is a 5 point smoother result Y(n). The resulting Y values are shown in the 'Y' column.

The table values have been plotted in the smoother plot Figure 7.4. The 1V event pulse creates a pyramid waveform response passing through the 5 point moving average. If our system was using the timing of the event pulse to correlate with other experiment sensor readings, we might have a problem. Assuming a timing threshold at 0.5V, as shown by the dotted line, the timing of the raw readings and the smoothed readings are different. The raw X(n) values time the front edge of the event pulse at n = 241 while the smoothed

Y(n) values time the front edge at n = 243. This is an offset error of 2 samples or two times the sample period, 1/fs in seconds.

[**Tech Note**: OK, the reader may suggest (and it is true) that if the 1V pulse had gone through an anti-aliasing filter, it would also be delayed and perhaps the shift seen here would be minor. Yes, this is why, for projects with critical timing issues, timing through analog filters must be calibrated.]

Great time to talk about "double sided" FIR filters using our same 5 point moving average. Let's rewrite the moving average as I would in a real measurement system I designed.

$$Y(n) = a_0X(n+2) + a_1X(n+1) + a_2X(n) + a_3X(n-1) + a_4X(n-2);$$

Where Y(n) is the result at 'n' while X(n+2) is the current ADC reading. The X(n+1) is the prior ADC reading and so on. The a_n values are the coefficients for the FIR filter. For the moving average of 5: $a_0=a_1=a_2=a_3=a_4=0.20$

Unlike before, we now have future n+2 and n+1 readings to work with. How do we get future readings? The current Arduino ADC reading is actually X(n+2) while calculating Y(n). Our filter equation still has one Y(n) for every X(n). We record the time stamp for reading result Y(n) as 2 sample periods behind the current measurement. Table 7.2 now has the new Y values. The Y values now have the same timing as the X values.

This is now a 'double sided' FIR filter with both positive and negative n values. The double sided FIR filter reduces measurement noise while protecting the relative timing relationship between sample X(n) and our result Y(n), see the plotted values in Figure 7.5. This is a significant advantage in signal processing. I have never run into an application preventing me from using a double sided moving average or FIR filter. This is an advantage over the IIR (Infinite Impulse Response) filter coming in the next section.

Table 7.2 Five point double sided average

Sample	Reading	Result
n	X	Y
239	0	0.2
240	0	0.4
241	1	0.6
242	1	0.8
243	1	1
244	1	1
245	1	0.8
246	1	0.6
247	0	0.4
248	0	0.2
249	0	0
250	0	0
251	0	0
252	0	0

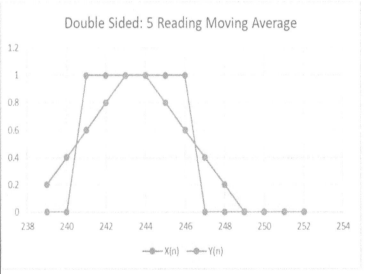

Figure 7.5 Plotted results from Table 7.2

The reader may have a couple of good questions as: what is the frequency response of a moving average filter? If a 5 point moving average is good, is a 10 or 20 point moving average better? The best way to consider the frequency response of the moving average is to convert the filter equation from the sample domain to the frequency domain. However, it's my opinion, Arduino users are better served by examples over pure calculations.

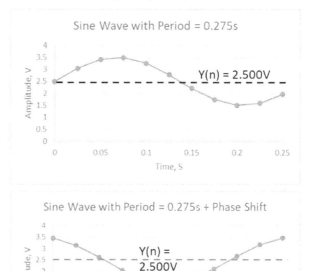

For example, the moving average has a unique feature for creating a 'zero' for frequencies with a period equal to the averaging time. If we are sampling at 40sps the time needed to average 11 readings is 11 * 1/40s or 0.275s. A sinewave of frequency 3.6364Hz (1/0.275s) sampled at 40sps with an 11 point moving average FIR filter will always average to 0V!

Continuing the example, assume we have a 3.6364Hz, 1Vpp (peak to peak Voltage) riding on 2.5V DC voltage, see Figure 7.6. When averaging 11 readings at a 40sps the averaging results in exactly 2.5V. The sinewave is zero'ed out of the input signal. The dots on the plot are the actual sample points. For every sample above 2.5V there are matching samples below 2.5V.

Figure 7.6 A sine wave with the same period as the average of samples. Top, sine wave in phase. Bottom, sine wave out of phase.

This is zero'ing out is independent of the phase or amplitude of the 3.6364Hz sinewave. The lower plot of Figure 7.6 has the 3.6364Hz shifted by nearly 90 degrees and the result is still 2.5V as if the sinewave riding on the 2.5V doesn't exist. If the 3.6364Hz wave is noise, GREAT.

Now, let's sample a sinewave that's 1.5 times 3.6364Hz or 5.4545Hz with the same 2.5V DC offset. With a 5.4545Hz sinewave in phase with our moving average, the Y(n) value is 2.6753V. In Figure 7.7, the higher frequency sinewave is NOT zero'ed out. Shifting the sinewave, changes the Y(n) value, in this case, Y(n) = 2.3246V. In fact, a sinewave at 1.5X the fundamental frequency of our sample period is NOT zero'ed out. There is some attenuation at this frequency but the signal is still there. If 5.4545Hz is unwanted noise, this is not a positive outcome.

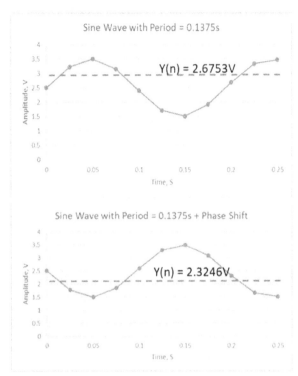

Figure 7.7 A sine wave with 1.5X period as the average of samples. Top, sine wave in phase. Bottom, sine wave out of phase.

In truth, the moving average is a poor filter. At DC, the filters gain is 1. As input frequencies approach the fundamental frequency created by the number of averaged ADC readings, those frequencies see their magnitude attenuated. At the fundamental frequency of the averaging period, the filter gain is 0. For that frequency, the moving average is a really great filter. However, as the input frequency increases past fundamental frequency, the filters gain partially recovers. At frequencies of 2X the fundamental frequency the filter provides another 0 gain but once again, there is a recovery of filter gain following frequencies above 2X. This processes repeats for integer values of the fundamental frequency up to the Nyquist frequency. A normalized plot of the 11 sample filter is provided in Figure 7.8. Unlike the anti-aliasing filters (or the IIR Filters in the next section), the stop band has large ripples. Unfortunately, increasing the number of samples averaged, does little to reduce the size of these ripples!

I was once in meeting where the researcher talked about the difficulty of removing noise from the measurement by saying, "We had to use a 100 point moving average to remove the noise." He was a good software engineer but WOW he really needed to understand how the moving average works.

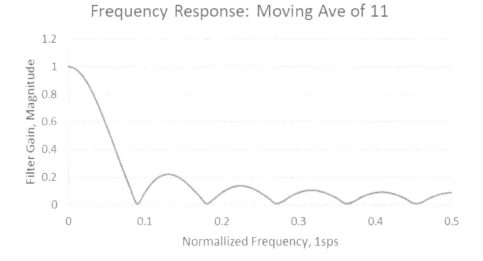

Figure 7.8 The frequency response of an 11 point moving average

Someone might ask, "Does the moving average need to be an odd number?" No, any number can be used. I always use odd number moving averages, because for every X(n) we have a Y(n). If an even number is used, then Y(n) is actually a calculated point between two samples periods. Not a big deal but why not simply go with an odd moving average?

Double sided FIR filters can be designed with cutoff frequencies for low pass, high pass, band pass or any type of filter needed. As shown in the moving average, FIR filters require a lot of terms.   It is not unusual to have a band pass FIR filter of 60 or more coefficients.   It takes time to process that many terms inside the Arduino when running real time measurements. For that reason, I suggest using IIR filters with the Arduino, which is the next section.

7.4 The IIR Filter

All the digital IIR filters discussed here are based on the Butterworth equations. The math for transforming these equations to digital sample domains is a bit too involved for this book. I will provide 'cookbook' solutions for IIR low pass, high pass and band pass that anybody can use with the Arduino or any other digital system. For people with a need to know, I will provide versions of the math via my website, www.onmeasurement.com for downloading.

7.4.1 Low Pass IIR Butterworth Filter

The Infinite Impulse Response (IIR) filter provides the type of filter response most people are looking for. What makes it different from the FIR filter is a $Y(n-1)$ term is used in the filter equation. The $Y(n-1)$ is a past result of our filter. Tying a past filter result to the filter equation makes all future results a partial product of all past results. This is why the IIR has an "infinite response".

Before providing a cook book set of equations to determine the IIR filter coefficients, I think a simple example will aid the reader. The following example is of a 1 pole, low pass IIR filter (as an RC filter). I will compare this filter with the 11 point moving average already discussed in the prior section.

The 1 pole, low pass digital IIR filter equation is below.

1 pole IIR filter equation: $Y(n) = a_0X(n) + a_1X(n-1) + b_1Y(n-1)$
Where $Y(n)$ is the result at n, $X(n)$ is the ADC reading at n, a_n are the coefficients for X values and b_n are the coefficients for the Y values.

We will cover how to calculate the 'a' and 'b' coefficients later. For now, let's use the following: $a_0 = 0.11216$, $a_1 = 0.11216$ and $b_1 = 0.77568$. Our filter equation is:

Example IIR equation: $Y(n) = 0.11216*X(n) + 0.11216*X(n-1) + 0.77568*Y(n-1)$

These coefficients were picked to create a ~1.6Hz low pass filter for a sample frequency, $fs = 40Hz$. This is approximately the same as the 11 point moving average for a system with an $fs = 40Hz$. Now look at the plot of the two filters seen in Figure 7.9.

Figure 7.9 Lab comparison of a moving average and IIR filter

The moving average has a faster roll-off but less total attenuation at higher frequencies compared to the 1 pole IIR. The IIR has only 3 coefficients compared to 11 in the FIR. We can increase the IIR filter roll-off by increasing the number of poles. Increasing the number of poles in an IIR filter doesn't shift the fc frequency. Increasing the number of averaged points shifts location of the zero frequency and does little to improve total attenuation at higher frequencies.

Remember the statement, "We had to use a 100 point moving average to remove the noise." It's easy to fall into thinking a moving average reduces noise (because it does), so more averaging must mean more noise reduction. The law of diminishing returns is in action for moving averages.

Let's now look at calculating our coefficients for the 1 pole, low pass IIR filter already discussed above.

7.4.2 One Pole, Low Pass IIR Filter

The 1 pole low pass Butterworth IIR difference equation is:

$$Y(n) = a_0X(n) + a_1X(n-1) + b_1Y(n-1)$$

Where $Y(n)$ is the result at sample n, $X(n)$ is the ADC reading at sample n, n is the sample index, 'a' terms are the coefficients for $X(n)$ and 'b' terms are the coefficients for the $Y(n)$ terms.

We need to calculate the coefficients a_0, a_1 and b_1. The coefficients will result in a low pass filter with an fc just like the RC filters already talked about in Chapter 4. The "general" IIR equations for the three coefficients are normalized for a sample frequency of 1Hz. Therefore in order to use the equations we must convert our desired digital filter's fc to a normalized value. Normalizing is simple. Knowing our fs and desired fc we can generate a normalized f'c as below.

Normalizing fc to a 1Hz sample frequency: $fc/fs = f'c/1Hz$
reducing to $f'c = fc/fs$
where f'c is our normalized frequency for use in IIR filter calculations

For the 1 pole example already used to compare to the 11 point moving average, I used fc = 1.6Hz. So, the f'c = 1.6/40 = 0.04Hz.

[**Tech Note:** f'c can only fall between 0 and 0.5Hz. The Nyquist frequency (fn) is the highest frequency any sampled system can represent. For the normalized 1Hz sample frequency, the Nyquist frequency is 0.5Hz. Also true that any fc value of any digital filter must be < fn.]

Now, we need to move our f'c from the continuous time domain to the digital sample domain as below:

Let $wa = tan(\pi*f'c)$
Where tan is the tangent function

The wa term is very important to the calculation of the IIR coefficients. Some authors refer to it as the critical frequency. For math junkies, wa is in radians.

For the 1 pole Butterworth low pass IIR filter the coefficients for the difference equation are:

$$a_0 = a_1 = wa/(1 + wa)$$

and
$$b1 = (1 - wa)/(1 + wa)$$

For fc = 1.6Hz and fs = 40Hz we have the IIR filter equation:

$$Y(n) = 0.11216 * X(n) + 0.11216 * X(n-1) + 0.77568 * Y(n-1)$$

The equation above is the same equation as before. For the low pass digital filter, the sum of the coefficients must equal 1. This can be used as a check of your work.

Check: 0.11216 + 0.11216 + 0.77568 = 1.0000? Yes, we're good. More on this check later.

7.4.3 Two Pole, Low Pass IIR Filter

Two Pole Digital Filter equation: $Y(n) = a_0 X(n) + a_1 X(n-1) + a_2 X(n-2) + b_1 Y(n-1) + b_2 Y(n-2)$. There are now 2 past Y(n) results. Guess how many will be needed for a three pole IIR. You're right, 3.

We need to calculated $f'c = fc/fs$ and $wa = \tan(\pi * f'c)$ as before.

For the 2 pole Butterworth low pass IIR filter calculate the coefficients as below.

$$a_0 = a_2 = wa^2/(1 + \sqrt{2}\,wa + wa^2)$$
$$a_1 = 2a_0$$
$$b_1 = 2(1 - wa)/(1 + \sqrt{2}\,wa + wa^2)$$
$$\text{and}$$
$$b_2 = -(1 - \sqrt{2}\,wa + wa^2)/(1 + \sqrt{2}\,wa + wa^2)$$

It would be good to take our IIR filter to an actual sketch program for a demonstration. In section 10.6, I used an SRAM and Arduino Due to demonstrate a 2 pole IIR filter in sketch "SRAM_LP". Taking the demonstration a bit further, I decided it would be good to compare an RC filter to a 2 pole IIR filter with the same fc. In the previous discussion regarding analog filters, the circuit in section 5.5.2, the A0 input had the RC filtered signal (fc = 570Hz) while A1 had the unfiltered signal.

Using the demonstration sketch, the Due A1 input is filtered by the 2 pole IIR filter. The results are shown in Figure 7.10.

Here is how the filter was implemented.

In the global variables, I defined the filter coefficients and variables. The coefficients were calculated using the equations above. The ADC readings from the Due were stored in the array of Xn integers. The array of Yn results were stored in the float array Yn.

```
//Filter coef for the low pass Butterworth, fc=570Hz,
fs=25KHz
const float a0 = 0.0047;
const float a1 = 0.0093;
const float a2 = 0.0047;
const float b1 = 1.7976;
const float b2 = -0.8163;
int Xn[3];   //Array of measured values for the filter
float Yn[3];   //Array of past values for the filter
```

Also run as part of the "setup()" loop, Xn and Yn reading are zero'ed out. In many cases, you may have better initial values knowing the nominal sensor output value. As a general rule, I assume all analog inputs were at 0V for all time until the system started taking data.

```
// Initialize at the start of collecting data
Xn[1]=0;
Xn[2]=0;
Yn[1]=0;
Yn[2]=0;
```

There isn't any need to initialize Xn[0] or Yn[0] variables as first measurement and first result respectfully. Below is the section reading the ADC and saving the results to the SRAM. This code is run in the main "loop()".

```
Chan1 = analogRead(A0);   //ADC reading at input A0
Xn[0] = analogRead(A1);   //ADC reading at input A1
// The filter equation is below.  This is a 2 pole LP IIR
filter
```

```
    Yn[0] = a0*Xn[0] + a1*Xn[1] + a2*Xn[2] + b1*Yn[1] +
b2*Yn[2];
 //  Save our data to the SRAM
    SPI.transfer16(Chan1);  //Save ADC readings to the SRAM
    SPI.transfer16(Yn[0]);  //This action truncates our float
value
 // Shift the past reading before making the next ADC reading
    Xn[2]=Xn[1];
    Xn[1]=Xn[0];
    Yn[2]=Yn[1];
    Yn[1]=Yn[0];
  // repeat until the designed number of data points is
reached
```

Looking at the code above, "Chan1" is the A0 analog input. The A0 input is following the RC filter. The Xn[0] is the A1 signal without any filtering coming directly from a function generator. The A1 input is going through the IIR filter. Using arrays for Xn and Yn and filter coefficients with the same names used in our IIR filter equations make the coded filter equation look familiar and hopefully easy to understand, see below:

 Coded filter equation:

$$Yn[0] = a0*Xn[0] + a1*Xn[1] + a2*Xn[2] + b1*Yn[1] + b2*Yn[2];$$

After calculating Yn[0], both Chan1 and Yn[0] are saved to the SRAM using the SPI transfer16 function. After Y[0] is calculated and saved, the arrays must be shifted in order to take on the next Xn[0] reading. This process continues until reaching the required number of readings, which for this example I stored only 125 readings for each A0 and A1. Using the "Serial Plotter" option under the "Tools" heading of the Arduino IDE, I captured data shown in Figure 7.10.

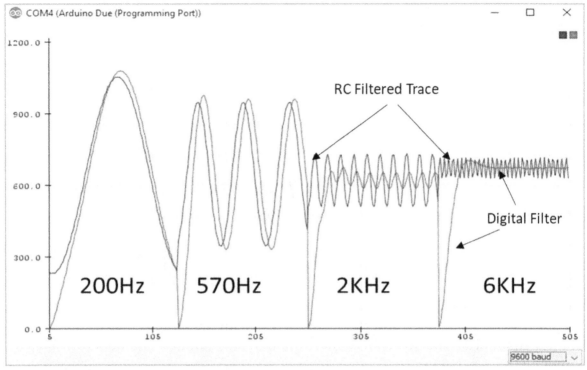

Figure 7.10 Comparison of a IIR 2 pole LP filter (red) and a RC analog filter both with fc =~ 570Hz

The Arduino serial plotter option displays your data as it comes in. By taking only a 125 readings with each trigger of "SRAM_LP", I was able to change the setting on the function generator to generate a new frequency. Figure 7.10 shows 4 different test frequencies. This is not an option on standard oscilloscopes. For illustration purposes, taking 125 readings using the serial plotter works very well.

In Figure 7.10, the A1 trace is starting at 0 with each trigger because it is going through the IIR filter. At 200Hz both the IIR and RC filters are passing the signal with little attenuation. At 570Hz both are showing attenuation on the order to -3dB (0.707X amplitude). So, we're happy with the filter's fc result. The IIR and the RC are doing their jobs and they are very comparable to this point. However, the IIR 2 pole filter will have a steeper roll-off. At 2KHz, the IIR filter (A1 trace) has more attenuation. At 6KHz, the IIR filter has virtually removed the input signal while the signal is still visible going through the RC filter. There are a couple of other differences between the two signals worth pointing out.

There is a greater phase shift in the IIR 2 pole filter. This shift becomes noticeable in the roll-off section of the filter, 570Hz. This can be "mostly" corrected as will be shown in section 7.5. Another difference between the two signals is caused by initializing the IIR values to 0. So each section of 125 samples starts at 0 and takes several input readings to catch up with the analog RC filter. This is a problem with all digital filters. The RC is in the continuous time domain. The distortion seen at the start of each set of 125 readings for the RC filtered input is caused by the random starting and stopping caused by the random trigger.

7.4.4 Three Pole, Low Pass IIR Filter

For the 3 pole Butterworth low pass IIR filter.

3 Pole Filter equation: $Y(n) = a_0X(n) + a_1X(n-1) + a_2X(n-2) + a_3X(n-3) + b_1Y(n-1) + b_2Y(n-2) + b_3Y(n-3)$

The calculations continue to grow time consuming so I have introduced variables A, B, C and D as intermediate steps.

Let $A = 1 + 2wa + 2\,wa^2 + wa^3$
Let $B = -3 - 2wa + 2wa + 3wa^3$
Let $C = 3 - 2wa - 2wa^2 + 3wa^3$
Let $D = -1 + 2wa - 2wa^2 + wa^3$
Now $a_0 = a_3 = wa^3/A$, $a_1 = a_2 = 3wa^3/A$, $b_1 = B/A$, $b_2 = C/A$, $b_3 = D/A$

Table 7.3 Three pole IIR Coef

f'c =	0.13334
Wa =	0.44525378
A=	2.3752814
B=	3.22918977
C=	-1.9778065
D=	0.41772232
a0=	0.0372
a1=	0.1114
a2=	0.1114
a3=	0.0372
b1=	1.3595
b2=	-0.8327
b3=	0.176
Sum =	1

An example of a 3 pole, LP Butterworth IIR filter would be useful. Let's say, we have a sample period of 6.667mS. Our Nyquist frequency is 74.996Hz. We have an input signal of 0.75Hz. However, at 50Hz there is 0.15Vpp of noise on our signal along with +/-25mV of just random noise. We want an IRR with an fc = 20Hz to reduce this noise. Table 7.3 shows the calculated values needed for our 3 pole, low pass IIR filter.

Using these values in our 3 pole IIR filter equation we can filter our signal. An example signal was created by summing a 1Vpp sinewave at 0.75Hz, a 0.15Vpp cosine wave at 50Hz and 0.025V random noise using Microsoft Excel.

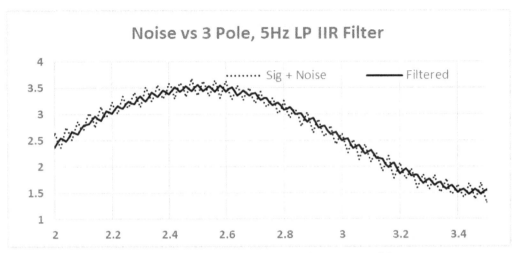

Figure 7.11 Three pole IIR, Butterworth low pass filter

This signal + noise was then filtered by our 20Hz low pass, 3 pole IIR filter. The results show a clear improvement, exposing the 0.75Hz signal under the noise in Figure 7.11.

7.4.2.1 Using Excel to Check Your Filter

It is easy to create a type-O or simple error when generating coefficients for the 3 pole IIR filter or any digital filter. To run a test of the 3 pole above, I created a test signal and noise using Microsoft Excel or another data spreadsheet. This type of filter testing is useful before programming your Arduino and powering up a function generator. Below are the Excel expressions to create the signal + noise used in the 3 pole IIR filter example shown in Figure 7.11.

The 0.75Hz was created in Microsoft Excel using the sin(2*pi()*n*sample period*f) function.

Where f is the 0.75 Hz frequency, n is the sample number, the sample period is the time between samples, the Excel default amplitude is 1Vpp

The 50Hz noise was created by 0.15*cos(2*pi()*n*0.006667*50) function.

The 0.15 is the Vpp amplitude of the cosine wave.

The random noise at 50mVpp was created with 0.05*(0.5 – RAND()).

The 0.05 is the amplitude multiplier. The function RAND() returns a random number between 0 and 1. By subtracting the random number from 0.5, we get random numbers between -0.5 and 0.5.

Now summing values from these functions gives us negative values which are not allowed by the Arduino ADC. So the sum was offset by adding 2.5.

Final summation is:
Signal(n) = sin(n) + cos(n) + Random(n) + 2.5V

Table 7.4 Excel signal + noise example

n	Sine	Cosine	Random	OffsetV	Sum
	0.75Hz	50Hz	0.05V	2.5V	Test Sig
0	0	0.15	-0.01309	2.5	2.636908
1	0.031412	-0.07501	-0.00777	2.5	2.448624
2	0.062794	-0.07497	0.024331	2.5	2.512152
3	0.094113	0.15	-0.01462	2.5	2.729488
4	0.125339	-0.07505	-0.01933	2.5	2.530957
5	0.156442	-0.07493	0.005519	2.5	2.58703

The final summation provided the 'raw' X values for the IIR filter. Table 7.4 shows an example of the first 5 values created in Excel.

7.4.2.2 Checking the LP IIR Coefficients

I entered the 3 pole IIR Butterworth equations for calculating the coefficients in to Excel. Clearly, I could have used a hand held calculator but with so many terms, a mistake is easy to make and hard to find.

In the 3 pole filter table of coefficients (Table 7.3), there was a 'sum' variable. The sum variable is an important check. For low pass digital filters both IIR and FIR, the sum of coefficients must equal 1.0 without rounding. Here 0.9999 is too low and 1.00001 is too high. Assume, we are measuring 2.5V for a 10 Million ADC reading passing through our IRR filter. If our coefficients sum to 0.9999, the eventual outcome of our filter is 0V. For a sum of 1.00001, the outcome of the filter over time is out-of-bounds. Only a prefect 1.0 sum means the outcome is 2.5V for all time.

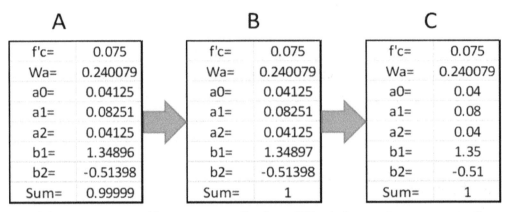

A			B			C	
f'c=	0.075		f'c=	0.075		f'c=	0.075
Wa=	0.240079		Wa=	0.240079		Wa=	0.240079
a0=	0.04125		a0=	0.04125		a0=	0.04
a1=	0.08251		a1=	0.08251		a1=	0.08
a2=	0.04125		a2=	0.04125		a2=	0.04
b1=	1.34896		b1=	1.34897		b1=	1.35
b2=	-0.51398		b2=	-0.51398		b2=	-0.51
Sum=	0.99999		Sum=	1		Sum=	1

Tables 7.5 A. Coefficients as calculated B. Adjusted to a sum of 1.0 C. Following extreme rounding

Correcting for a less than perfect summation of coefficients is easy. For example, I have calculated the coefficients for a 2 pole, IIR low pass filter as shown in Table 7.5A.

In Table 7.5A, all we need to do is add 0.00001 to one of the coefficients to make a perfect 1.0 summation. Here, the b1 term was bumped up for Table 7.5B coefficients. This small change has virtually zero impact on the poles location and improves the DC response to 1.0 for all time.

Since the sum of the coefficients must = 1 means our coefficients are really just ratios or a weighting of the contribution of the X(n-K) and Y(n-k) values. As fc moves toward fn, the a_n coefficients become larger and the b_n coefficients become smaller. This allows the filter to respond quicker to changing X(n) values. As fc moves toward 0Hz, the b_n coefficients become increasingly dominate. This lags the signal as it takes more time for changes in X(n) to have an impact on the resulting Y(n).

As ratios, we can round our coefficient values with little change of fc. Table 7.4C

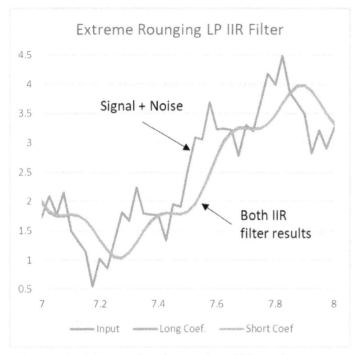

Figure 7.12 Example of rounding IIR coef.

above has severely rounded values from Table 7.4B. Remember, at DC, there is no change as the sum always = 1.0. However, in the filters transition frequencies there will be slight filter output differences between using Table 7.4B and Table 7.5C. I used both set of coefficients on the test signal generated in section 7.4.2.1. For this case, Table 7.5C coefficients had a difference (error) in Y(n) values of ~+/- 0.05V compared to using the 7.4B coefficients. At high frequencies in the band stop regions, there isn't any difference. Using shorter coefficients is a benefit for the 8 bit Arduino in processing time.

Figure 7.12 is an expanded look at the raw signal + noise and two filter output traces using Table 7.5B and 7.5C coefficients. The trace labeled "Long Coef" and the trace labeled "Short Coef" are shown with the original trace of signal + noise values. Even with this blowup plot, there are no significant differences in the two filter outputs.

Again, the amplitude differences will be found in the digital filters transition band. At DC, there is no difference (each sum to 1.0) and in the stop band any small error is virtually zero anyway. For real time processing inside the Arduino, consider rounding the coefficients for a more manageable real time calculation.

7.5 Time Shifting the IIR LP Filter

Like the 5 point smoothing function discussed in the FIR filter section 7.3, the IIR filter will cause a lag in your timing of fast rising signals. The double sided FIR filter has an advantage over the IIR filter in this respect. However, there is a little trick which can recover most of the timing error. This is a simple trick and can only be performed in post processing of your data, not in real time data capture.

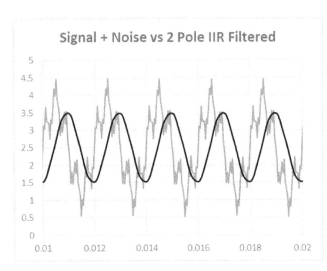

Figure 7.13 Two pole, LP IIR filter

The trick is to run the filter as described in real time while making the measurements. Then in post processing, run the same IIR filter only reversing the order of the measured values.

Perhaps an example of running the data in reverse order needs an example. Let's use a 2 pole, IIR filter. The sample frequency, fs = 25KHz and we want an fc = 570Hz. Our f'c = 0.07175 so we can use the coefficients from section 7.4.3 above.

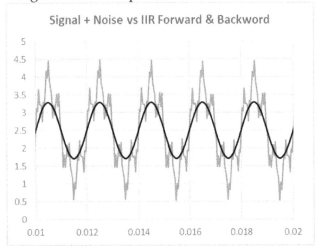

Figure 7.14 Same IIR filter run backwards

To test this filter, I created an input signal with a sum of sine waves. One of the test frequencies is near the fc with noise in the stopband. The noisy signal is run through the IIR filter, see Figure 7.13. The filter is doing its job of removing the high frequency part of the signal. Clearly, there is significant lag time between the input signal and the filtered output.

Now in post processing, the same filter (using the same coefficients) is used to process the filtered readings starting with the last reading. The filter is now working toward the first reading taken, n=0.

Working backwards we have:

$$Y(n) = a0X(n) + a1X(n+1) + a2X(n+2) + b1Y(n+1) + b2Y(n+2)$$
Where n starts at the max value n and is decremented for each new Y(n) value.

By running the same IIR filter backwards through the data, much of the signal lag has been corrected for. The signal lag in Figure 7.14 is virtually zero'ed out. Also, the filter's attenuation at frequencies above fc is independent of the direction the values are run. So, the second backward pass results in a **4 pole, low pass IIR filter of your measurements!**

Unfortunately, we cannot claim to have fully recovered the lag in X(n). All we can claim is that we have recovered much of the timing. Lag is a function of the step increase in X(n) values. The first pass, reduced the step values as any low pass filter will do. So, the second pass is working with a smoothed step response. It is fair to suggest the timing within the lower part of the filters passband is really, good. Good enough for most timing applications. However, not technically, as good as a double-side FIR low pass filter.

7.6 High Pass IIR Filters

Just like the low pass Butterworth IIR filters there are high pass and band pass versions of the Butterworth filters. High pass is good for removing unwanted low frequencies (including DC) found in some signals. There are sensors with frequency responses below the desired signal frequency. MEM accelerometers are normally sensitive to DC position such as slow moving changes in tilt. Tilt isn't of much interest when looking for mechanical vibration in an aircraft wing during a test flight.

Just like the IIR low pass Butterworth filters, we start with the normalized Butterworth equation and use the same $f'c = fc/fs$ and $wa = \tan(\pi*f'c)$. The high pass IIR is no more difficult than the low pass IIR.

7.6.1 One Pole High Pass IIR Filter

The Butterworth high pass IIR filter equation and coefficient calculations are given below.

The 1 pole, HP IIR filter equation is: $Y(n) = a_0X(n) - a_1X(n-1) + b_1Y(n-1)$
The coefficients are: $a_0 = a_1 = 1/(wa + 1)$ and $b_1 = (1 - wa)$

Note, the a_n coefficients are equal and of the opposite sign in the high pass IIR filter. The filter is taking the difference of $X(n)$ and $X(n-1)$. As such, only the difference between the current reading and the past reading is accepted. The b1 coefficient is always less than 1. Clearly, this filter is removing any DC value in the signal. The check for a summation of 1.000 is not working to work here.

7.6.2 Two Pole High Pass IIR Filter

The Butterworth 2 pole, high pass IIR filter equation and coefficients are given below. The solution for coefficients is more difficult than the 1 pole high pass. To make these calculations easier for the user, I have interim variables, A, B and C.

The 2 pole IIR high pass filter equation is: $Y(n) = a_0X(n) - a_1X(n-1) + a_2X(n-2) + b_1Y(n-1) - b_2Y(n-2)$

The coefficients are:
$$a_0 = a_2 = 1/A$$
$$a_1 = 2/A$$
$$b_1 = B/A$$
and
$$b_2 = C/A$$
Where $A = 1 + \sqrt{2}\,wa + wa^2$, $B = 2*(1 - wa^2)$ and $C = 1 - \sqrt{2}\,wa + wa^2$

It's good to have a means to check our calculations. Here the summation of all coefficients must be < 1. As noted in the low pass section, a summation of samples less than 1 degrades any DC value to 0.

To provide an example, let's design a high pass IIR filter assuming we have fs = 100Hz and we want fc = 3Hz in order to pass most of our sensors MEM accelerometer data.

$$f'c = fc/fs = 0.03$$
$$wa = \tan(\pi * f'c) = 0.09452783$$

We need to carry a lot of digits

$$A = 1.14262$$
$$B = 1.98213$$
$$C = 0.87525$$
$$a_0 = 0.87518$$
$$a_1 = 1.75036$$
$$a_2 = 0.87518$$
$$b_1 = 1.7347$$
$$b_2 = 0.7660$$

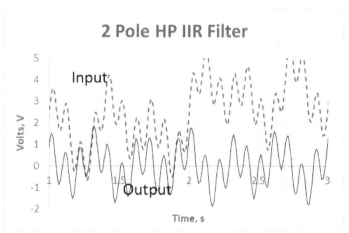

Figure 7.15 Two pole HP IIR filter results

Checking the coefficients using the signs from high pass filter equation:

Sum = a0 – a1 + a2 + b1 –b2 = 0.87518 – 1.75036 + 0.87518 + 1.7347 – 0.7660 = 0.9687 < 1.0 check

To further test our high pass IIR filter, a 2.5V DC signal has four 1Vpp sinewaves at 0.5Hz, 1.5Hz, 3Hz and 10Hz were summed. The IIR filter is applied and the results can be seen in Figure 7.15.

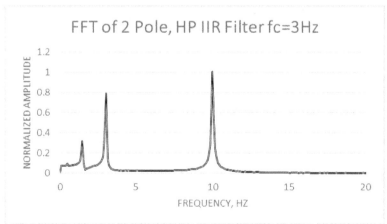

Figure 7.16 The IIR filters output Fourier Transform

The input trace is riding on 2.5V DC. The high pass has removed the DC level. The 0.5Hz sinewave also appears to be removed from filtered signal. Taking the magnitude values from the Fourier Transform (FFT) of the filter's output measures the filter's response frequency to the input.

All input sinewaves were at the same voltage levels, 1Vpp. Figure 7.16 is the FFT of the filters output. It can be seen that the filter did its job. The frequencies below 3Hz were attenuated and the 10Hz above 3Hz was passed. The 3Hz component is at the high pass filter's cutoff frequency, fc.

For users with access to Microsoft's Excel, the Fourier Transform (FFT) can be loaded as an option. See the Excel "Help" for information on how to do it.

7.7 Band Pass Butterworth IIR Filter

A band pass filter has both a high pass and low pass filter functions, see Figure 7.17. Having two, 1 pole filters isn't very useful while the calculations are difficult. For this reason, only the 4 pole (2 high pass and 2 low pass), Butterworth IIR filter will be presented here.

We now must normalize two pole frequencies. For the HP fc I will use f'cl and ωL. For the LP fc, I will use f'ch and ωh. The center frequency is ωo. The sample frequency, fs is the same for both.

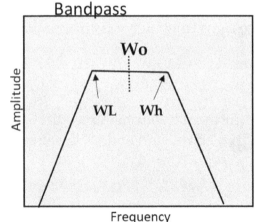

Figure 7.17 Bandpass filter

f'cl = fcl/fs at the HP pole
f'ch = fch/fs at the LP pole
$$\omega L = \tan(\pi * f'cl) \text{ and } \omega h = \tan(\pi * f'ch)$$
Where fc is the desired corner frequency for each location and fs is the sample frequency.

$$\omega o = \sqrt{\omega L * \omega h}$$
Where ωo is the center frequency of the two poles

As might be imagined, having twice as many pole locations and with two poles at each location, the calculation of the filter equation coefficients is long and prone to errors when using a handheld calculator. It is best to use Excel or other program to aid in filter coefficient equations. However, nothing worth doing is ever easy. The detailed solution of this filter along with the other filters in this book are available to the interested reader at the author's web site, www.onmeasurement.com.

The IIR Butterworth band pass filter equation is:

$Y(n) = a_0 X(n) - a_2 X(n-2) + a_4 X(n-4) - b_1 Y(n-1) - b_2 Y(n-2) - b_3 Y(n-3) - b_4 Y(n-4)$

Coefficients: $a_0 = a_4 = \alpha^2/A$, $a_2 = 2a_0$, $a_1 = a_3 = 0$, $b_1 = B/A$, $b_2 = C/A$, $b_3 = D/A$, $b_4 = E/A$

Where:

$\alpha = (wh - wL)$

$A = 1 + \sqrt{2}\alpha + 2wo^2 + \alpha^2 + \sqrt{2}\,\alpha wo^2 + wo^4$

$B = -4 - 2\sqrt{2}\alpha + 2\sqrt{2}\,\alpha wo^2 + 4wo^4$

$C = 6 - 4wo - 2\alpha^2 + 6wo^4$

$D = -4 + 2\sqrt{2}\alpha - 2\sqrt{2}\,\alpha wo^2 + 4wo^4$

$E = 1 - \sqrt{2}\alpha + 2wo^2 + \alpha^2 - \sqrt{2}\,\alpha wo^2 + wo^4$

An example of a band pass IIR filter calculation will aid the reader needing to check their calculation process against the author's.

So, let the high pass fc = 3Hz and the low pass fc = 15Hz and a sample frequency of fs = 100Hz. Remember, each of these two frequencies are normalized by dividing by fs, each result must be positive and less than 0.5 (Nyquist). I'm showing a lot of digits in this example, so that the reader can use this example to check out their calculations before undertaking their own band pass problem.

$$wL = \tan(\pi * fc/fs) = 0.0945278$$
$$wh = \tan(\pi * fc/fs) = 0.5095254$$
$$wo = \sqrt{wL * wh} = 0.2194637$$

Now we have all the critical frequencies in radians. Calculating the intermediate solutions:

$\alpha = (wh - wL) = 0.4149976$

$A = 1 + 0.5868952 + 0.09632863 + 0.1722230 + 0.02826742 + 0.0023198 = 1.88603412$

$B = -4 - 1.17378869 + 0.056534841 + 0.009279213 = -5.10797464$

$C = 6 - 0.19265734 - 0.34444605 + 0.013918819 = 5.47681543$

$D = -4 + 1.173791 - 0.0565348 + 0.0092792 = -2.8734651$

$E = 1 - 0.58689526 + 0.09632867 + 0.17222302 - 0.02826742 + 0.0023198 = 0.65570882$

Wow, entering those and double checking took a few hours of work. Now the actual coefficients can be calculated.

$a_o = a_4 = \alpha^2 / A = 0.0913149$

$a_2 = 2a_o = 0.1826298$

$a_1 = a_3 = 0$

$b_1 = B / A = -2.708156$

$b_2 = C / A = 2.90388$

$b_3 = D / A = -1.5235488$

$b_4 = E / A = 0.3476654$

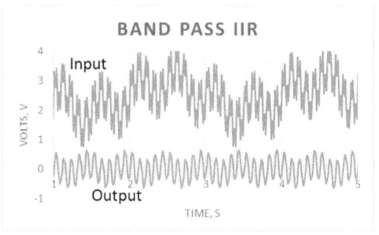

Figure 7.18 Band pass, 4 pole IIR filter results

Finally, the IIR band pass equation for a high pass knee at 3Hz and a low pass knee at 15Hz with a sample frequency of 100sps is below.

$$Y(n) = 0.0913*X(n) - 0.1826*X(n-2) + 0.0913*X(n-4) + 2.7082*Y(n-1) - 2.9039*Y(n-2) + 1.5235*Y(n-3) - 0.3477*Y(n-4)$$

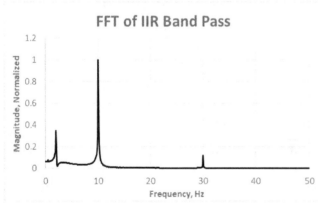

Figure 7.19 FFT of the band pass filter output

To test the band pass filter, a signal comprised of 3 frequencies at equal amplitude was created. The three frequencies were at 2Hz, 10Hz and 30Hz along with a 2.5V DC value.

The plot of the input and filter output in Figure 7.18 show the output has removed the 2.5V DC component. The low 2Hz is less noticeable and the 30Hz seems greatly attenuated.

Taking the magnitude of the Fourier Transform of the filtered results is shown in Figure 7.19. The filter is working. The 10Hz signal is passing through while the 2Hz and 30Hz are attenuated.

Because the 4 pole band pass IIR filter has so many terms, I compared the filter output with significantly rounded coefficients. Normally when post processing your readings, use the full coefficient values as calculated. When real time processing the Arduino ADC readings, rounding the coefficient values is a time saver. Rounding the coefficients of a band pass filter is a little more risky than a low pass or high pass filter because there are two filter transition zones. The above filter example was re-run with rounded coefficients. The maximum observed difference in y(n) was <+/-20mV with our signal frequency at 10Hz.

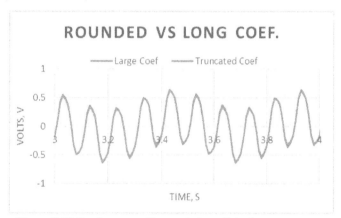

Figure 7.20 Small errors with rounded coefficients

The filter equation with rounded coefficients used for Figure 7.20 is given below.

Y(n) = 0.091*X(n) - 0.182*X(n-2) + 0.091*X(n-4) + 2.708*Y(n-1) - 2.904*Y(n-2) + 1.524*Y(n-3) - 0.348*Y(n-4)

7.8 The Median Digital Filter

There is a class of powerful digital filters which are not linear. Many of these filters will transform the measured values based on user supplied knowledge of the signal and on the type of noise encountered when making a measurement. I view the median filter as one of the most useful and easiest to use with the Arduino.

For example, look at the 20 point data set plotted in Figure 7.21. Most people can look at those readings and say, looks like noise on a 0.2V input. Those people would be right. I simply added +/-40mV of random noise to a constant 0.2V.

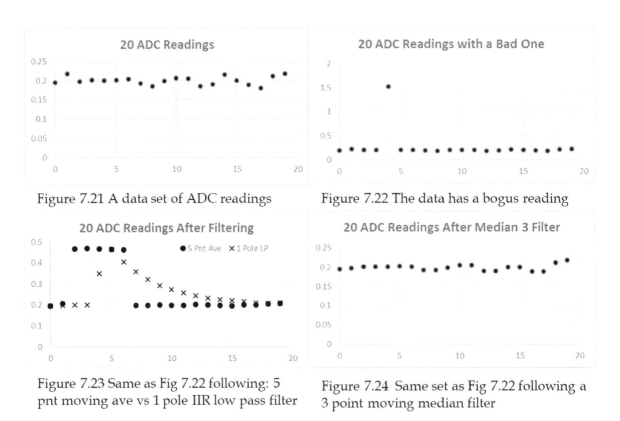

Figure 7.21 A data set of ADC readings

Figure 7.22 The data has a bogus reading

Figure 7.23 Same as Fig 7.22 following: 5 pnt moving ave vs 1 pole IIR low pass filter

Figure 7.24 Same set as Fig 7.22 following a 3 point moving median filter

However, in the real world, when making very high resolution ADC readings, there is something called shot noise. Shot noise is evident when a single ADC reading is well out of alinement with neighboring readings. In short, if the same person looked at the same set of 20 points shown in Figure 7.22 now questions, "What happened here, looks like a bogus reading?" It's the same set but I greatly altered the 4th ADC reading. Most people would quickly agree with their eyes, the 4th reading must be an erroneous reading.

Now, look at those same 20 data points following digital signal processing using either a 5 point moving average or a 1 pole, IIR low pass filter in Figure 7.23.

Both linear filters reduced the size of the error measurement but they also greatly increased its base. In short, the bogus reading now looks a lot more like real measured event. The viewer is unlikely to see these as simply errors in the measurement but some type of event in our experiment.

Enter the 3 point median filter. The median filter has completely removed the bogus measurement and also smoothed the readings. Figure 7.24 plot the 3 point moving median filter. Our 20 points once again look like a 0.2V signal again.

How does a median filter work? Given a set of ADC readings, the median value is the ADC reading in the center of those readings. The median is not the average (or mean) value of the set. For example, given the set of 3 numbers [45, 32, 36], the median value is 36. For the set [0.1, 0.13, 0.099] the median value is 0.1. In a set of 3, the median value is the value in the middle. For a set of 5 as [8, 9, 10, 11, 89034] the median value is 10. It's not a mathematical calculation but logical operation, hence non-linear.

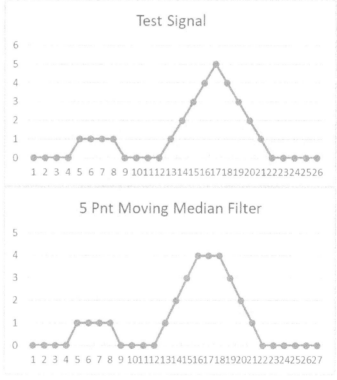

Going back to the 20 readings with the 4th reading being bogus and applying a moving median 3 filter, we get the following results shown in Figure 7.24. The bogus reading was removed and replaced with either the reading before (3rd) or after (5th). No artificial values are ever created, every reading in the set of 20 is still an actual ADC reading from the sensor. A simple moving median filter of 3 or 5 is a powerful filter for removing shot noise.

Figure 7.25 Top, test signal Bottom the results of using a 3 point moving median filter

Because a median filter is a logical operation not a linear calculation there isn't any good way to describe the median filter in terms of a frequency or bandwidth. I will provide some examples to aid in understanding how the median filter effects your measurement.

The test signal of data points was created as shown top of Figure 7.25. This is a simple set of points with a pulse input 4 readings wide and a triangle wave of increasing values followed by declining values.

A 5 point moving median filter is applied to the test signal and is shown in Figure 7.25 bottom plot. First note, the median filter is not time shifting the test signal events. Good. The median filter is not changing the test pulse or the rising or falling values in the test signal. Great! The only change is the loss of the peak of the triangle wave. The 5 point median filter will remove any signal events shorter than 3 data points. The 3 point median filter removes signal events of only 1 data point. So, as electronic measurement designers, we need a high enough ADC sample rate (fs) to insure any expected signal events are captured and can pass through a median filter. The fs must be fast enough that they are sampled more than ½ plus 1 of the median filter set size.

[**Tech Note:** There is no logical upper limit to median filters. A median filter of 21 points or more is possible. However, going past 5 or perhaps 7 is dangerous. In the case of median of 21 points, ask yourself, is there any real reason for two ADC measurements separated by 20 samples to be exchanged? If you take a signal of all random noise and pass it though a large median filter, the filter will create something visually acceptable as a signal. That's the danger of this filter.]

Chapter 8 Plotting Your Measurements

Some help on passing inspection

No experiment is done until the documentation is done. If it's not documented, it doesn't exist. The part of the documentation created by yourself and your team is the display of the data. Creating good and honest data plots is just as important as the effort in conducting the experiment! In this section, I try to present some of my biases on data presentation. These are one dimensional data plots of a sampled signal event. However, what is true for 1-D is also true for 2-D and 3-D images.

Again, these are my prejudices. Every industry or research topic will have generally accepted data presentation norms. I suggest following those accepted norms before anything I say here.

8.1 Some Good and Bad Examples

As a reviewer of test results, there were a few things I'm hoping not to see. There are as many ways to present data as there are colors in the rainbow. I will provide some classic examples of what I might look for in your presentation. Hopefully, this will help the reader build some confidence in presenting their measurement plots. The following examples were all produced using Microsoft Excel.

My test results 'A' is simply plotting each measurement as a point. This a good means of presenting event data. Assuming your plotted points appear close. In this case, as a reviewer, I might ask about the sample period. Since there is a large displacement between measurements, I might ask about the anti-aliasing filter. If they can rerun the test, how much effort is needed to increase the over sample?

My test results 'B' places a straight line between points. For data points being <u>zoomed in on</u>, this is a good way to go. I like seeing some peak points in the measurement. I feel it implies measurements have not been over processed.

My test results 'C' has a problem. Note, the measurement went negative near the start. Notice the nice rounded curves where the other plots have points. Here the measurement has been plotted using the Microsoft 'smoother' option. This smoothing is simply a cosmetic treatment of the measurements in order to look nice. In doing so, it is interpolating between the real data points making the trace look like it was sampled much faster than it was. The small negative values can be a real problem depending on the sensor or application to the reviewer. For example, say this is a pressure measurement. The reviewer might ask, is your calibration off because your test should never pull a vacuum? As a reviewer, I normally suggest,

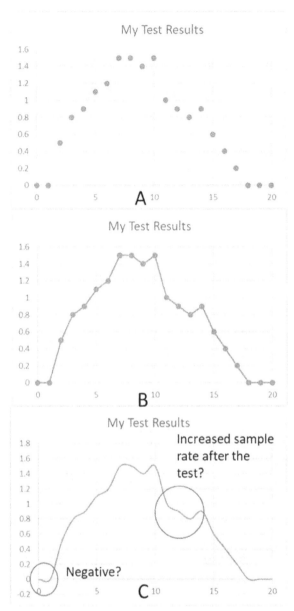

Figure 8.1 Three examples of plotted data.

redoing this plot. I feel the Microsoft smoother option should be left to the business school graduates.

[STORY: The phrase, "typical results shown" is too commonly found in technical papers. Most researchers don't have the luxury of performing so many tests they can establish "typical results". A research physicist once told me, the term "typical results" really means "the best *%#@" results we could find. I avoid the phrase in my documents.]

8.2 Correlation Between Two Measurements

Often an experiment is posing a simple question, if one parameter is changed what happens to a second parameter. In this case, the experimenter has control over the initial parameter. The measurements of the parameters are plotted as a pair of readings. We have already seen such plots. Section 4.6, Figure 4.17 is of 3 typical voltage reference ICs change in output voltage as temperature changes. Temperature was the parameter controlled to create this voltage response plot. These are easy to do.

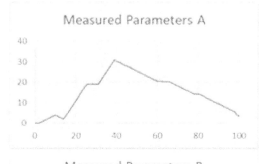

Figure 8.2 Two sets of data with a potential relationship between them

However, the correlation between two variables where the researcher doesn't have any control of either parameter are more difficult. Environmental measurements are often this type of data. Researchers may plot the two measured parameters 'A' and 'B' independently, placing one above the other as shown in Figure 8.2. Here the parameter A could be the speed of a car or the angle of an aircraft wing flap. The parameter B could be vibration of a car tire or aircraft wing. Not shown, are the other often unknown environmental parameters as wind speed and direction, road conditions or plane altitude. The reviewer is asked to visually validate how the two parameters are correlated. Does the data support the claims or assumptions made by the researchers?

As a reviewer, I have a real problem with using two plots with one above the other. I have seen cases where this method was used to mask a problem. I suggest having the measurements normalized and plotted together. I believe any data set can be normalize. Normalizing ranges the data values between 0 and 1. Commonly, this is performed by dividing the measured values by the maximum measured value.

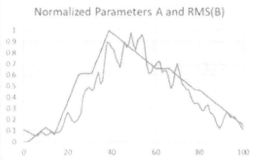

Figure 8.3 Normalized to show the correlation between sensor measurements

Figure 8.3 has normalized the A and B measured parameters of Figure 8.2. I also used the RMS value of parameter B. By converting B measurements to RMS (or other form of intensity), it is easier to see the potential impact of A on B. Plotting on the same graph also makes it much easier to see the phase relationship between the two parameters. It may assist in determining if parameter A is driving parameter B or the other way around.

[**Tech Note:** There are correlation coefficients and covariance values for placing a numerical value on the relationship of two or more parameters. However, a picture is worth a 1000 words.]

Chapter 9 Reducing Electronic Noise

Defense is the best offence

Reducing electronic noise is a huge topic to undertake in an Arduino based book. The typical Arduino bread board circuit looks like a rat's nest of wires. Even so, there are several design elements every measurement circuit builder can do to reduce noise in their circuits.

Most authors start noise discussion on the 4 modes electronic noise enters your circuits: Conductive, Magnetic, Capacitive and RF. They then start working on models where there is a noise source and a noise receiver. In the case of making electronic measurements, the measurement system is the noise receiver. However, I will take a more pragmatic view. I will look at basic concepts for reducing the most common noise sources from getting in to the measurement system. In truth, the measurement system designer does not normally have control over the noise sources. So, let's work on making the measurement circuit a poor receiver of electronic noise.

9.1 Arduino Power Supply

Wall plugin DC power converters are great for everything but powering low noise circuits. These DC converters normally run between 30K to 100KHz. The DC output voltage has a ripple voltage from the conversion process. They are also well known for magnetic noise. Shielding is normally required for running a power converter inside the instrumentation box. However, they are inexpensive and convenient. Consider one with the converter electronics close to the power plug end as shown in Figure 9.1.

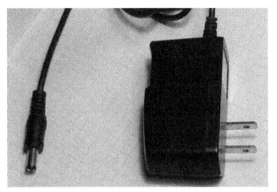

Figure 9.1 Power Plug for Arduino

The USB 5V power from a PC is not much better. The PC power is normally from a power converter even when a laptop is running from its internal battery. In section 3.3, there was a lot of discussion on the ill effects of using the USB to power your Arduino.

Using clean battery power is by far the easiest and best means for reducing noise in the data. A battery does not generate electronic noise. The battery can isolate the Arduino from earth ground. (More on this topic is coming.) In most cases, this will reduce electrical noise coupling from other electrical systems using wall power and earth ground. Batteries can have a higher internal resistance than electrical power devices. It is always best to keep battery wires short and to have a large valued capacitor (>22μF) near the circuits being powered from the battery.

9.2 Conductively Coupled Noise

Conductively coupled noise is noise coming in to our circuits via a hardwired path. Conductive noise frequencies range from DC to infinite. I have found conductively coupled noise as the dominate noise in most electronic measurement systems created by the novice. Removing conductively coupled noise will go a long way to making professional electronic measurements.

The good news, conductively coupled noise is the easiest to remove. The major source of electronic noise conductively coupling into sensor circuits is from the digital circuit power supply. The digital power is the 5V pin the Uno and Mega. On the Due it's the 3.3V pin.

9.2.1 Noisy Supply Voltage (Vsup)

An example of conductive coupling of noise has already been discussed. In section 6.3.1, I discussed RC filters (also called bypass capacitors) on the power supply input pins for analog signal amplifiers and sensors. The Arduino Vsup voltage supply is naturally noisy. All DC voltage supplies for large digital circuits are noisy. Let's look at an example of why.

Let's take "Blinky" program as an example. The blinky sketch comes installed with the Arduino IDE. It simply blinks an LED on the Arduino circuit board. The current draw for the LED is ~4mA. The Arduino microcontroller will turn the LED on and off. The Uno power circuit has a 47µF capacitor at the 5V supply regulator. Looking at a comparable 47µF capacitor, the manufacturer lists an effective series resistance (ESR) of 4 to 9.5 ohms at 120Hz. Using this information, we can estimate the voltage drop when the LED is turned on.

$$\text{delta Vsup} = I_{led} * C_{esr} = 4mA * 4 \text{ ohm} = 0.016V$$

Where LED current is I_{led}, Capacitor internal resistance is C_{esr}

The change in Vsup is 16mV for a short period as the LED is toggled on and off. This 16mV is noise on the Vsup. For the Uno, 16mV noise is approximately 3 cnts on the ADC. For the Due, it's ~20 cnts. Obviously, this is a very simple illustration. There are more capacitors than just the 47µF inside the Uno. Also, the voltage regulator will respond to correct this drop. However, no analog voltage regulator can respond at digital clock speeds. Yes, there are more capacitors but, the microcontroller has 1000s of internal digital gates all timed from one clock. At any clock transition, there are hundreds if not thousands of logic transitions requiring current. Also, the drive current rating for the Uno digital IO is 20mA. There could be 20mA loads coming on and off with an IO pin.

The following section offer some ideas on reducing noise from the supply voltage.

9.2.1.1 The RC Device Supply Filter

Most sensors draw very little current and we can take advantage of this fact. An RC circuit as shown in Figure 9.2 can be used to clean up the supply voltage going to a sensor and/or the sensor's amplifier circuit. Just be mindful of the RI voltage drop. The use of two capacitors was discuss in section 6.3.1. The goal of the RC power supply filter is to have a very low fc; the lower, the better. However, the minimum useful fc should be below 160KHz for the Uno and Mega. That provides 2 decades of attenuation for the 16Mhz Arduino clock frequency.

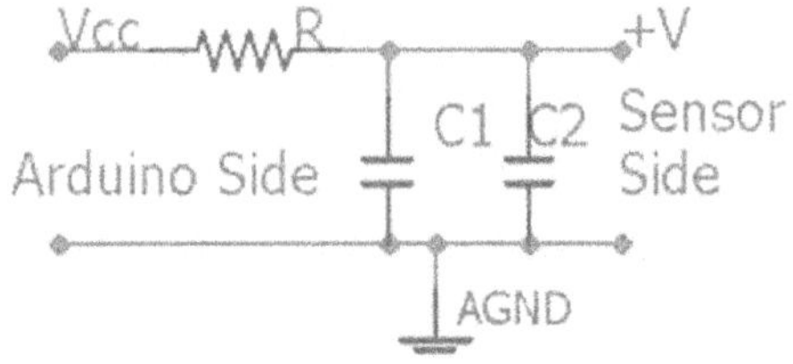

Figure 9.2 RC power filter

For larger circuits drawing more DC current where the IR drop is too much, the world famous π filter can do the job. The π filter is two capacitors and an inductor (choke) in the shape of the symbol π as seen in Figure 9.3.

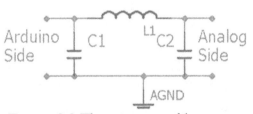

Figure 9.3 The pi power filter

The π filter has a double pole created by the inductor and capacitors. The inductor impedance increases with frequency while the capacitance impedance decreases. The C1 shown in Figure 9.3 may not be an actual capacitor in your circuit but assumed to be inside the Arduino. The fc of the LC low pass circuit is as below.

$$fc = 1/(2*π*\sqrt{L * C})$$

Where L is the inductance and C is the C2 capacitance

When working with LC filter circuits, we want a large capacitor and small inductor. Inductors have three important parameters needed for power circuit filters as illustrated in Figure 9.4:

1. Saturation current,
2. DC internal resistance,
3. Self-resonant frequency.

The saturation current is the current at which the inductor's ferrite material saturates with magnetic flux. The inductor will not work correctly after that point. The analog circuit current draw (including peak signal currents) must be below the saturation point of the inductor.

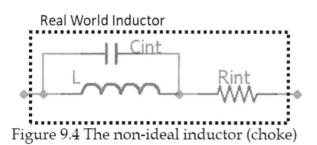

Figure 9.4 The non-ideal inductor (choke)

The DC resistance of the inductor is simply the internal resistance used to calculate the voltage drop when supplying current to your analog circuits. Inductors are built using small wire. The smaller the wire, the higher the internal resistance.

Finally, the self-resonance frequency of the inductor is the frequency where the internal capacitance (Cint) and inductance (L) match and the coil will resonate. At the self-resonance frequency, the inductor will not work as a filter. We want the self-resonance frequency to be above the 16MHz of the Arduino.

Sometimes it is difficult to find the ideal inductor. There is a simple trick I have used several times. Inductors in series add while the internal capacitance of the sum is less than either internal capacitance. Two series 22µH inductors are better than a single 44µH inductor for this type of application. In fact, there are inductors manufactured as a series of 3 individual sets of windings, see Figure 9.5.

Figure 9.5 Bourns 6310-RC Choke composed from 3 inductor coils

To clarify, consider the following example; I found a 22µH inductor with a DC resistance of 0.7ohms, a saturation current of 40mA and a self-resonance frequency of 20MHz in a small 805 package. What is the low pass fc if I use a 220µF capacitor with it?

$$fc = 1/(2\pi\sqrt{L * C}) = 1/(2\pi\sqrt{22u * 220u}) = 2.288KHz$$

9.2.1.2 A Second Supply Regulator

There is one more circuit which may not be in the tool box of most Arduino users. However, I use it most of the time when building a measurement system. A second voltage regulator for the analog side. The best way to isolate the digital side from the analog side is as shown in Figure 9.6.

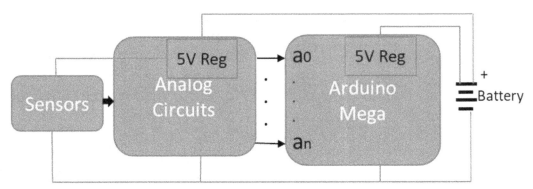

Figure 9.6 Block diagram of the Arduino and analog circuits using independent 5V regulators

The diagram of Figure 9.6 shows one power source (a battery) and two sets of power leads. One set of leads for the Arduino and one for a 5V regulator used by the analog circuits. Now the analog circuits are comprised of the anti-aliasing filter, signal amplifiers, interface circuits and the system sensors have their own clean supply voltage. Even if the sensors have digital interfaces as SPI, they should be powered by the low noise power supply. Also, high gain amplifiers and high resolution ADCs should have additional RC filters near their DC voltage input pins even when powered by the analog supply.

To highlight the importance of this concept, the following is a real world example. I was once asked to review a project to measure a small vibration signal traveling down miles of pipe. The engineer building the system had really great stuff. He had an 8 pole anti-aliasing filter, low noise high gain amplifiers, an expensive high resolution, high speed ADC and a custom accelerometer sensor attached to the pipe. Unfortunately, he could not measure the vibration at the other end? It took only one look. We applied a second power supply for the analog circuit and RC filtered the analog amplifiers. The vibration was captured.

9.2.1.3 Star Ground

Star ground is a religion for many in the electronic measurement business. I'm both a believer and a critic. In the block diagram shown in Figure 9.7, there are two sets of "+" power leads from the battery and a common grounding wire back to the battery. Each wire has an impedance to the flow of current. The sensor current (Isen) and analog circuit current (Iana) and Arduino digital currents (Idig) are summed in the last wire going to the battery.

Every wire has an impedance. When all grounds are connected in series, the currents sum and create a noisy voltage drop at each wire. The currents are summed creating a noise voltage as below:

Voltage drop (noise) at R1 = (Isen + Iana + Idig)*R1
Where currents I are illustrated in Figure 9.7

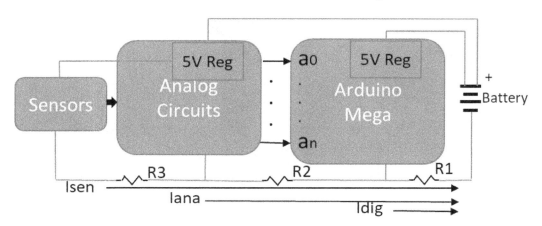

Figure 9.7 Block diagram illustrating the flow of ground currents in a circuit with grounds connected in series

Like the digital voltage supply, the Idig currents are noisy. The voltage drop at R1 is noisy and that noise effects everything upstream. The star ground reduces this effect by having parallel grounding wires as seen in Figure 9.8.

However, for Arduino users using the internal ADC to the Arduino microcontroller, the star ground may not provide a measureable improvement. This is because the ADC is on the R1 grounding wire. So, I recommend using the Arduino GND pin for the analog and sensor circuits when using the internal ADC and keeping the power wires short.

Now, someone is going to suggest, "What's the big deal, the wire resistance is almost 0 ohms. In fact, most handheld digital multi-meters cannot read any resistance in the small wires used in prototype boards." However, the wires impedance is more than DC resistance. The impedance of the wire is a function of the DC resistance (~0 ohms) and transmission impedance which is a function of wire length, loop area and current frequency. Digital circuits running at MHz, "see" prototype jumper wires as a much higher impedance than their resistance value. So, the voltage drop (noise) across R1 going to the battery will be larger than the DC resistance value at digital clock speeds.

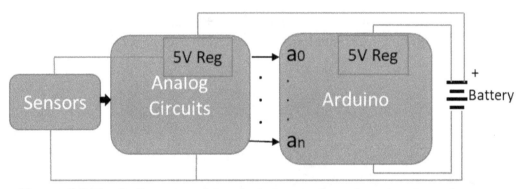

Figure 9.8 Block diagram of the Arduino and analog circuits using star ground going back to the battery.

[**Tech Note:** The consideration for separate analog and digital power & ground is often manufactured in the ADC IC. Many high resolution ADC devices come with separate analog and digital power & ground pins. This is needed as the ADC is a device with an analog input side and a digital output side.]

9.2.2 Impedance: Keeping it Low to Reduce Noise

One of my math professors told me, "All mathematics is a form of geometry". In my career, I have been unable to prove him wrong. The same is true for all wire impedances. The impedance of a wire is dependent on its geometry. To reduce the reception of noise or to reduce the transmission of noise from wires in your circuit, watch your wire geometry.

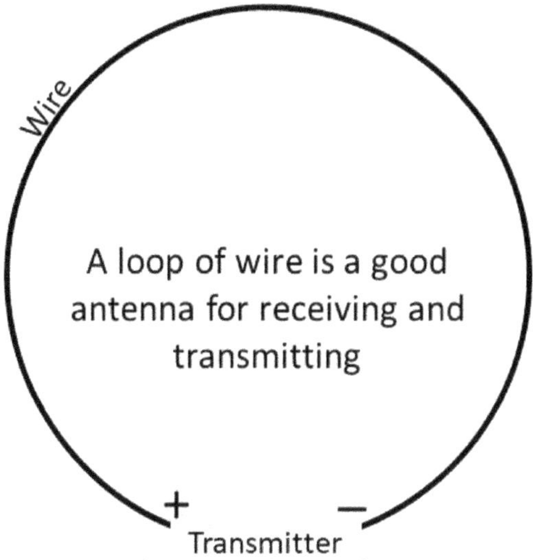

For example, a wire is always a loop or it does not conduct current. Obviously, the power and ground return discussed in the last section is also a loop. The impedance of any loop of wire is comprised of three elements: resistance, capacitance and inductance. This is a complex concept. I hope to make it easier by simply considering wire geometry.

A loop of wire is a good antenna for receiving and transmitting

Wire

+ −

Transmitter

Figure 9.9 The impendence of a wire at high frequencies is based on the loop area

The impedance of a common wire is dominated by the inductance and resistance. The resistance is small but the inductance reacts to increasing signal frequency. The inductance of a wire is based on the loop area of the wire. The larger the loop area, the larger the inductance. The larger the wires inductance, the higher the impedance to signal current.

A loop of wire is also an antenna. A loop antenna can transmit and receive electrical signals. The larger the loop, the better transmitter/receiver works at lower frequencies. Figure 9.9 is a loop of wire connected to a transmitter.

All this talk about inductance and antennas is simply to say, there is every reason for minimizing the loop area of signal and power wires. Reduced loop area: reduces noise generation, reduces noise reception, and increases the ease for passing current without noisy voltage drops. More detail will be provided on loop size in the magnetic coupling section.

Images in Figure 9.10 show an LED connected using a pair of wires. Each pair of wires creates a loop of wire. Pair "A" has the minimum loop area while pair "B" has a large loop area. Turning the LED on and off using loop "A" creates less electrical noise in surrounding circuits than using loop "B".

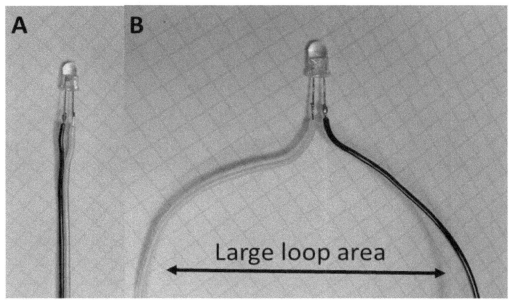

Figure 9.10 A. Wires close together and B. wires far apart

Assume the LED is now a sensor. The sensor wires going to the Arduino are either loop "A" or loop "B". Sensor wires from loop "A" will receive less electrical noise from other electrical circuits over using loop "B" sensor wires. For hooking up sensors use cables minimizing the loop area.

9.2.2.1 Sensor Cables

Three common sensor hook up cables are: coax, twisted pair and twisted pair shielded, see Figure 9.11. Each offers an advantage over the other for reducing noise coupling into the sensor circuit. Coax is best used when there is only a single signal and a common ground between the Arduino and the sensor. Many accelerometers

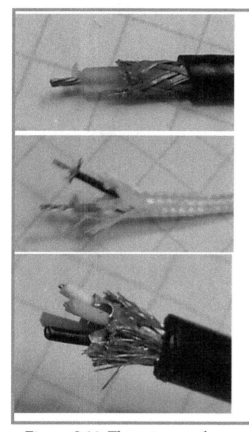

Coax: Provides a shielded center conductor wire. Good for sensors with a common ground to the Arduino.

Twisted Pair: Two insulated wires of equal size and twisted around each other. Good for sensors without a common ground with the Arduino.

Twisted Pair Shielded: Two insulated wires of equal size, twisted around each other with an outer conductive shield. This photo is of 2 pairs of twisted shielded wire. A 4 wire system like this is good for stain sensors or sensors with a power and signal wire requirement.

Figure 9.11 Three types of common wire cables for connecting sensors

operate this way. This type of sensor signal is often referenced as "single-ended".

The twisted pair is perhaps the most common sensor hook up cable. The two wires are matched in size, length and experiencing the same temperature giving each wire the same resistance value. This is important when measuring sensor signals which are "differential". Differential sensors (such as thermocouples or strain sensors) are commonly connected to the measurement system with twisted pair. The other advantage of twisted pair is the twisting action. As the wire moves through an electrically noisy environment, each twisted wire has an equal exposure to electrical noise. This noise is common mode to the cable. Common mode voltage is rejected by a differential amplifier.

Twisted pair with a shield allows for the user to ground the shield reducing electrical noise getting to the wires. The most common shield grounding point is at the receiver's end. For Arduino users, the receiver's end is normally the Arduino ground pin (GND). More on cable shield grounds later in this chapter.

The Figure 9.11 image of the twisted pair with shield has two sets of twisted pairs, a red-black pair and white-green pair. This is a very useful cable for strain sensors. Here the red-black pair can be used for a clean DC voltage to power the stain sensors. The white-green pair can be used for the differential signal coming back from the strain sensor.

9.2.2.2 Printed Circuit Board Circuits

In section above, the goal of reducing noise entering the measurement circuits was to keep the loop area of connecting wires low. The exact reasoning holds true for printed circuit board circuits. Keep the loop area small to reduce inductance and circuit impedance low.

For example, most Arduino shields are built with sensors on 2 layer printed circuit boards. In fact, most Arduinos themselves are built on two layer circuit boards.

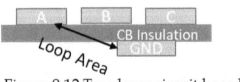

Figure 9.12 Two layer circuit board

Figure 9.12 shows copper circuit traces on a circuit board (CB insulation). This is a two layer circuit board. Getting all the circuit traces on the board requires running only a few ground "GND" traces. As such, circuit trace "A" has a large loop area because the ground return trace is some distance away.

Also, notice that circuit trace "B" is located between "A" and its return ground trace. This encourages the signal on "A" to create noise on trace "B".

Now look at Figure 9.13. This is a multi-layer circuit board with a copper ground plane, "GND". The ground plane is placed on a middle layer. Now, all the signal traces have a signal return trace right below or above. This reduces the loop area of all signal traces where GND return is required.

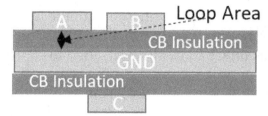

Figure 9.13 Multi-layer circuit board with a ground plane

[**Tech Note:** While discussing ground planes, often there are two ground planes: digital and analog. Two ground plans are often used in large circuit boards with complex circuits.]

9.2.2.3 Resistor Noise

All forms of electrical resistance generates a small amount of electronic noise. Resistance is found in all circuit elements and by design, circuits will require actual resistors. There is no means for eliminating this type of noise from any circuit design. The only action is to minimize resistance generated electronic noise and apply analog signal filters to reduce bandwidth.

The good news, electrical resistance generated noise levels generally fall well below the detection levels of the Arduino's internal ADC with 10 or 12 bit resolution. The noise generated by resistance is a function of:

- Resistance values; more resistance increases noise levels,
- Resistor temperature; hotter temperatures increases noise levels,
- Current flow; higher currents in a resistor increases noise levels,
- Circuit bandwidth; limiting bandwidth is always good for reducing noise.

To minimize noise created by circuit resistance means to keep it cool. For example, keep the measurement circuits away from hot engines. Given a choice in resistor values for sensor circuits, favor lower resistor values over higher ones. For example, the resistor divider circuit in section 4.1, can be done with two 5K ohm resistors or two 50K ohm resistors or even 5M ohm resistors. Chose resistor values offering the highest circuit performance with the lowest resistance value.   Finally, going back to choosing cutoff frequencies for filters, noise is always proportional to bandwidth. Use as little bandwidth as needed to capture the measurement.

In general, when choosing resistor values I prefer values between 5K – 50K ohms when working with low voltage Arduino circuits assuming there are no other driving requirements.

9.3 Wireless Coupled Noise

I believe most people fear wireless coupled noise the most. Perhaps, because there is a feeling of helplessness? Perhaps there is a feeling it comes from everywhere and anywhere? This section should help the reader gain an understanding of wireless couple noise, help identify where it is coming from and how to best deal with it.

I hope to illustrate how wireless noise couples into measurement circuits. Knowing how is critical to understanding the best method to minimize receiving this unwanted signal.   I will look at capacitance, magnetic and RF (radio frequency) noise coupling to electronic circuits. Capacitance and magnetic coupling are considered "near field" effects. They have a limited coupling range. While RF coupling is consider far field, meaning RF can cross great distances. Near field coupling contains more signal power than far field. The first step in reducing wireless coupled noise is reducing the near field wireless coupling.

For example, while listening to the radio in the car, you drive up to the radio-stations antenna. If the station is an AM station with a 300ft tower and your car comes within 600 to 1200ft of the tower, your radio becomes overwhelmed and the sound is horribly corrupted.   Driving away again and the sound returns. The radio continues to work fine many miles distant from the antenna as far field RF is low power. The lesson learned when making electronic measurements, take care of the near field effects first.

9.3.1 Capacitive Coupled Noise

Capacitive coupled noise is generally the easier to deal with than magnetic noise. A typical demonstration of capacitive coupled noise is to consider the lighting system of a lab. The overhead lighting system in the USA is 60Hz at ~120Vac. The 120Vac given is the RMS value, while the peak-to-peak value is ~170Vpp.

Capacitance coupling requires a modulating electric field. Figure 9.14 shows overhead lights running at 60Hz and 170Vpp. This power sees the earth ground below the lab as a power return conductor going back to the power plant. So, we have a capacitor made up of the air between the lights above and the ground below. Thankfully, air is a good insulator and a poor dielectric. The capacitance between the lights and ground is small. However, the Arduino sensor circuit is sitting on a bench with a power supply grounding the Arduino circuit back to mother earth.

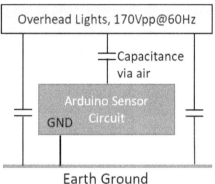

Figure 9.14 Capacitive coupled noise from over head lighting

The capacitance between the overhead lights and the Arduino is very small. However, the Arduino is measuring sensor voltages at 1mV resolution with our circuit amplifiers and ADC. The voltage difference across the air capacitor is 170Vpp – 0.001V. That is a huge voltage difference across even a small capacitor.

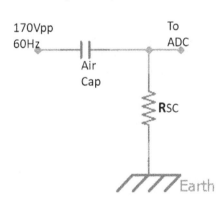

Figure 9.15 Lighting power coupling into the sensor circuit

Capacitive coupled noise is simply a high pass RC circuit as show in Figure 9.15. Here Rsc is the sensor's circuit resistance to ground at 60Hz. The air cap is the air capacitor illustrated in Figure 9.15. The clear issue here is the magnitude of the input signal at 170Vpp. The required RC high pass filter to prevent measureable noise entering the sensor circuit is -105dB at 60Hz. The simple RC filter has a roll-off of -20dB per decade, so we need an RC with a stop band at (~105/20) 5.25

frequency decades below 60Hz. Doing the math, we need a high pass RC with the fc at ~600µHz! This is why, local wall power is a common noise source found in sensitive electronic measurement systems.

There are three plans of action to remove this noise from our measurements.

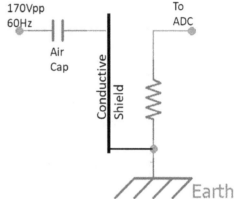

1. Shielding is the most common solution, see Figure 9.16. Placing a grounded electrical conductor (shield) between the measurement system and the lighting system will short the air capacitor to ground. Effectively providing a better path to ground than the measurement circuit. For most Arduino measurement systems, this means placing the Arduino inside a metal, grounded box. In the list of sensor cables in Figure 9.11, use a shielded cable with a conductive box thus providing a path to ground for cables running outside of the box.

Figure 9.16 Metal shield is shorting out the air capacitor from our circuit

2. Remove the earth ground connection of the measurement system. This is not always an option. There might be sensor requirement for connecting to earth ground. However, if the measurement system ran from a battery, the path to earth ground is broken. The measurement system is now floating somewhat like a bird sitting on a high voltage wire. In other words, all conductive surfaces of the measurement circuit are moving up and down with the electric field at the same time. The Arduino GND and all analog signals are at the same potential inside the electric field. Without a voltage difference, the ADC does not see the electric field. This concept may take a moment to realize.

3. Filtering out the 60Hz. This option is often used with 1 and 2 above. Here an analog filter is used to reject 60Hz. It needs to be placed very near the ADC such that there is very little exposure to the capacitive electric field between the filter's output and the ADC input. It is possible to digitally remove the 60Hz, if the sample rate of the system is fast enough and the end user will accept this filtering.

In reference to option #1. When using a shielded cable, there is a tendency to attach ground connections at both ends of the cable shield. This could create a problem. The shield might see high ground currents. For example, in Figure 9.17, the shield cable is seen as a lower impedance than the actual earth ground. These ground current can be large and couple into the signal or transmit into other signals. As such, it is normally best to connect the shield at only one end, leaving the other end open circuit. I normally start with the shielding grounded to the end where the ADC is located. In most cases, this would be at the Arduino end. This points to a weakness in using coax for sensitive

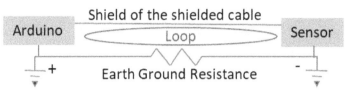

Figure 9.17 A ground loop can be a problem

measurements. Coax has only 1 signal wire and an outer conductive shield. Normally, coax must be grounded at both ends.

In reference to option #2. Sometimes, floating the circuit without a system ground connection is not an option. Some sensors require connection to the local system ground. If there is no requirement for the measurement system to be grounded, the battery solution normally proves the best solution for capacitive coupled noise. If running off a battery and there is still local capacitive couple noise, check for a missed grounding terminal. Often circuit boards ground the mounting hardware to the case. The case is bolted to a steel rack and the rack's power plug runs to ground.

Last words on option 1 and 2. The designer has a choice: float above the noise or to grab the system ground hard and tight. For example, assume the measurement system is placed inside a shielded and grounded metal enclosure. It may appear we have a good shielded system until noticing the enclosure ground connection is through a 200ft extension cable! Remember, impedance is more than the resistance of the wire. Having a 200ft power cord will read as a very small resistance on an ohm meter but the loop inductance is huge. The grounded enclosure will not work as a good shield without a good ground. So float above or grab on tight with a very low impedance ground connection.

When looking for noise sources in large systems (for example: commercial aircraft), I start by identifying all the grounds used by all electrical sub-systems. It is not enough to say, "Grounded to the air frame". Where electrical systems are tied to the air frame or to earth or to which battery return makes a difference. In short, the perfect ground does not exist. There isn't a true 0V location anywhere on planet earth or even the solar system. Current is running through any ground and all grounds offer some resistance to current. Finding the effects of ground currents and capacitive coupling is not easy. In every case, taking the time to identify where and how electrical systems are grounded has proved to be time well spent.

9.3.2 Magnetic Coupled Noise

Magnetic lines of force created by a magnet or by the flow of current inside a wire are the same thing. A field of magnetic lines of force is called an H-field. Anytime a wire passes through an H-field, an electrical signal is created in the wire

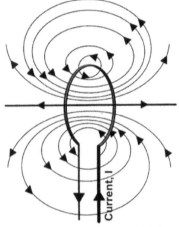

proportional to the strength of the H-field and speed of the wire. Generating an electrical signal in a wire using the H-field is called magnetic coupling. A noise signal created by magnetic coupling is both wireless and independent of signal ground. Magnetic coupling is the same if created by a wire passing through an H-field or a stationary wire inside an oscillating H-Field. Any wire passing through the Earth's magnetic field will also see a small voltage based on the speed of the moving wire and location inside the Earth's H-field. A transformer magnetically couples a primary side to a secondary side by oscillating current in the primary side.

Figure 9.18 The H-field is strongest in the center of a current caring loop

Unlike capacitive coupling, shielding is less effective at blocking magnetic lines of force. Shielding which is both ferrous (magnetic) and conductive will reduce the strength of the H-field reaching the shielded wire. However, having a ferrous material around a signal wire can create other signal problems.

Any loop of wire with current flowing in it generates an H-field proportional to the current and loop area. Figure 9.18 shows the H-field created by a loop of wire containing a current, I. As the current changes so does the H-field. If the current reverses direction, so does the H-field. If the current is in the form of a sinewave, the H-field grows and collapses and reverses direction in response to the current. So any wire near the loop shown in Figure 9.18, will have a noise signal at the same frequency and shape as the current in the loop. If the second wire passed through the center of the loop, the noise signal would be the strongest. If the second wire was outside the center, the noise signal will be weaker. Move the second wire some distance away and the noise signal becomes smaller. This magnetic coupling is a near field effect.

OK, the best means for reducing magnetic coupling is to keep your measurement circuits and sensors away from magnetic sources. If the H-field is static (a constant current in a wire or simply a magnet) and your circuit is static inside the H-field, no problem. We deal with that every day here on magnetic planet Earth. For high current, magnetic rich circuits as DC-DC converters, keep them as far away as possible from the sensitive sensors and measurement circuits. If the DC-DC converter must be inside the same enclosure as the Arduino; consider building the DC-DC inside its own secondary metal enclosure. This will reduce the distance of the H-field travels because the H-field creates a current inside the conductive metal enclosure, effectively loading down the H-field.

[**Tech Note:** Current created inside metal housing or shielding by oscillating H-fields is referenced as Eddie Current. The properties of Eddie current are interesting but outside the scope of this book. However, consider having magnetic ferrous shielding material to protect a signal wire from magnetic coupling. The signal wire must also conduct current (generating its own magnetic field) to send a signal.]

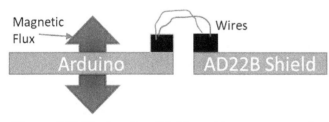

Figure 9.19 Placing the shield next to not on top of

A really good question is: what is a good distance for keeping my sensitive measurement circuits from the current loop? I have a general answer. Based on years of experience, I found the loop diameter to be the main parameter for predicting magnetic coupling distance. The size of the loop is dominate over the magnitude of the current. In the general case, if the loop is 2 inches in diameter, the measurement circuit should be 2X or 4 inches removed. It is also true that the orientation of the loop makes a difference. Looking at Figure 9.19, the digital traces of the Arduino create a magnetic loop perpendicular to the Arduino circuit board. Placing the high resolution ADC shield, as the AD22B, next to the Arduino is better than placing it above the Arduino.

9.3.3 RF Coupled Noise

Radio frequency (RF) noise is a far field coupled noise, meaning it can travel very, very long distances. The good news, RF noise has very low power and normally very high frequency. Any conductor is a potential receiver of RF, so sensor wires are subject to catching RF signals. Fortunately, RF coupling is weak and not able to drive normal sensor impedances. Most sensor output impedance is a few K ohms or lower. As such, the RF noise signal is normally attenuated below concern.

Even if the sensor circuit has a high impedance, a small valued capacitor can short out the high frequency RF signal. For example, a 0.1μF on a temperature signal will normally short out the RF without any effect on the temperature measurement.

There is always some discussion about building the measurement system inside a Faraday Cage. A Faraday Cage is an enclosure build out of a conductive screen or even solid metal. The screen must provide 100% coverage; no gaps between any of the 6 walls of the enclosure. Such an enclosure prevents RF signals (with wavelengths too large to fit through the screen's holes) from entering. In all my years, I have never had the opportunity to build a laboratory measurement system inside a Faraday Cage. The reason, a true Faraday cage cannot have a wire penetrate the enclosure. No wires coming out of the enclosure for communication or wires coming out of the enclosure for connecting sensors. The sensors and measurement system must be fully enclosed and self-contained inside the shielding of the Faraday Cage.

Even if a true Faraday Cage cannot be used, building the measurement system inside a conductive enclosure covering 90% of the measurement electronics does benefit noise reduction. Not RF, but a reduction in noise from near field effects both capacitive and magnetic will be realized.

9.4 Found Noise on the Signal?

The measurement looks noisy. Where to start looking for a solution? First, the wrong answer: start working on a digital filter to remove the noise. Use digital filtering only as the last resort.

First, consider what type of noise is it. To aid in noise identification, I created some noise examples to help.

Figure 9.20 is simply bit chatter created as the analog signal is at an ADC transition between two digital values. For the 10 ADC used in Uno and Mega this is a common occurrence. This is not noise entering the measurement system. Here is one example where digital filter will improve the appearance of the measurement. If this is an issue, increasing ADC resolution is the only real solution.

Figure 9.21 is of low level, random noise. Here an external high resolution ADC is being used with the Arduino. If the noise is random (non-periodic) and appears across the full bandwidth, it might simply be thermal resistive noise level of the

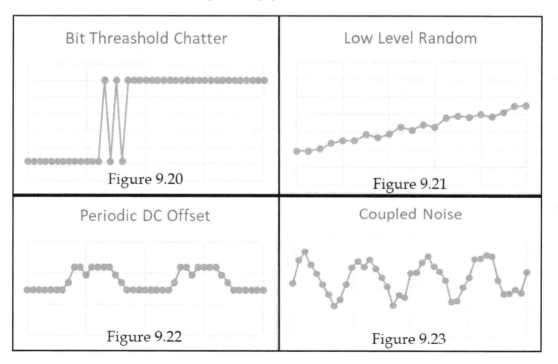

Bit Threashold Chatter	Low Level Random
Figure 9.20	Figure 9.21
Periodic DC Offset	Coupled Noise
Figure 9.22	Figure 9.23

system. Every system has a noise floor. This might be it. Consider reducing resistor values used in the signal path, consider finding lower noise amplifiers, possibly reducing the operating temperature of the system or reducing signal bandwidth.

Figure 9.22 is an example of period noise with a DC offset to the noise signal. The only noise which can create a DC offset is noise conductively coupled to the signal. Look for the conductive noise locations such as the DC supply voltage, voltage resistive dividers and such. Note, conductively coupled noise can also have ac like noise components. Look for frequencies used by digital circuits or multiples of digital circuits.

 Figure 9.23 is a periodic ac noise signal. This is most likely the result of capacitive or magnetically couple noise. The good news, by looking at the period of the wave form, it is normally easy to identify the source. Most DC-DC converters run at 30-100KHz. Pulse Width Modulators have periodic waveforms with changing pulse width. The local wall power has a constant and well known frequency.

Figure 9.24 is something like the noise seen on an oscilloscope. The standard oscilloscope has a high noise floor. Normally much higher than a custom built measurement system using the Arduino. The standard scope has an 8 bit ADC with little if any input filtering. They are made for the highest possible bandwidth. It is not possible to have a low noise anti-aliasing filter on a general purpose oscilloscope.

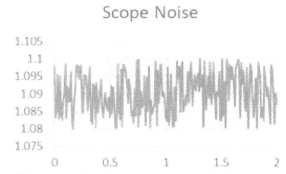

Figure 9.24 Scopes generally have no or limited filtering and high noise floors

If the noise problem is large enough to be seen on a scope, then everything above applies. However, using a scope to determine the measurement circuit's noise floor is normally not possible. In fact, using the techniques provided in this book, the reader could build a good, low noise system for measuring the floor of other systems.

9.5 Concluding Notes on Reducing Noise

Below is a check list of ideas for reducing noise found in electronic measurements. When designing a measurement system, this list will aid in making good measurements from the start.

1. The first rule of reducing noise is to reduce the bandwidth of the incoming analog signal. The total amount of noise in any measurement system is proportional to the bandwidth.
2. All measurement systems need to ensure the analog incoming signal has a maximum frequency below the sample system's Nyquist frequency. Every measurement system benefits from an anti-aliasing filter.
3. To reduce conductive coupled noise, isolate the supply voltage used by analog circuits from those used by digital circuits. Consider a second voltage regulator and/or RC filters on all analog IC power pins. Consider a star ground when connecting analog circuits.
4. Keep analog signal wires (including power wires) close together to reduce loop area. The smaller the loop area, the less noise will be received or transmitted. When placing wires either on a prototype board or on a circuit board, work to keep the signal and signal return wires close together (consider twisting low level signal wires together). If designing printed circuit boards, consider using a ground plane to aid in reducing loop area.
5. Test Arduino circuits using wall power for function but consider using a battery to reduce noise for the actual test. The battery improves the Arduino internal voltage reference.
6. Determine if the measurement system must use a common system ground. Using a battery may allow for your system to float above the system ground, thereby reducing capacitive coupled noise. However, if the measurement system ground is common with the system ground, make a good connection. There is no perfect ground.
7. Shielding wire and the measurement system inside conductive enclosures generally reduces capacitive and magnetic coupling. A Faraday Cage requires an enclosure without wires penetrating the enclosure.

8. When investigating the source of noise on a signal line, looking at the wave form of the noise aids in finding the source. Keep in mind, noise coupling either by conduction, capacitive or magnetic, doesn't changes the frequency of the noise. As such, the source of the noise can be tracked back by determining the frequency of the noise and looking for that frequency in your measurement system or near it.

Chapter 10 Programming Examples

Getting a jump start

A selection of complete sketches are provided. These will enable the reader to get a head start on creating their own sketches. Most of these sketches were written using basic Arduino program statements. As the Arduino has become more popular, there are more and more third party libraries. These libraries can greatly increase the readability and efficiency in coding instructions for your Arduino. However, they become increasingly difficult to maintain as time goes by. So, I opted to KISS it keep it simple.

These examples, updates and additional programming examples can be found at www.onmeasurements.com.

10.1 Auto-Ranging the Mega

The UNO and Mega offers options for choosing an internal voltage reference. There is a software statement for setting the ADC voltage reference to an internal 1.1V reference. The Mega 2560 goes one better with two internal references: 1.1V and 2.56V. Using the Arduino default 5.0 voltage external reference, the Mega has 3 ADC ranges.

This program exploits the Mega to create an auto-ranging voltage meter to maximize measurement resolution.

The nominal resolutions for Mega's 3 reference options are:

1.1Vref: ADC V/Cnts = $1.1V/2^{10}$ = 1.074mV/Cnts
2.56Vref: ADC V/Cnts = $2.56V/2^{10}$ = 2.5mV/Cnts
5.0Vref: ADC V/Cnts = $5.0/(2^{10})$ = 4.883mV/Cnts

The program sets the Vref based in the analog input voltage. If the input is between 0 and 1.1V, the resolution is ~5X improved over the 0-5V range. If the input is between 1.1 and 2.56V, the resolution is ~2X using the 2.56V reference.

I calibrated my Arduino Mega 2560 using this program. The voltage difference between my calibrated lab meter and the Arduino are plotted in Figure 10.1. The auto-ranging of the ADC's voltage reference does improve the Arduino's resolution at lower voltages. In some sensor measurements, this could reduce the need for a signal amplifier.

There is a cost for auto-ranging in measurement speed. Changing between reference voltages takes time. For the program, MegaAutoRange, I used the following three statements every time the reference voltage was changed.

```
analogReference(DEFAULT);// or INTERNAL1V1 or
INTERNAL2V56
  int junk = analogRead(A0);
  delay(25);
```

In the above statements, "analogReference(DEFAULT)", instructs the Arduino to use the 5Vsup as the reference. Before the reference is actually changed in hardware, an "analogRead()" statement must be run. The value returned is under the variable "junk" because it will be discarded. Now that the Vref has been changed, there is a delay to allow for voltage settling. I tried both "delay(10)" and "delay(25)" for a delay of 10mS or 25mS respectfully. The longer delay appeared slightly better and it was used for calibration.

Along with changing the reference voltage and measuring an input voltage, the program provides a simple histogram of 100 ADC readings. This allows the user to see the measurement noise (uncertainty) of any one ADC reading using the three reference voltage options. In my testing, the 1.1V reference did have a slight increase in noise but not enough to offer any reason for not using it.

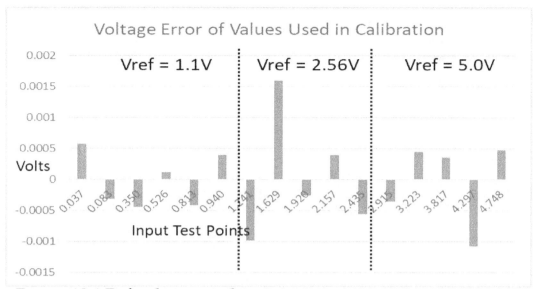

Figure 10.1 Ref voltages and error in measurements

The code below was used to capture a 100 point histogram of the readings with a constant DC input test voltage. In short, an average of 16 readings is made to find the "center" value for our histogram. The value of "center" is an integer. The divide by 16 is an integer divide not a floating number. It is the closest integer to the actual input value. Next, 100 ADC readings are made. Each reading has the "center" value removed. The result is a small integer, either positive or negative. If the difference is an integer between 4 and -3 then that value in the Jitter array in incremented. If the difference is outside of 4 to -3, then the variable "Outside" in incremented. In testing the Mega, I only had zero values for "Outside".

```
total = 0;
for (int i=0; i<16; i++)
{
   total = total + analogRead(A0);
}
int center = total/16 ;   //Estimate ADC reading
for (int i=0; i<100; i++)
{
  int Cnt = analogRead(A0) - center; //dif in counts
  switch (Cnt)
     {
       case 4:  Jitter[7]++; // Add 1 to the value;
```

```
    break;                          // Found it, we're done
    case 3:   Jitter[6]++;
    break;
    case 2:   Jitter[5]++;
    break;
    case 1:   Jitter[4]++;
    break;
    case 0:   Jitter[3]++;
    break;
    case -1:  Jitter[2]++;
    break;
    case -2:  Jitter[1]++;
    break;
    case -3:  Jitter[0]++;
    break;
    default:  Outside++;
  break;
    }  //switch
 }  // for sum
```

The program prints out the results of the histogram to the "Serial Monitor" provided with the Arduino IDE. I plotted the result with input of 0.0472V using MS Excel as seen in Figure 10.2. It was common to see the zero difference Jitter[3] with a huge value. Sometimes the results were split between the zero difference and

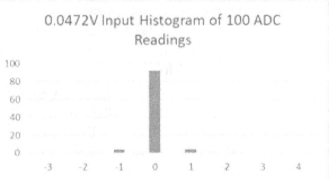

Figure 10.2 Histogram for low voltage input using the 1.1V internal reference

either +1 or -1 results. Once again, the Arduino proves to have a very good, 10bit ADC.

10.1.1 Test Circuit

A 5K potentiometer across the 5v supply works to create an input analog test DC voltage. From the center wiper, an RC filter was used to reduce noise. I used a 5.1K resistor with a 220uF capacitor. The input was to A0. A calibrated volt meter with a 5.5 digit resolution was connected parallel to A0 to calibrate the Mega.

The Arduino was powered from a 9V battery pack of "AA" size cells. After the Arduino was powered up, the USB cable was connected. This procedure enabled the Arduino to power itself from the battery while allowing the user to view data via the Arduino IDE "Serial Monitor". Powering from the battery improves calibration as discussed in Chapter 3.

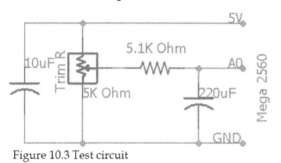

Figure 10.3 Test circuit

10.1.2 MegaAutoRange Sketch

```
// Program Constants
int Jitter[8];  //Array of ADC values for any measurement
int Outside;  //ADC values not falling in the range of Jitter
int total = 0;  // the running total of our analog input summation is a 'long' integer
int sum = 100;  // # of reading to be summed for our readings
float Slp;  //Slope of cal equation
float Int;  // Intercept of cal equation
int inputPin = A0;

void setup()
{
  // initialize serial communication with computer:
  Serial.begin(9600);
}
void loop() {
```

```
// look for input at A0 using default reference voltage of 5V
analogReference(DEFAULT); //Set AREF to system 5.0V
int junk = analogRead(A0); // Required to change the AREF
delay(25); //a delay is needed to settle the AREF voltage
total = 0; //zero out summation variable
for (int i=0; i<8; i++)
  {
  Jitter[i] = 0; //set all values to zero
  }
Outside = 0;
// FirstRead is the reading used to determine which voltage reference will be used.
int FirstRead = analogRead(A0); // This reading uses the default 5.0V reference
// Choose which AREF to use and create a histogram
if (FirstRead > 500) //Use the 5V ref if FirstRead > or near 2.56V
{
  Slp = 0.004883; // Default = 0.004883 or replace with calibration values
  Int = 0.0; // Default = 0.0 or replace with calibration values
  for (int i=0; i<16; i++)
  {
    total = total + analogRead(A0);
  }
  int center = total/16 ; //Estimate the ADC reading
  for (int i=0; i<sum; i++)
  {
   int Cnt = analogRead(A0) - center;//Difference for the Histogram
   switch (Cnt)
    {
    case 4: Jitter[7]++;
    break;
    case 3: Jitter[6]++;
    break;
    case 2: Jitter[5]++;
    break;
    case 1: Jitter[4]++;
    break;
    case 0: Jitter[3]++;
```

```
      break;
      case -1: Jitter[2]++;
      break;
      case -2: Jitter[1]++;
      break;
      case -3: Jitter[0]++;
      break;
      default:  Outside++;//Difference too great!
    break;
    } //switch
  } // for sum
} else if (FirstRead > 210)// Choose the 2.56V reference for AREF or else...
  {
    analogReference(INTERNAL2V56); //Set AREF to 2.56V
    int junk = analogRead(A0); // must perform an analogRead to update AREF
    delay(25); //Give time for AREF to reach it's new value
    Slp = 0.0025; // Default 0.0025
    Int = 0.0; // Default 0.0

    for (int i=0; i<16; i++)
    {
      total = total + analogRead(A0);
    }
    int center = total/16 ; //Our average ADC
    for (int i=0; i<sum; i++)
    {
     int Cnt = analogRead(A0) - center;//Difference for the Histogram
     switch (Cnt)
      {
      case 4: Jitter[7]++;
      break;
      case 3: Jitter[6]++;
      break;
      case 2: Jitter[5]++;
      break;
      case 1: Jitter[4]++;
```

```
        break;
        case 0:  Jitter[3]++;
        break;
        case -1:  Jitter[2]++;
        break;
        case -2:  Jitter[1]++;
        break;
        case -3:  Jitter[0]++;
        break;
        default:  Outside++;
      break;
      } // end switch
      } // sum samples
} else
  {
    analogReference(INTERNAL1V1);  //set AREF to 1.1V
    int junk = analogRead(A0);
    delay(25);
    Slp = 0.001074;  // Default 0.001074
    Int = 0.0;  // Default 0.0

    for (int i=0; i<16; i++)
    {
     total = total + analogRead(A0);
    }
  int center = total/16;
    for (int i=0; i<sum; i++)
    {
     int Cnt = analogRead(A0) - center;
     switch (Cnt)
      {
       case 4:  Jitter[7]++;
       break;
       case 3:  Jitter[6]++;
       break;
       case 2:  Jitter[5]++;
```

```
          break;
          case 1: Jitter[4]++;
          break;
          case 0: Jitter[3]++;
          break;
          case -1: Jitter[2]++;
          break;
          case -2: Jitter[1]++;
          break;
          case -3: Jitter[0]++;
          break;
          default: Outside++;
        break;
        } // end switch
        } // sum samples
      } //if else statement on input voltage size

// Display Results inside the IDE
 Serial.println("Jitter -3,-2,-1,0, +1, +2, +3, +4, Outside Range");
  for (int i=0; i<8; i++)
    {Serial.print(Jitter[i]);
     Serial.print(", ");
     }
 Serial.println(Outside);
 float RelTotal = total/16.0;
 float X = RelTotal*Slp + Int;
 Serial.print("Cal: ");  //Tell user which cal is being used
 Serial.print(Slp,6);
 Serial.print(" Input: ");// Tell user measured voltage
 Serial.print(X,4);
 Serial.print("V ");
 Serial.print(" ADC: ");// Tell user ADC value + 1 digit
 Serial.println(RelTotal,1);

 delay(5000);  //Let the user see the valued in the screen
} //End the sketch program
```

10.2 SD_Logger

This sketch uses a SD memory card to save ADC readings. It creates a text file on the SD card compatible with MS Excel. The sample frequency (fs) timing uses the "millis()" function. This program works well for data logging at 1Hz = fs. The default fs in the program is 33Hz which is described in section 5.1.2.

In the "void setup()" section of the sketch, the SD card is verified by creating a junk file, "TstFile.jnk" and writing the integer value 680 to it. The file is then closed. The file is reopened and the integer value saved in the file is read back out. If the value read back out is 680, then the SD card is functioning. If not, an error message is sent to the user. The "TstFile.jnk" is then removed from the SD card.

I prefer to validate removable memory by writing and reading. Too many times in my past, tests have been run but for some reason the data was not saved to memory. Apparently, there are cases where the memory is verified as being installed while being dysfunctional.

 SD cards offer a huge memory for any 8 bit data collection system. In this program, the user must remove the SD card to delete the data file, "simlog.csv". If the file is not deleted, every time the system restarts, the existing file has the new data appended to the file. This makes the file a series of data sets. This is a better option than having the Arduino delete the data file. Again, some level of effort needs to be performed to reduce the probability of deleting a valuable scientific data file.

It is important to start every data set with a good header. It will be needed to separate the files later. Here, the header is written in the "void setup()" section. It lists the program's name that created the new data set, as SD cards are often reused. The user can add a program version number or other comment to the header. After that, a listing of ADC reading names is extremely useful. It is easy to forget this type of information. If a real time clock is available, date and time is another important parameter.

Along with the list of ADC reading names is the time stamp of each set of readings. The time is recorded by saving the millisecond counter.

10.2.1 Test Circuit

The Arduino web site has instructions on connecting SD card shields to the Arduino. To use the built in Arduino IDE library "SD.h" those connections must be used. The only exception is the chip select pin for the SD card. The programmer must define the Arduino connection (pin 53 in this case) for the chip select signal with the statement below.

const int chipSelect = 53; // User defined for SD card

Once the chip select connection is defined, the programmer no longer needs to worry about that pin. This is unlike other SPI interfaces.

Below are the connections used in the example program for either the Uno or Mega.

Analog sensors inputs on analog pins 0, 1, and 2
SD card attached to SPI bus on the Uno as follows:
MOSI - pin 11
MISO - pin 12
CLK - pin 13
CS - pin 10
SD card attached to the Mega as follows:
MOSI - pin 51
MISO - pin 50
CLK - pin 52
CS - pin 53

I greatly appreciate using the names MOSI and MISO for SI or SO. SI means Serial In and SO means Serial Out, however, it's not clear which way the serial bits are running. MOSI means Master Out – Slave In and MISO means Master In – Slave Out. Now that label describes the wire connection because the master is the Arduino and the slave is the device.

10.2.3 SD_Logger Sketch

```
#include <SPI.h>  //Both libraries are required for using the SD card
#include <SD.h>

const int chipSelect = 53;  // User defined for SD card, assuming the Mega 2560 is
used here
unsigned long TimeS;      // Starting time
unsigned long TimeF;      // Final time
unsigned long TimeP;       // Sets the sample period
unsigned long n = 0;      // Our ADC sample count
int sensor0;            // Input ADC value from the sensor A0
int sensor1;            // Input ADC value from the sensor A1
int sensor2;
String dataString = "";   // string to hold our data to be written to the SD card

void setup() {
  // Open serial communications and wait for port to open:
  Serial.begin(9600);

// Verify the SD card is working
  Serial.print("Initializing SD card...");
  // see if the card is present and can be initialized:
   if (!SD.begin(chipSelect)) {
   Serial.println("Card failed or not present");
   // Unknown Problem!!
   }
   else  { //verify working SD card with file creation and read
     Serial.println("Creating test file on the SD card");
     File tstFile = SD.open("TstFile.jnk", FILE_WRITE);
     int jnkIn = 680;  //This is a test value could be any unique number
     if (tstFile) { tstFile.print(jnkIn); }
     tstFile.close();
     tstFile = SD.open("TstFile.jnk", FILE_READ);
     int jnkOut = 123;  //Dummy value to be over written
```

```
   if (tstFile) {
     while (tstFile.available()) {
      jnkOut = tstFile.parseInt();
     }
     Serial.print("Reading jnkOut: ");
     Serial.println(jnkOut);
     tstFile.close();
     SD.remove("TstFile.jnk"); }
   if (jnkOut == jnkIn) {
     Serial.print("SD Card verified ");
     Serial.println(jnkOut);
     tstFile.close();
     SD.remove("TstFile.jnk"); //remove our test file from the SD card
   }
   else { Serial.println("SD Card Verification Failure"); }
  }

  // open the file and write the file header
  File dataFile = SD.open("simlog.csv", FILE_WRITE); //File name must be 8.3
format
   dataFile.println("SD_Logger Program");
   dataFile.println("Chan 0, Chan 1, Chan 2, Sample t");
   dataFile.close();
}

void loop() {
  TimeS = millis(); // Get the starting time used to measure through put of the
system

  for (n=0;n<100;n++)  //This for statement is used to test the measurement through
put
  {
  TimeP = millis() + 30;
  dataString = ""; // Reset dataString for new readings
  // read three inputs and append to the dataString:
   sensor0 = analogRead(0);
```

```
  sensor1 = analogRead(1);
  sensor2 = analogRead(2);
  dataString += String(sensor0);
  dataString += ",";
  dataString += String(sensor1);
  dataString += ",";
  dataString += String(sensor2);
  dataString += ",";
  dataString += String(millis()); //save millis() clock as our timer

 // Open the file. Write the data string and close the file
 File dataFile = SD.open("simlog.csv", FILE_WRITE); //File name must be 8.3
format
  dataFile.println(dataString);
  dataFile.close();
  while (millis()<TimeP){ delayMicroseconds(100);}
 } //End the timing test of writing 3 ADC reading to the SD card in a Excel format

 // Report results to the user
 TimeF = millis(); // How long did this take to run?
 TimeS = TimeF - TimeS; //TimeS should now = the time used

 Serial.println(dataString); //Show the operator a dataString example
 Serial.print("Time to run: ");
 Serial.print(TimeS);
 Serial.println(" mil-sec");
 delay(5000); //Give us time to look at the results
}
```

10.3 SRAM Scope2 Sketch

This sketch is working with the Arduino Due. The reader can use this sketch do things an expensive oscilloscope cannot do. This is a fun program.

This program uses the 23LC1024 SRAM chip as a fast memory storage device supporting fast data capture. (See section 5.1.2 for more information.) The SRAM is 1MBit. The program stores one ADC reading as a 16 bit integer. So the SRAM can store 62.5K ADC readings. The 23LC1024 has a SPI interface device capable of 20MHz. The Due is the fastest Arduino running at 84MHz. ADC readings can be captured, processed and stored quickly using the SRAM.

The internal ADC of the Due is 12bits, not 10bits like the other Arduinos. However, to use all 12bits requires the programming statement shown below.

analogReadResolution(12);

The default Arduino SPI clock speed is 4MHz. To speed up the writing of data to memory the program statement below increased the SPI clock to 14MHz.

SPI.setClockDivider(6);

The SPI interface is great for fast transfer of serial information. However, the SPI specification defines the device pins but allows the device manufacturer to define how the interface logic works. For example, the serial data bits can be valid on either a rising or falling edge of the SPI clock. As such, the Arduino IDE has a default SPI interface which often needs to be altered. Knowing how to alter the interface requires digging into the device specifications.

The good news, the default SPI mode works for the 23LC1024. For future reference, I placed the correct SPI set up commands in the sketch but commented them out.

In the "void setup()" section of the sketch and after the SPI setup statements, the SRAM chip is set up. The 23LC1024 has a number of modes of operation. For this program, the SRAM is set up as a large serial memory for writing 16 bit integers. Each time the program writes an ADC reading, the SRAM automatically increments its memory address and is immediately ready for another ADC reading. This is the simplest mode for the Arduino processor. Also, when reading from the SRAM, the memory address starts at zero and each 16bit read increments the memory. So, the SRAM is always being written to or read from as an entire block of 16bit integers. Each time the sketch is run, the first readings saved are also the first readings out, FIFO.

While still in the setup() section of the sketch, the program verifies the SRAM by writing a unique integer number to the device and then reading it back. I suggest doing the same activity on an SD card. Nothing verifies the memory device is connected and working like using it before your program (or scientific test $$$) is run.

The program is using the "SPI.h" library to read and write to the SRAM. The program must chip select the SRAM before writing or reading. This is done because the "SPI.h" doesn't know what device it will be writing or reading. So, it's up the programmer to keep track of the chip select IO pins. In this program, the SRAM select chip is IO pin 10. It can be changed by the programmer to any digital IO pin. The other SPI pins cannot be changed by the programmer. The IO statements below are used to control the chip select line.

```
digitalWrite(SRAM_CS, LOW); // Selects the SRAM chip
digitalWrite(SRAM_CS, HIGH); // deselects the SRAM chip to free up the
SPI bus
```

The read and write instructions are below.

```
SPI.transfer(0X01); //Writes the 8 bit hex byte 01 (0000 0001)
SPI.transfer16(0x0200); // Writes the 16 bit hex word 0200 (0000 0010 0000
0000)
SPI.transfer16(Chan1); // Writes the 16 bit ADC reading saved in "Chan1" to
memory
```

tst = SPI.transfer(0x00); //Reads an 8 bit hex byte from the SRAM, 0X00 is a dummy
Chan1 = SPI.transfer16(0x0000); //Reads a 16bit word from the SRAM, 0X0000 is a dummy

In this sketch, two analog inputs are read and saved as raw integers from the ADC. The timing is maintained as shown in section 5.1.2.2 using the "micros()" and "delayMicrosecond()" functions. This works reasonable well while using the Due. Inside the measurement timing loop there is a "delayMicroseconds(value)" statement The value hard coded into the instruction determines the sample frequency, fs. Table 10.1 was developed running this program.

Table 10.1

fs in KHz	Delay
55.64	None
49.99	2
25	22
10	82
0.999	982

Commenting out the delay statement and the program ran at 55.64KHz. For a desired fs, set the delay value and download to the Due.

I assume this will work with the Uno and Mega at significantly slower sample frequencies. I also did a 4 channel version of this program. It can be downloaded from www.onmeasurement.com.

In the program, a manually operated switch is use to trigger the start of data collection. The switch could be replaced by a comparator circuit (see Figure 2.1, replace R1 and R2 with a potentiometer) to generate a trigger as found on a real oscilloscope.

For each trigger, the program runs until "samp" sets of ADC readings have been saved to the SRAM. For two sets of readings, the maximum value for "samp" is 31,000. I used the program to capture waveforms and plot them using the Arduino IDE "Serial Plotter". The screen on the plotter only holds 500 samples for two traces.

The serial plotter worked well with integer ADC values. It wasn't as good working with floating values. It worked with floating points but the auto-scaling was off. In the example code, "samp" is 125. This value let me capture 4 triggers and display the results in the serial plotter. Many of the data plots in this book were created with this program, the serial plotter and the screen capture button on my laptop.

Going back to the serial plotter. At the time of my writing this book, Arduino hasn't provided much detail on this option. Here are a few details I learned. You can transmit any floating or integer value to the serial plotter and it will auto range to display received values. When sending two data channels as in this program, separate the two values by a space. Separate sets of readings with a line return. The statements below illustrate writing to the serial plotter.

```
for (int i  = 1; i <=samp; i++) {
Chan1 = SPI.transfer16(0x0000);
Chan2 = SPI.transfer16(0x0000);
Serial.print(Chan1);
Serial.print(" "); //Need a space between variables for the Serial Plotter
Serial.println(Chan2); // Line feed needed to term data set
j++;
delay(10); //Simple delay to make watching the serial plotter more
interesting
```

I learned normal text is ignored by the serial plotter. This is great. I can use the same code for sending a waveform to the serial plotter or programming variables to the serial monitor. If you have a number within some text, to keep the serial plotter from acting on it, don't leave any spaces between the text and the number.

10.3.1 Test circuit

The 23LC1024, SRAM was connected as shown in Figure 10.4 below. For more details of the demonstration circuit see section 5.2.2 of this book.

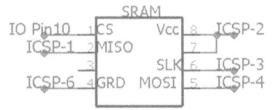

Figure 10.4 Pinout and connections for the SRAM

10.3.2 SRAM_Scope2 Sketch

```
// inslude the SPI library:
#include <SPI.h>

// define Pins
const int SRAM_ CS = 10;
const int Trigger = 13;

// define gobal veriables
float slope = 0.0008057; // 0.004883 for Uno, Mega and 0.0008057 Due
float intercept = 0;

void setup() {
  //Setup USB to display events to the user
  Serial.begin(9600);

  //For the Due use the statement below for all 12 bits
  analogReadResolution(12);

  // put your setup code here, to run once:
  // set the SRAM CS Pin as an output:
  pinMode (SRAM_ CS, OUTPUT);
  pinMode (Trigger, INPUT);
  digitalWrite(SRAM_ CS,HIGH);  //Start with SRAM not selected.
  pinMode(4, OUTPUT);
  digitalWrite(4,HIGH);

  // initialize SPI:
  SPI.begin();
  delay(5); // Give the system some power up time

  //Speed up the SPI clock
  // SPISettings(20000000, MSBFIRST, SPI_MODE0);  //Not nornally needed
  SPI.setClockDivider(6);  //Speed up the Due SPI clock to 14MHz for Due
```

```
// SPI.setClockDivider(SPI_CLOCK-DIV2) //Use for Uno or Mega to speed up to
8MHz

// Set the SRAM in to Sequential Mode for reading/writing
digitalWrite(SRAM_ CS, LOW);
// send in the address and value via SPI:
SPI.transfer(0X01);// send the command to write to the Mode Reg
SPI.transfer(0x40);// select sequential mode for the SRAM
// take the SC pin high to de-select the SRAM:
digitalWrite(SRAM_CS, HIGH);

//Verify the SRAM chip is working by reading the Mode Reg back out
digitalWrite(SRAM_ CS, LOW);
SPI.transfer(0x05);
int tst = SPI.transfer(0x00); // tst should now = 0x40
if (tst==0x40) Serial.println("SRAM passed."); else Serial.println("SRAM failed.");
delay(3000); //Provide time for the user to see the result
digitalWrite(SRAM_SC, HIGH);
}
// ////////////////////////////////////////////////////////////////
void loop() {
// The data collection loop runs a bit faster with local variables
int Chan1 = 0; //define analog inputs
int Chan2 = 0;
int samp = 125; // samp/(#byte writes) = number of samples saved
//The SRAM can only save 2^16 (65536) 16bit ADC readings.  The number of ADC
reading
// times the #samp above must be less than 65,000.  If 2 channels and samp = 1000,
// we have 2000 integers.

unsigned long timeS; //Used to track time taken
unsigned long timeF;

// Set the SRAM in Write mode and the starting memory address of 0x000000
digitalWrite(SRAM_ CS, LOW);
SPI.transfer16(0x0200);// first 16 bits are start to write next 24 bits is the address
```

```
SPI.transfer16(0x0000);// this is the address starting from

//wait for user to push the trigger button, logic LOW
do{
} while (digitalRead(Trigger) == HIGH);

//Read analog inputs and save to the SRAM
timeS = micros(); //millis();
// digitalWrite(4, LOW); //Using pin 4 for timing with a scope
for (int i = 1; i <=samp; i++) {
  Chan1 = analogRead(A0);
  Chan2 = analogRead(A1);
  SPI.transfer16(Chan1);
  SPI.transfer16(Chan2);
  // kill time
  delayMicroseconds(22);// Change delay to change fs as 22:
  } // end 'for' statement
//   digitalWrite(4, HIGH);  //Used by my scope to validated timing

//Stop writing
digitalWrite(SRAM_CS, HIGH);

// record time spent
timeF = micros(); //millis();
unsigned long  timeT = timeF - timeS;
Serial.print("Timer=");  //Don't leave spaces between letters and the number
Serial.print(timeT);  //To get uS
Serial.println("uS.");
delay(2000);//Give the user time to see the timer value

// Set memory to Read mode
digitalWrite(SRAM_CS, LOW);
SPI.transfer16(0x0300);// first 8 bits set read next 24 bits is the address
SPI.transfer16(0x0000);
int j=0;
//Read from the SRAM all the saved data.  The auto scale of the Serial Plotter
```

```
//seams to work better with integers than real voltages.  So, I calculate the
//real voltage but send the ADC values to the Serial Plotter.
   for (int i  = 1; i <=samp; i++) {
   Chan1 = SPI.transfer16(0x0000);
   Chan2 = SPI.transfer16(0x0000);
   Serial.print(Chan1);
   Serial.print(" ");  //Need a space between variables for the Serial Plotter
   Serial.println(Chan2); // Line feed needed to term data set
   j++;
   delay(10);  //Simple delay to make watching the serial plotter more interesting
   } // end of the 'for' statement
Serial.print("# of readings=");
Serial.print(j);
Serial.print("time used=");
Serial.println(timeT);
   // Stop reading
   digitalWrite(SRAM_CS, HIGH);
}
```

10.4 Saving to a PC w RTC

Thanks to Joe Henfling for spending some of this time developing this sketch. I had been using the RTC (Real Time Clock) examples found on the web. They all lacked an easy means to set the Arduino RTC to the same time as the laptop without compiling the Arduino sketch. Joe modified "realtimeclock" Adruino sketch written by Jack Christensen, Aug 8, 2013. Joe also created a simple PC program to be run with this sketch. The program is called, "RTC_Software_Rev2.exe". Joe's program is available by emailing the author or going to www.onmeasurements.com.

The PC software allows the Arduino to sync its RTC to the PC without reprogramming the Arduino. This means any PC can set the time because the Arduino IDE is not required. In fact, the Arduino IDE needs to be off so that the PC software can connect to the Arduino via the USB port.

After the time is sync'ed, the user has an additional option to have the Arduino measurements recorded on the PC. The default file name is "myData.csv".

The program includes a couple of features the RTC. The DS3232/DS3231 offers reading the temperature of the RTC chip and turning on an output frequency (SQW pin). The program sets the frequency to 4096 Hz, but the options include; no frequency (default if commented out the "RTC.squareWave(4096)" statement if no frequency is needed), 1 Hz, 1024 Hz, 4096 Hz, or 8192 Hz.

In general, here is how the system works:

- Build up the measurement system with a RTC, either DS3231 or DS3232.
- Program the Arduino with "RTC_Rev5".
- Kill the Arduino IDE running on the PC.
- Reset the Arduino.

- Run the PC program "RTC_Software_Rev5.exe" on a Windows PC
- Connect the Arduino. The software should find the Arduino.
- Press the button labeled "Sync to PC Time"
- View the text box that displays the return messages and data from the Arduino to make sure the new time is displayed
- When ready, start to record data by pressing the "Record Data" button.
- The data file is called, "myData.csv". The file size text box will increase with each reading and indicates data is being stored on the PC. Since the created files is a CSV file, it can be opened and viewed with MS Excel.

Run the test and review the data. The Arduino program has a few basic functions to help demonstrate logging with the RTC and includes monitoring 4 A/D channels on the Arduino. The program sends out a comma delimited data packet comprised of: Date, Time, loop count, ADC channel 1, ADC channel 2, ADC channel 3, ADC channel 4. Every 1 minute, the temperature of the RTC is added to the end of the data packet.

The Arduino is also triggered by the RTC to take data reading every 1 second. Every time the clock "ticks", the program performs the tasks within the loop. Within the loop, the serial port is checked to see if commands came in and if so, performs the tasks for the entered command. If other data intervals are desired, the sketch could be modified by adding a variable to count how many one second loops are desired between readings and then execute the inner loop at that time.

To demonstrate using the serial interface to communicate with the Arduino, along with setting the RTC, a routine was included to read a "serial number" from the Arduino. If the user sends the command "SN" through the serial port, the Arduino will respond ":1234". The PC demo program searches for a connected Arduino and once a valid port is found, verifies the connected device is an Arduino by sending out this command and reading the response. The returned response is displayed in a text box. Setting the time is performed in a similar manner. The button in the PC program initiates a command to the Arduino. In this case, it is "ST" followed by the PC time. The PC time is formatted before it is sent to reflect the defined input string the Arduino expects. The complete command sent to the RTC is STyyMMddhhmmss, where yy = year, MM = month, dd = month, hh = hour, mm =

minute, ss = second. Additional commands could be added to perform other functions such as a programmable data interval, number of ADC channels you want to use to take data, etc.

The RTC shield usually includes a backup battery. Once, the clock is set, it will retain the time with no power to the shield with the battery installed.

10.4.1 Test Setup

The RTC is an IC2 device. The connections are below.

DS3231/DS1307 SDA → Pin A4, UNO; Pin 20, Mega2560; Pin 20, Due
DS3231/DS1307 SCL → Pin A5, UNO; Pin 21, Mega2560; Pin 21, Due
DS3231/DS1307 VCC → 5V (In some shields the 3.3V is used)
DS3231/DS1307 GND → GND

10.4.2 RTC_Rev5

```
#include <DS3232RTC.h>      //http://github.com/JChristensen/DS3232RTC
#include <TimeLib.h>         //http://playground.arduino.cc/Code/Time
#include <Wire.h>          //http://arduino.cc/en/Reference/Wire

static time_t tLast;
time_t t;
tmElements_t tm;


String inString = "";   // string to hold input
String inTime = "";   // string to hold input
int intTimeArray[20];
int LoopCnt = 0;
String inCommand = "";
String inMessage = "";
```

```
String stringReadSP;

//A/D variable
String stringADchan1 = "";
String stringADchan2 = "";
String stringADchan3 = "";
String stringADchan4 = "";
String stringIndex1 = "";

int i = 0;
int forDelay = 0;


void setup(void)
{

   Serial.begin(115200);
   //turn on squarewave
   RTC.squareWave(SQWAVE_4096_HZ);      // options include: SQWAVE_1_HZ,
SQWAVE_1024_HZ, SQWAVE_4096_HZ, SQWAVE_8192_HZ, SQWAVE_NONE

   RTC.writeRTC(RTC_STATUS, 8);         // write 8 to status registor to turn on
32kHz and 0 to turn off

   setSyncProvider(RTC.get);
   Serial.println("RTC Sync");
   if (timeStatus() != timeSet) Serial.println(" FAIL!");

}

void loop(void)
{

   t = now();              //Get time from Real time clock

   if (t != tLast) {       // if time increments, then proceed
```

```
      i++;
      // get A/D readings
      stringADchan1 = String(analogRead(1));
      stringADchan2 = String(analogRead(2));
      stringADchan3 = String(analogRead(3));
      stringADchan4 = String(analogRead(4));
      stringIndex1 = String(i);

      tLast = t;
      printDateTime(t);
      Serial.print("," + stringIndex1 + "," +stringADchan1 + "," + stringADchan2 + ","
+ stringADchan3 + "," + stringADchan4);
      if (second(t) == 0) {      // when seconds roll over, send out the temperature of
the real time clock
          float RTCTempc = RTC.temperature() / 4.;

          Serial.print(",");
          Serial.print(RTCTempc);

      }
      Serial.println();


    ckSerial();
  }

}

//print date and time to Serial
void printDateTime(time_t t)
{
  Serial.print(':');
  printDate(t);
  Serial.print(',');
  printTime(t);
}
```

```
//print time to Serial
void printTime(time_t t)
{
   printI00(hour(t), ':');
   printI00(minute(t), ':');
   printI00(second(t), ' ');
}

//print date to Serial
void printDate(time_t t)
{
   printI00(day(t), 0);
   Serial.print(monthShortStr(month(t)));
   Serial.print(year(t));
}

//Print an integer in "00" format (with leading zero),
//followed by a delimiter character to Serial.
//Input value assumed to be between 0 and 99.
void printI00(int val, char delim)
{
   if (val < 10) Serial.print('0');
   Serial.print(val);
   if (delim > 0) Serial.print(delim);
   return;
}

void ckSerial(void)
{

   // RS232 read test begin
   while (Serial.available() > 0) {
    int inChar = Serial.read();
    inString += (char)inChar;    //get complete message
```

```
    if (inChar == 13) {                   // if CR is received, check if valid
command came in

        inCommand = inString.substring(0,2);

        // following 3 lines are for troubleshooting
        //Serial.print(inString);
        //Serial.print(" command is ");
        //Serial.println(inCommand);

        if (inCommand == "ST")         // Set time command, from terminal, send
STyyMMddhhmmss, then a CR,
                            //where yy = year, MM = month, dd = month, hh = hour,
mm = minute, ss = second
        {
            //year
            stringReadSP = inString.substring(2,4);
            intTimeArray[0] = stringReadSP.toInt();

            //month
            stringReadSP = inString.substring(4,6);
            intTimeArray[1] = stringReadSP.toInt();

            //day
            stringReadSP = inString.substring(6,8);
            intTimeArray[2] = stringReadSP.toInt();

            //hour

            stringReadSP = inString.substring(8,10);
            intTimeArray[3] = stringReadSP.toInt();

            //minute
            stringReadSP = inString.substring(10,12);
            intTimeArray[4] = stringReadSP.toInt();
```

```
//second
stringReadSP = inString.substring(12,14);
intTimeArray[5] = stringReadSP.toInt();

// following 6 lines are for troubleshooting
//Serial.println(intTimeArray[0]);
//Serial.println(intTimeArray[1]);
//Serial.println(intTimeArray[2]);
//Serial.println(intTimeArray[3]);
//Serial.println(intTimeArray[4]);
//Serial.println(intTimeArray[5]);

//now set the clock with values received

    tm.Year = y2kYearToTm(intTimeArray[0]);

    tm.Month = intTimeArray[1];
    tm.Day = intTimeArray[2];
    tm.Hour = intTimeArray[3];
    tm.Minute = intTimeArray[4];
    tm.Second = intTimeArray[5];
    t = makeTime(tm);
    RTC.set(t);      //use the time_t value to ensure correct weekday is set
    setTime(t);
    Serial.print("RTC set to: ");
    printDateTime(t);
    Serial.println(" ");


        inString = "";

    }
    else if (inCommand == "SN")
    {
        // can add routines here to load variables, etc. by using the serial port as
input
```

```
            // change the command to reflect the task
            // this is an example of setting a serial number for the Arduino
electronics
            Serial.flush();
            delay(100);     // add time delay to ensure the terminal receives the data
            Serial.println("$1234");
            delay(1000);    // add time delay to ensure the terminal receives the data

            inString = "";
        }


        else
        {
        Serial.print("Serial Data Received ");
        Serial.println(inString);
        inString = "";
        }
    }

  }
} // RTC_Rev5 Sketch
```

10.5 AD22B and DAC12B Sketch

Sketch AD22B_DAC12B_Test demonstrates writing to a DAC (Digital-To-Analog Converter) and reading back the output value using analog input A0 on the Uno and the AD22B shield. The DAC12B shield is designed to be used as a precision, low noise sensor power supply. A low noise power supply for sensors is critical for scientific measurements. The AD22B is a 22 bit ADC improving the resolution, also critical for many scientific measurements.

With an input supply voltage of 12V, the DAC12B can be programmed by the Arduino for output voltages from 0 to 10V. The DAC chip inside the DAC12B is the MCP4921. The DAC12B supplies the MCP4921 its own precision 2.5V reference. The MCP4921 is a 12bit DAC with a nominal calibration as below.

$$\text{DAC resolution is } 0.61mV/Cnts = 2.5/2^{12}$$

A low noise, non-inverting amplifier increases the DAC12B output from 0 to 2.5V to 0 to 10V. The amplifier also drives an output power transistor so that the output current of the DAC12B is rated to 50mA.

The DAC12B circuit has a current sense amplifier. The output of the current sense amplifier can be used to monitor sensor current by either the AD22B or any Arduino analog input.

The AD22B is based on the MCP3550 ADC. The AD22B circuit uses a low pass π circuit to filter power going to the MCP3550. The circuit also has its own 2.5V reference. This combination provide a clean, noise reduced environment in order the high resolution ADC to do its best conversions.

The AD22B has a number of input options. The input options are: differential, 0 to 2.5V and 0 to 5V. These options are selected using jumpers on the input header pins. The option used in this sketch is the 0 to 5V option. The 5V input uses a voltage divider circuit with two 500K ohm, 0.1%, 25ppm/C precision resistors. The voltage divider reduces the input from 0 to 5V to 0 to 2.5V for the MCP3550 ADC.

The nominal calibration of the AD22B for 0 to 5V input is:

$$\text{Input 0 to 5V resolution: } 2.38418\mu V/Cnts = 5V/2^{21}$$

The main program is a simple loop. The programmed output voltage of the DAC12B circuit starts low and goes high with increments of 10 counts. The final DAC12B output is near 10V. As the input to the AD22B is limited to 5V, there is an external voltage divider of ½ using two 10K ohm resistors.

For every new step of the DAC12B, the new output voltage is monitored by both the AD22B and the Arduino A0 analog input. This allows for the user to compare the results.

Once the DAC12B programming variable "DAC_V" is >4030cnts, variable is reset to 0 and the ramping of the system starts over.

The function "DAC_Write(unsigned int Val)" is used to write a new value to the DAC12B. This function formats the "Val" by adding MCP4921 required control bits. Once in the right format, the bits are transmitted using the pin assignment for the SPI provided by the programmer.

The function "AD_Read(long int &Val)" is used to read the ADC value from the AD22B. The ADC reading is returned in the variable "Val". The actual reading from the MCP3550 is 24 bits. The first two bits are error indications. These bits are removed and the 22bit value is transferred to "Val" used by the program.

10.5.1 Test Circuit

A prototype board is needed along with some resistors and capacitors. I plugged AD22B and DAC12B shields into the prototype board to connect the power and SPI wires back to the Arduino. The SPI connections I used are below. The user can easily choose other SPI pins. The program is not using the Arduino SPI library to control these two shields.

CS_AD → Pin 39 MEGA; Pin 11 UNO; Chip select AD22B

CS_DAC → Pin 43 MEGA; Pin 7 UNO; Chip select DAC

MI_SO → Pin 28 Mega; Pin 12 UNO; Using MI_SO as MISO is already used by Arduino's IDE

MO_SI → Pin 30 Mega; Pin 6 UNO; Using MO_SI as MOSI is already used by Arduino's IDE

SPI_Clk → Pin 32 Mega; Pin 13 UNO;

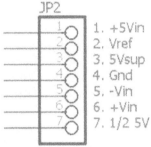

JP2

1. +5Vin
2. Vref
3. 5Vsup
4. Gnd
5. -Vin
6. +Vin
7. 1/2 5V

Figure 10.5 AD22B Input

The input pins for the AD22B offer a number of options. See the pin header shown in Figure 10.5.

Each of the MCP3550 input pins are available at the pin header at pins 5 and 6. The voltage reference is also provided at pin 2. This can be used to bias a sensor or create a precision offset voltage for the ADC. The 5Vsup on pin 3 is provided as a filtered 5V for low current sensors.

The +5Vin is used with this sketch. So, on the AD22B input header, place a jumper across pins 4 and 5 and a jumper across pins 7 and 6. The jumper on 4 (Gnd) and 5 (-Vin) makes the ADC single ended. The jumper on 6 (+Vin) and 7 (1/2 5V) connects the 1M ohm voltage divider to the positive input of the ADC. Now, pin 1 (+5Vin) is the input for the analog voltage we are interested in measuring.

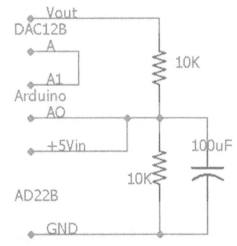

Figure 10.6 External circuit for measurement testing

In order to get 0 to 10V out of the DAC12B, the 12V supply input requires 12V. The other proto board circuits are shown in Figure 10.6. The Arduino analog inputs A0 and A1 are used. The A0 input is shared with the +5Vin on the AD22B.

10.5.2 AD22B_DAC12B_Test Sketch

```
#include <SPI.h>
#include <SD.h>

// Pin assingment for Uno
const int CS_AD = 2;  // Digital IO pins
const int CS_DAC = 3;
const int CS_SD = 10;
const int MO_SI = 4;
const int MI_SO = 5;
const int SPI_Clk = 6;
const int LED2 = 7;
const float DAC_Cal = 2.502E-3; // 5v/4096, this is the default cal
const float AD_Cal = 2.384186E-6; // 5V/2^21, the default cal, MSB is a sign bit
unsigned int DAC_V = 100;

void setup() {
// initialize serial communication at 9600 bits per second:
 Serial.begin(9600);
// see if the card is present and can be initialized:
 Serial.println("Checking for SD Card");
 if (!SD.begin(CS_SD)) {
  Serial.println("Card failed");
  }
  else { //verify working SD card with file creation and read/write
   Serial.println("Creating test file on the SD card");
   File tstFile = SD.open("TstFile.jnk", FILE_WRITE);
   int jnkIn = 860;
   if (tstFile) { tstFile.print(jnkIn); }
   tstFile.close();
   tstFile = SD.open("TstFile.jnk", FILE_READ);  // Now to read back our value
```

```
  int jnkOut = 123;  //setup value to read from the new file
  if (tstFile) {
   while (tstFile.available()) {
    jnkOut = tstFile.parseInt();  //We are reading an interger our of the file
   }
   Serial.print("Reading tstFile should see 860: ");
   Serial.println(jnkOut); //Show the user what value was readout
   tstFile.close();
   SD.remove("TstFile.jnk"); }
   // now test what we read out is the same as what we wrote in
  if (jnkOut == jnkIn) {
   Serial.print("SD Card verified: Opening AD_DAC2.CSV ");
    //write program variables on to the SD card
   File dataFile = SD.open("AD_DAC2.csv", FILE_WRITE);
   dataFile.print("AD22B_DAC12B_Test Sketch by RAN");
   dataFile.print("DAC Target, AD22B, A0, A1, A3");
   dataFile.close();
  }
   else { Serial.println("SD Card Verification Failure"); }
 }
// setup IO pins
 pinMode(CS_AD, OUTPUT);
 digitalWrite(CS_AD,HIGH);
 pinMode(CS_DAC, OUTPUT);
 digitalWrite(CS_DAC,HIGH);
 pinMode(LED2, OUTPUT);
 digitalWrite(LED2, LOW);
 pinMode(MI_SO, INPUT_PULLUP);// places a 20K pull on this pin use
INPUT_PULLUP
 pinMode(MO_SI, OUTPUT);
 pinMode(SPI_Clk, OUTPUT);
 digitalWrite(SPI_Clk,LOW);
}

void loop() { //Main program loop
 DAC_Write(DAC_V);
```

```
String dataString = String(DAC_V); //Start string for SD card
dataString += ", "; // we are using ',' as the data delimiter for Excel
delay(600); //give DAC time to charge the filter capacitor normally 100uF
int long AD22 = 0; //define the variable for the 22bit ADC readout
AD_Read(AD22); //Get the 22bit ADC readout
float DAC_Volt = DAC_V * DAC_Cal; //basic calibration for input V from the
DAC
dataString += String(AD22); //adding AD22 binary reading to the SD file string
dataString += ", "; //delimiter agian
float AD_Volt = AD22 * AD_Cal; //Convert AD22 readout to volts
long A0 = 0; //Get A0 value
for (int i=0;i<149;i++)
  { A0 = A0 + analogRead(0);}
float AA0 = (A0/149.0)*4.883E-3;
dataString += String(A0);
dataString += ", ";
Serial.print("DAC Tar="); //Report to the screen real time the DAC target voltage
Serial.print(DAC_Volt,4); // In the normal set up DAC_Volt reaches 10V
Serial.print(", AD22= ");
Serial.print(AD_Volt, 4); // In the normal set up, AD_Volt and AA0 are 1/2 DAC
Tar
Serial.print(", A0=");
Serial.print(AA0, 4);
int A1 = analogRead(1); //Read A1 input which is normally attache to the DAC
feedback pin
AA0 = A1*4.883E-3;
dataString += A1; // attach the A1 reading to the SD string for saving
dataString += ", ";
Serial.print(", FB=");
Serial.print(AA0, 4);
int A2 = analogRead(2); // Normally attached to the current output of the DAC
AA0 = (A2 * 4.883E-3)/100;
dataString += A2;
dataString += ", ";
Serial.print(", I=");
Serial.print(AA0, 4);
```

```
Serial.println("Amp");

//Save our data to the SD card
File dataFile = SD.open("AD_DAC2.csv", FILE_WRITE);
    dataFile.println(dataString); // Save our data string to the SD card file
    dataFile.close();

DAC_V = DAC_V + 1;
if (DAC_V > 4045) {DAC_V = 200;}

digitalWrite(LED2,HIGH); // Tell user valid readings
delay(400);
digitalWrite(LED2,LOW);

}// end main loop

//-------------------------- AD_Read Function -------------------------
/* This function reads the 22bit AD (MCP3550) and returns an unsigned value.
 * the lower 22 bits are the value and bits 23 and 24 are over, under flow errors.
 * Bit 22 is OVH over Vref.  The AD is still in spect at 10%over voltage
 * Bit 23 is OVL under Vss.  The AD will not work in this case.
 */
void AD_Read(long int &Val)  //the & tell the compiler this veriable will be altered
by the function
{
digitalWrite(SPI_Clk, HIGH); //AD expects a high clock at start of convert
digitalWrite(CS_AD,LOW);// select AD and start conversion
delay(85); // provide time for conversion
digitalWrite(SPI_Clk, LOW); // clears a flag or use the program below.

/* while (digitalRead(MISOad) == HIGH) // could be used to reduce conversion
time for max rate
 {
 Serial.print("-");
 delay(10); // if this line is used with delay of 10, I get 7 dashes
 } */
```

```
for (int i=1; i<25; i++) // Read 24 bits from the AD
  {
  digitalWrite(SPI_Clk, HIGH);  // clock SPI

  Val = Val*2;// really a shift left to move bits up 1
  if (digitalRead(MI_SO)== HIGH)
    { Val = Val + 1;
    // Serial.print("1");
    }
    else {
    //  Serial.print("0");
    }
  if (i==12) {Serial.print(", ");}
  digitalWrite(SPI_Clk, LOW);
  //delay(1);
  if (i>23) {
    Serial.print(", ");
    Serial.println(Val);}
  }// End for i
 digitalWrite(CS_AD,HIGH); //release the AD
 //delay(2);
}


//--------------------------- DAC_Write Function --------------------------
/* This function sends a unsigned int value to the DAC, MCP4921.  This is a 12 bit
DAC.
 * The upper 4 bits of the 16 bit word sent to the DAC are control bits.  In most cases
they
 * will never change.
*/
void DAC_Write(unsigned int Val) {
  digitalWrite(CS_DAC, LOW);
  Val = Val + 0b0011000000000000;// Control bits (0011) to be sent out infront of the
  //12 bit value.
  // Lower 12 bits are Vout = value*5v/4096
```

```
unsigned int Mask   = 0b1000000000000000;// used to mask 1 bit at a time for SPI
MO_SI
 for (int i=0; i<16; i++)
 {
   if ((Val & Mask) > 0) //set MO_SI bit out to the pin
   { digitalWrite(MO_SI, HIGH);
   }
   else
   { digitalWrite(MO_SI, LOW);
   }

 digitalWrite(SPI_Clk, HIGH); // clock out the data to the slave
 delay(1); // time to see it
 digitalWrite(SPI_Clk, LOW);
 Mask = Mask >> 1;// Mask ready for next bit
 delay(1);
 } // end for i
 digitalWrite(CS_DAC, HIGH);//Release the DAC
}// end DACwrite, end of AD22B_DAC12B_Test Sketch
```

10.6 SRAM Low Pass Butterworth

Sketch SRAM_LP demonstrates:

> 1. using the "micros()" function to time sets of 2 analog channels.
> 2. using the SRAM 23LC1024 memory for fast data recording using SPI.
> 3. a 2 pole, low pass Butterworth IIR filter (fc at 570Hz with fs = 25KHz).

The analog input at A0 is the raw signal (no digital filtering). The analog input at A1 is passed through a low pass Butterworth IIR filter.

This sketch can work with either the Serial Monitor or Serial Plotter.

The Arduino "serial plotter" function will plot out the ADC readings. Each reading is sent to the plotter as an integer. This allows for easy auto-scaling of the measurements. Each ADC reading in the string sent to the serial plotter is separated by a comma. Each set of points is separated by a line feed.

> The Arduino "serial Monitor" will display the calculated fs and sample period followed by all the measured data points. These values are ignored by the serial plotter. The serial plotter ignores numbers when mixed with text.

The sample frequency is determined by setting the global variable "period" in the program. For the Due, if period = 40, the sample frequency (fs) equal to 1/period * 1MHz or 25KHz. This is because "period" is an integer counting micro-seconds. Setting period = 100, sets the fs = 10KHz.

The SRAM can only hold ~65,000 integer values. This sketch reads two integer ADC values with each pass. So, the number of data sets is limited to 32,500. By setting the value of "samp" in the global variables, the programmer sets the number of data sets to be taken. The Arduino serial plotter can only display two channels and at 500 samples each. I used this program to work like a scope using the serial plotter and normally limited the number of samples to "samp = 500;" or less.

There might be problems with taking 10,000 sample sets. At some point, the repeated reading of the "micros()" function seems to develop an error. If this is true, consider the sample timing used in 10.3 SRAM Scope2. This timing will work without errors.

Digital IIR filter. This is a 2 pole, Butterworth IIR. The fc is 570Hz with fs = 25KHz. The filter coefficients are global constants a0, a1, a2 and b1, b2. Two arrays are used to hold the filter input values. The Xn integer values coming from the ADC are stored in "Xn[3]". The past results of the filter, Yn floating values are stored in "Yn[3]".

With each run of "samp" sets of readings, the filter values start at 0. This means the filter output is 0 and it takes some time before the filter is up and running.

The data collection loop is a "do – while" loop. The two inputs A0 and A1 are collected. The filter output is calculated by the statement below.

$$Yn[0] = a0*Xn[0] + a1*Xn[1] + a2*Xn[2] + b1*Yn[1] + b*Yn[2];$$

After the new filter output Yn[0] is calculated, the values in the Xn and Yn arrays are shifted making room for the next Xn[0] measured value and new calculated yn[0].

For more information on this sketch, see sections 5.1.2.2 and 5.2.2 of this book.

10.6.1 Test Circuit

This sketch is using the same SRAM as described in 10.3 SRAM Scope2.

10.6.2 SRAM_LP Sketch

```
// include the SPI library:
#include <SPI.h>

// define Pins
```

```
const int SRAM_SC = 10;
const int Trigger = 13;  //Input trigger to start taking data

//Filter coef for the low pass Butterworth filter with
fs=25KHz, this is a 2 pole, 570Hz filter
const float a0 = 0.0047;
const float a1 = 0.0093;
const float a2 = 0.0047;
const float b1 = 1.7976;
const float b2 = -0.8163;
int Xn[3];  //Array of measured values for the filter
float Yn[3];  //Array of past values for the filter

// define gobal veriables
int Chan1 = 0;  //define analog inputs
int Chan2 = 0;
unsigned long timeS;  //Used to track time taken
unsigned long timeF;
unsigned long timeP;
const float slope = 0.0008057; // 0.004883 for Uno, Mega and
0.0008057 Due
const float intercept = 0;
const int samp = 500;  //The number of samples to be taken
const int Period = 40;  //Time in uS between samples

void setup() {
  //Setup USB to display events to the user
    Serial.begin(9600);

 //For the Due use the statement below for all 12 bits
  analogReadResolution(12);

  // put your setup code here, to run once:
  // set the SRAM CS Pin as an output:
  pinMode (SRAM_SC, OUTPUT);
  pinMode (Trigger, INPUT);
  digitalWrite(SRAM_SC,HIGH);  //Start with SRAM not selected.

  // initialize SPI:
  SPI.begin();
```

```
  delay(5); // Give the system some power up time

  // Set the SRAM in to Sequential Mode for reading/writing
  digitalWrite(SRAM_SC, LOW);
  // send in the address and value via SPI:
  SPI.transfer(0X01);// send the command to write to the Mode
Reg
  SPI.transfer(0x40);// select sequential mode for the SRAM
  // take the SC pin high to de-select the SRAM:
  digitalWrite(SRAM_SC, HIGH);

  //Verify the SRAM chip is working by reading the Mode Reg
back out
  digitalWrite(SRAM_SC, LOW);
  SPI.transfer(0x05);
  int tst = SPI.transfer(0x00); // tst should now = 0x40
  if (tst==0x40) Serial.println("SRAM passed."); else
Serial.println("SRAM failed.");
  delay(3000); //Provide time for the user to see the result
  digitalWrite(SRAM_SC, HIGH);
}

void loop() {
  // put your main code here, to run repeatedly:

  Xn[1]=0;
  Xn[2]=0;
  Yn[1]=0;
  Yn[2]=0;

  // Set the SRAM in Write mode and the starting memory
address of 0x000000
  digitalWrite(SRAM_SC, LOW);
  SPI.transfer16(0x0200);// first 8 bits are start to write
next 24 bits is the address
  SPI.transfer16(0x0000);

  //wait for trigger to go low
  do{
  // int val = digitalRead(Trigger);
```

```
  } while (digitalRead(Trigger) == HIGH);

  //Read analog inputs and save to the SRAM
  long totalS = 0;  //The sample counter can only save 2^16
(65536) 16bit ADC readings
  timeS = micros(); //millis();// save the starting time to
verify the sample frequency
  timeP = timeS + Period;  //Set the sample period before
doing the data collection loop
  do {
    Chan1 = analogRead(A0);
    Xn[0] = analogRead(A1);
    Yn[0] = a0*Xn[0] + a1*Xn[1] + a2*Xn[2] + b1*Yn[1] +
b2*Yn[2];
    SPI.transfer16(Chan1);
    SPI.transfer16(Yn[0]); //This action is truncating the
result
    totalS += 1;  //Counting measurement sets
    Xn[2]=Xn[1];// shift the readings, ready for the next
sample
    Xn[1]=Xn[0];
    Yn[2]=Yn[1];
    Yn[1]=Yn[0];
    do {
      delayMicroseconds(2);}// delay waiting on time to pass
    while (micros() < timeP);
    timeP += Period;  //add another period time for taking
another data set
  } while ( totalS < samp);  //Test to see if we are done
filling memory with sets of data points

  //Stop writing
  digitalWrite(SRAM_SC, HIGH);

  // record time spent
  timeF = micros(); //millis();
  unsigned long timeU = timeF - timeS;  // time used in uS by
the
  timeU = timeU/samp;  // average time for each sample set
  Serial.print("Sample Period=");
```

```
  Serial.print(timeU);   //In uS when using micros() function
in the period
  Serial.print("uS ");
  Serial.print("Sample Freq=");
  float fs = (1.0/timeU)*1E6;   //timeP is an integer in uS
  Serial.println(fs,2);
  delay(2000);//Give the user time to see the timer value

  // Set memory to Read mode
  digitalWrite(SRAM_SC, LOW);
  SPI.transfer16(0x0300);// first 8 bits set read next 24 bits
is the address
  SPI.transfer16(0x0000);
  totalS = 0;

  do {
  Chan1 = SPI.transfer16(0x0000);
  Chan2 = SPI.transfer16(0x0000);
  totalS += 1;
  //Serial.print("Chan1= ");
  float Vread = Chan1*slope + intercept;
 // Serial.print(Vread,3);
 Serial.print(Chan1);
  Serial.print(" ");   //Need a space between variables
  //Serial.print(" Chan2= ");
  Vread = Chan2*slope + intercept;
//  Serial.println(Vread,3);
  Serial.println(Chan2);
  delay(50);
  } while (totalS < samp);

  // Stop reading
  digitalWrite(SRAM_SC, HIGH);
}// End SRAM_LP Sketch
```

Index--

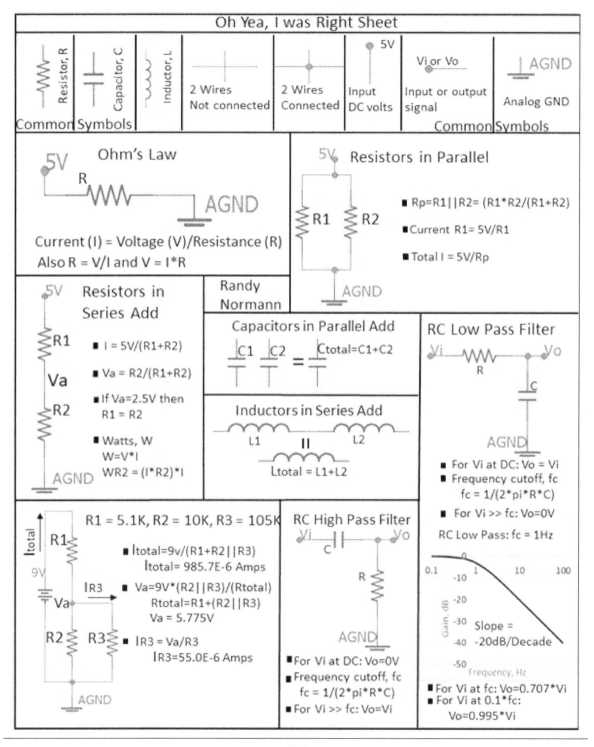

Oh Yea, I was Right Sheet

Common Symbols — Resistor, R; Capacitor, C; Inductor, L; 2 Wires Not connected; 2 Wires Connected; Input DC volts 5V; Input or output signal Vi or Vo; Analog GND AGND — Common Symbols

Ohm's Law

Current (I) = Voltage (V)/Resistance (R)
Also R = V/I and V = I*R

Resistors in Parallel

- Rp=R1||R2= (R1*R2/(R1+R2)
- Current R1= 5V/R1
- Total I = 5V/Rp

Resistors in Series Add

- I = 5V/(R1+R2)
- Va = R2/(R1+R2)
- If Va=2.5V then R1 = R2
- Watts, W
  W=V*I
  WR2 = (I*R2)*I

Randy Normann

Capacitors in Parallel Add

C1 C2 = Ctotal=C1+C2

Inductors in Series Add

L1 || L2

Ltotal = L1+L2

RC Low Pass Filter

- For Vi at DC: Vo = Vi
- Frequency cutoff, fc
  fc = 1/(2*pi*R*C)
- For Vi >> fc: Vo=0V

RC Low Pass: fc = 1Hz

Slope = -20dB/Decade

R1 = 5.1K, R2 = 10K, R3 = 105K

- Itotal=9v/(R1+R2||R3)
  Itotal= 985.7E-6 Amps
- Va=9V*(R2||R3)/(Rtotal)
  Rtotal=R1+(R2||R3)
  Va = 5.775V
- IR3 = Va/R3
  IR3=55.0E-6 Amps

RC High Pass Filter

- For Vi at DC: Vo=0V
- Frequency cutoff, fc
  fc = 1/(2*pi*R*C)
- For Vi >> fc: Vo=Vi
- For Vi at fc: Vo=0.707*Vi
- For Vi at 0.1*fc:
  Vo=0.995*Vi

These circuits assume nominal IC values. Data sheets should be consulted before using the circuit.

Comparator

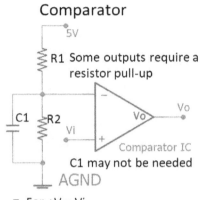

R1 Some outputs require a resistor pull-up

C1 may not be needed

AGND

- For +V = Vi
  If Vi > -V: Vo is HIGH
  If Vi < -V: Vo is LOW
- No loading on input signal

Non-Inverting Amplifier

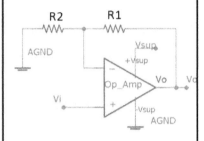

- $G(ain) = 1 + R1/R2$
- Offset voltage error:
  Offset error = $G*(input\ offset)$
- No loading on input signal

DC Offset

Vo to Arduino Analog input

- At DC: $Vo = Vsup*R2/(R1+R2)$
- $fc = 1/(2*pi*(R1||R2)*C1)$
- Loading on input signal
  At Vi>>fc Rload = R1||R2

Single input, In-Amp Circuit w 2 RC Poles

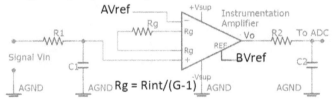

Rg = Rint/(G-1)

Assumes: R1*C1 = R2*C2 and three op-amp design as AD623
AVref is a low noise input voltage
BVref is a low noise input voltage must source or sink current

- $G(ain) = 1 + Rint/Rg$; See data sheet for Rint
- To ADC = $G*(+V - Avref) + BVref$
- Offset voltage error for high gain:
  Offset error = $\sim G*(input\ offset)$
- $fc = 1/(1.554*(2*pi*R*C))$

Assumes:
R1 = R2
C1 = C2
C3 >> C1 or C2
Three op-amp IC version

- $G(ain) = 1 + Rint/Rg$;
  See data sheet for Rint
- ADC = $G*(+Vi - -Vi) + Vref$
- $fc = 1/(1.554*(2*pi*R*C))$
  Where R = R1 + R2 and
  C3 for the first RC

Differential In-Amp Circuit w 2 RC Poles

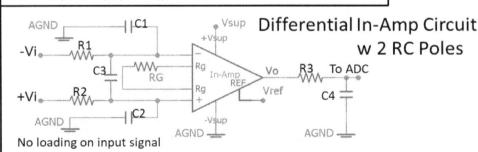

No loading on input signal

www.ingramcontent.com/pod-product-compliance
Lightning Source LLC
Chambersburg PA
CBHW080551060326
40689CB00021B/4823